MY SOUL
HAS GROWN DEEP

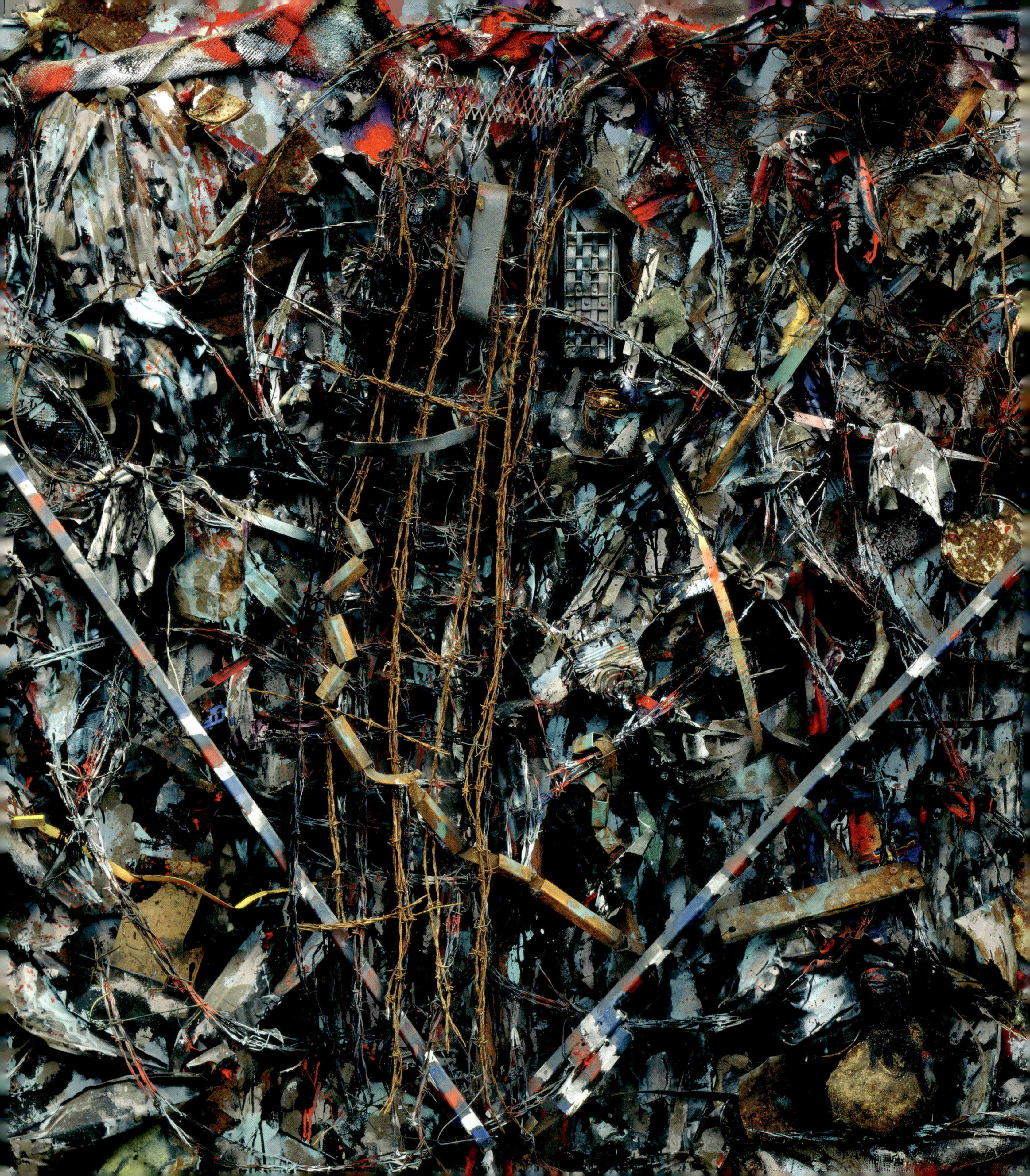

MY SOUL HAS GROWN DEEP

BLACK ART FROM THE AMERICAN SOUTH

CHERYL FINLEY

RANDALL R. GRIFFEY

AMELIA PECK

DARRYL PINCKNEY

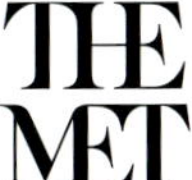

THE METROPOLITAN MUSEUM OF ART, NEW YORK

DISTRIBUTED BY YALE UNIVERSITY PRESS, NEW HAVEN AND LONDON

This catalogue is published in conjunction with "History Refused to Die: Highlights from the Souls Grown Deep Foundation Gift," on view at The Metropolitan Museum of Art, New York, from May 22 through September 23, 2018.

This publication is made possible by The Andrew W. Mellon Foundation.

Published by The Metropolitan Museum of Art, New York
Mark Polizzotti, Publisher and Editor in Chief
Gwen Roginsky, Associate Publisher and General Manager of Publications
Peter Antony, Chief Production Manager
Michael Sittenfeld, Senior Managing Editor

Edited by Kamilah Foreman
Designed by Bethany Johns
Production by Lauren Knighton
Bibliography edited by Jayne Kuchna
Image acquisitions and permissions by Elizabeth De Mase

Photographs of works in The Metropolitan Museum of Art's collection are by the Imaging Department, The Metropolitan Museum of Art, unless otherwise noted. Additional photography credits appear on page 116.

Typeset in Fakt Pro and Stanley
Printed on 65 lb. Sterling Premium Matte

Separations by Professional Graphics, Inc., Rockford, Illinois
Printed and bound by Puritan Capital, Hollis, New Hampshire

Jacket illustrations: front, Thornton Dial, *The End of November: The Birds That Didn't Learn How to Fly*, 2007 (detail, pl. 22); back, Lucy T. Pettway, *Housetop and Bricklayer with Bars quilt*, ca. 1955 (detail, pl. 34)
Frontispieces, page 2: Thornton Dial, *Victory in Iraq*, 2004 (detail, pl. 14); page 6: Nellie Mae Rowe, *Woman Scolding Her Companion*, 1981 (detail, pl. 17); page 8: Lucy Mingo, *Blocks and Strips work-clothes quilt*, 1959 (detail, pl. 30); page 10: Purvis Young, *Locked Up Their Minds*, 1972 (detail); page 12: Thornton Dial, *January 20, 2009*, 2009 (detail, pl. 12); page 20: Mary Proctor, *The Keys*, 1996 (detail, pl. 26); page 52: Willie "Ma Willie" Abrams, *Roman Stripes quilt*, ca. 1975 (detail, pl. 29); page 92: Walker Evans, *Washstand with Pail, Bowl, and Mirror in Dog Run of Burroughs Home, Hale County, Alabama*, 1936. Film negative, 8 × 10 in. (20.3 × 25.4 cm). The Metropolitan Museum of Art, New York, Walker Evans Archive, 1994 (1994.258.46)

First printing

The Metropolitan Museum of Art
1000 Fifth Avenue
New York, New York 10028
metmuseum.org

Distributed by
Yale University Press, New Haven and London
yalebooks.com/art
yalebooks.co.uk

Cataloguing-in-Publication Data is available from the Library of Congress.
ISBN 978-1-58839-609-9

CONTENTS

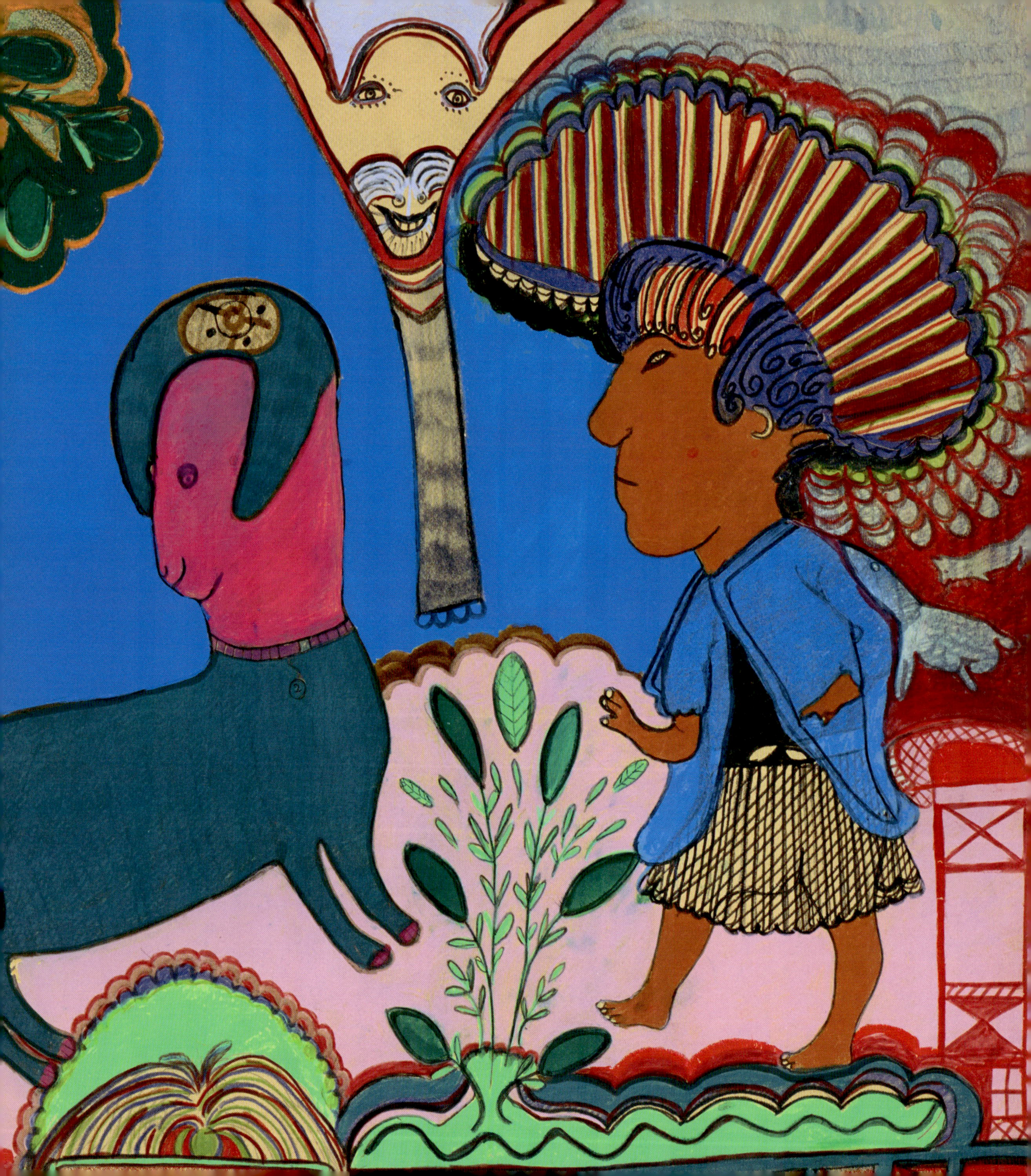

FOREWORD

This publication, like the exhibition "History Refused to Die" it accompanies, celebrates the remarkable gift to The Metropolitan Museum of Art of fifty-seven artworks by contemporary African American artists from the Souls Grown Deep Foundation, Atlanta, in November 2014. Included in this generous gift are key works by Thornton Dial, Lonnie Holley, and Nellie Mae Rowe, among other artists. Twenty important quilts created by women artists based in the area around Gee's Bend (now Boykin), Alabama, were also part of the gift, including works by Annie Mae Young, Lucy Mingo, Loretta Pettway, and other members of the extended Pettway family. Linked by geographic region, these artists are all connected by common legacies of slavery and post-Reconstruction histories of oppression under the Black Codes and Jim Crow laws, experiences and issues their work often invokes. Variously described as "self-taught" or, less desirably, as "outsider," they frequently employ everyday or discarded materials to create art for themselves and for their communities, often in the context of elaborate yard installations. Boldly patterned quilts might be viewed by visitors on the family clothesline. These artists and quilt makers had few expectations that their work would be seen in galleries or museums. Over the past decades, owing to growing interest in self-taught art in museums and galleries as well as university art-history programs, several of these artists have garnered increasing recognition in the mainstream art world. The paintings, sculptures, assemblages, and quilts within the gift serve as a powerful collective testament to humanity's creative urge to make art, even amid sometimes difficult circumstances—and perhaps even because of or in response to them.

The Souls Grown Deep Foundation gift supports the Museum's goal to convey a broad view of contemporary art practice to its many visitors, widening the collection's scope aesthetically, geographically, and culturally. Moreover, the gift expands the canon as a whole by furthering The Met's commitment to art by African American artists, evident in recent acquisitions of works by Mark Bradford, Beverly Buchanon, Aaron Douglas, Ellen Gallagher, Arthur Jafa, Kerry James Marshall, and Stanley Whitney in the Department of Modern and Contemporary Art, and by William A. Harper, Joshua Johnson, Edmonia Lewis, and Charles Ethan Porter in the American Wing. Joining The Met's collection, these new acquisitions complement a rich and deep trove of works on paper—especially prints—by African American artists, the majority of which were given by Reba and Dave Williams in 1999.

I wish to express our deepest gratitude to the Souls Grown Deep Foundation cofounder and former board president William S. Arnett and the foundation's board members, particularly Michael Sellman, for his ongoing support and remarkable insight into the work. Scott Browning, collection manager of the Souls Grown Deep Foundation, was very helpful throughout the process of selecting the group of works, and many thanks are merited to President Maxwell L. Anderson. At The Met I would also like to acknowledge Sheena Wagstaff, Leonard A. Lauder Chairman of Modern and Contemporary Art, who four years ago instigated the effort to bring this gift into the collection. Former Met curators Robert Nicholas Cullinan and Marla Prather were integral to the selection process, with Prather serving as the originating curator of the exhibition. Randall R. Griffey, Curator in the Department of Modern and Contemporary Art, and Amelia Peck, Marica F. Vilcek Curator of American Decorative Arts in the American Wing, saw through the exhibition's execution and contributed essays to this catalogue. Finally, I would like to thank The Andrew W. Mellon Foundation, whose support helped to bring this important publication to life.

As our nation continues to wrestle with the complex, painful history and present-day reality of discrimination along the lines of race, gender, religion, immigration status, and more, in addition to the stark financial inequities endemic to the postindustrial economy, these affecting works of contemporary American art offer cause for deep reflection and a means of fostering increased understanding. In so doing, this collection fulfills two of the highest functions art can serve.

Daniel H. Weiss
President and CEO
The Metropolitan Museum of Art

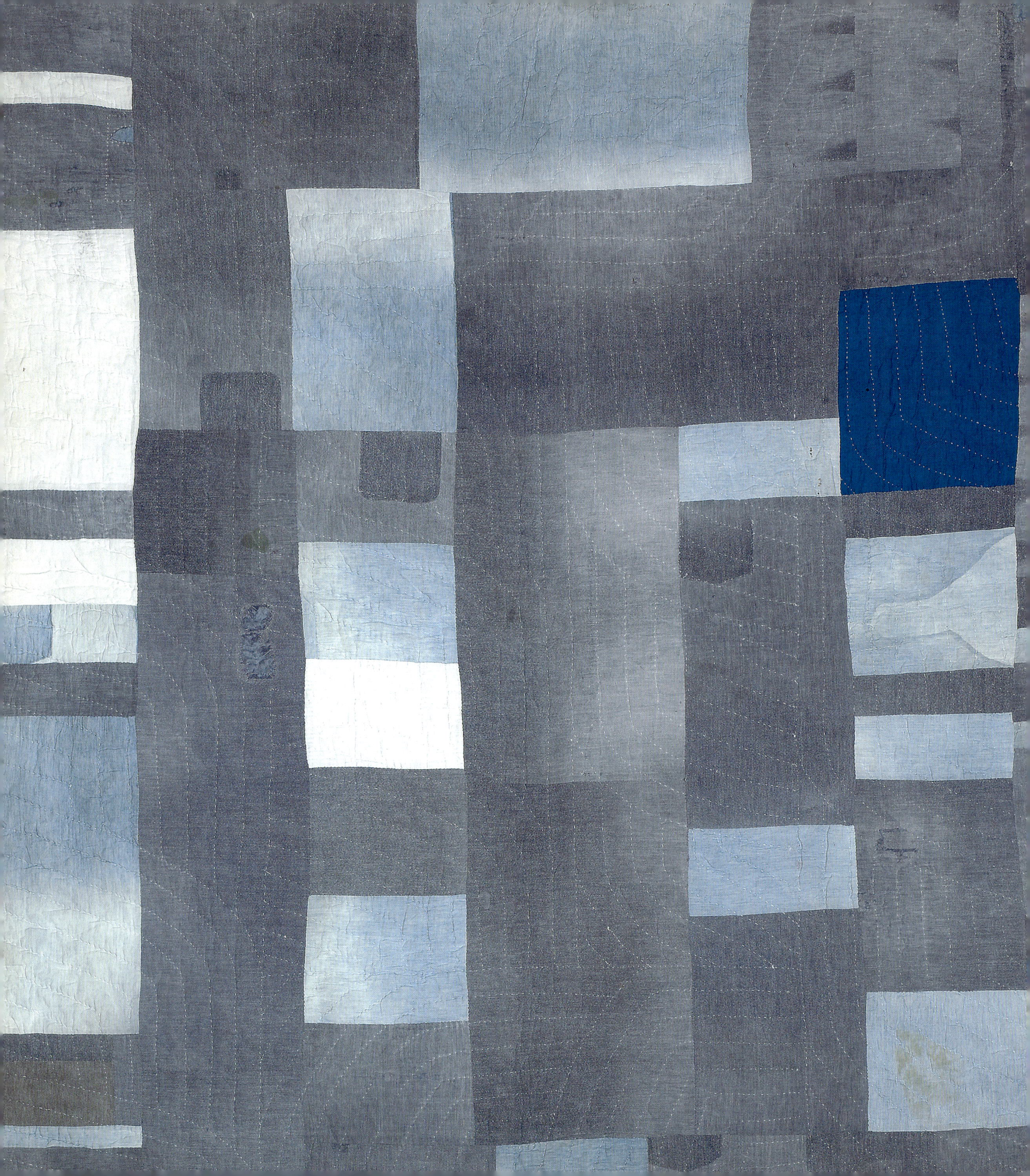

ACKNOWLEDGMENTS

It has been an honor and a privilege to work with, learn from, and share the extraordinary sculptures, assemblages, paintings, and quilts in the Souls Grown Deep Foundation gift to The Metropolitan Museum of Art.

First and foremost, we wish to echo President Daniel H. Weiss's thanks to the Souls Grown Deep Foundation. To bring the catalogue and the exhibition "History Refused to Die" to fruition at The Met, we are indebted to many of the Museum's talented and dedicated staff members. Sheena Wagstaff, Leonard A. Lauder Chairman of Modern and Contemporary Art, initiated this gift for the collection, with the intent of stretching its parameters with a lesser-known story of American art within the broad scope of twentieth-century art history. Former curators Robert Nicholas Cullinan and Marla Prather were essential to the selection process. We extend our gratitude to Pari Stave, Senior Administrator; Cynthia Iavarone, Collections Manager; Rebecca Tilghman, Collections Specialist; Anthony Askin, Supervising Departmental Technician; Jeff Elliott, Senior Departmental Technician; and Sandie Peters and Brooks Shaver, Principal Departmental Technicians, all in the Department of Modern and Contemporary Art. We would also like to thank, in the American Wing, Sylvia Yount, Lawrence A. Fleischman Curator in Charge; Leela Outcalt, Senior Collections Manager; Sean Farrell, Supervising Departmental Technician; Dennis Kaiser, Principal Departmental Technician; and Chad Lemke and Mary Beth Orr, Senior Departmental Technicians, for their expertise in installing quilts.

Because many of the works in the gift are made of nontraditional and sometimes fragile materials, we especially relied on the expertise of colleagues in the Museum's conservation departments, particularly Isabelle Duvernois, Conservator for paintings; Rachel Mustalish, Conservator for drawings; and Kendra Roth, Conservator for objects. The quilts were studied and prepared for exhibition by Kristine Kamiya, Conservator; Christina B. Carr, Conservator; and Yael Rosenfield, Associate Conservator. Appreciation is also extended to Quincy Houghton, Deputy Director for Exhibitions, and her team, including Rachel Ferrante, Exhibitions Project Manager, and Sophie Golub, Assistant for Administration. Aileen Chuk, Chief Registrar, and Bryanna O'Mara, Associate Registrar, coordinated many necessary viewings of works in the collection over the course of manuscript and exhibition preparation. Zoe Alexandra Florence, Senior Exhibition Designer, and Chelsea Amato, Graphic Designer, combined their talents to create the exhibition's elegant design.

For the publication, we thank Mark Polizzotti, Publisher and Editor in Chief; Gwen Roginsky, Associate Publisher and General Manager of Publications; Peter Antony, Chief Production Manager; and Michael Sittenfeld, Senior Managing Editor. We are grateful as well to other members of the Publications and Editorial Department who were indispensable to this book: Anne Rebecca Blood, Assistant Managing Editor; Sophia Bruneau, Editorial Coordinator; Elizabeth De Mase, Image Acquisition Manager; Kamilah Foreman, Senior Editor; Lauren Knighton, Production Manager; and Briana Parker, Associate Editor. The volume's beautiful design is the work of Bethany Johns. Jayne Kuchna, independent bibliographer, edited the notes and selected readings.

Our coauthors Cheryl Finley, Associate Professor of Art History, Cornell University, Ithaca, New York, and novelist and essayist Darryl Pinckney contributed illuminating essays. Museum Fellow Aleesa Pitchamarn Alexander, who closely studied the artists included in the Souls Grown Deep Foundation gift, improved this publication in numerous ways.

This catalogue and exhibition are part of a series of incredibly rewarding collaborations between curators from the Department of Modern and Contemporary Art and the American Wing. This collegial spirit, a special feature of The Met's rich curatorial resources, allows us to present to our visitors works of art like those in the Souls Grown Deep Foundation gift in all their dazzling complexity. We are grateful for this new inclusivity both in our daily work and its resultant impact on our permanent collection. This catalogue and exhibition attest to the expansive vision of The Metropolitan Museum of Art today.

Randall R. Griffey, Curator, Modern and Contemporary Art
Amelia Peck, Marica F. Vilcek Curator of American Decorative Arts, The American Wing

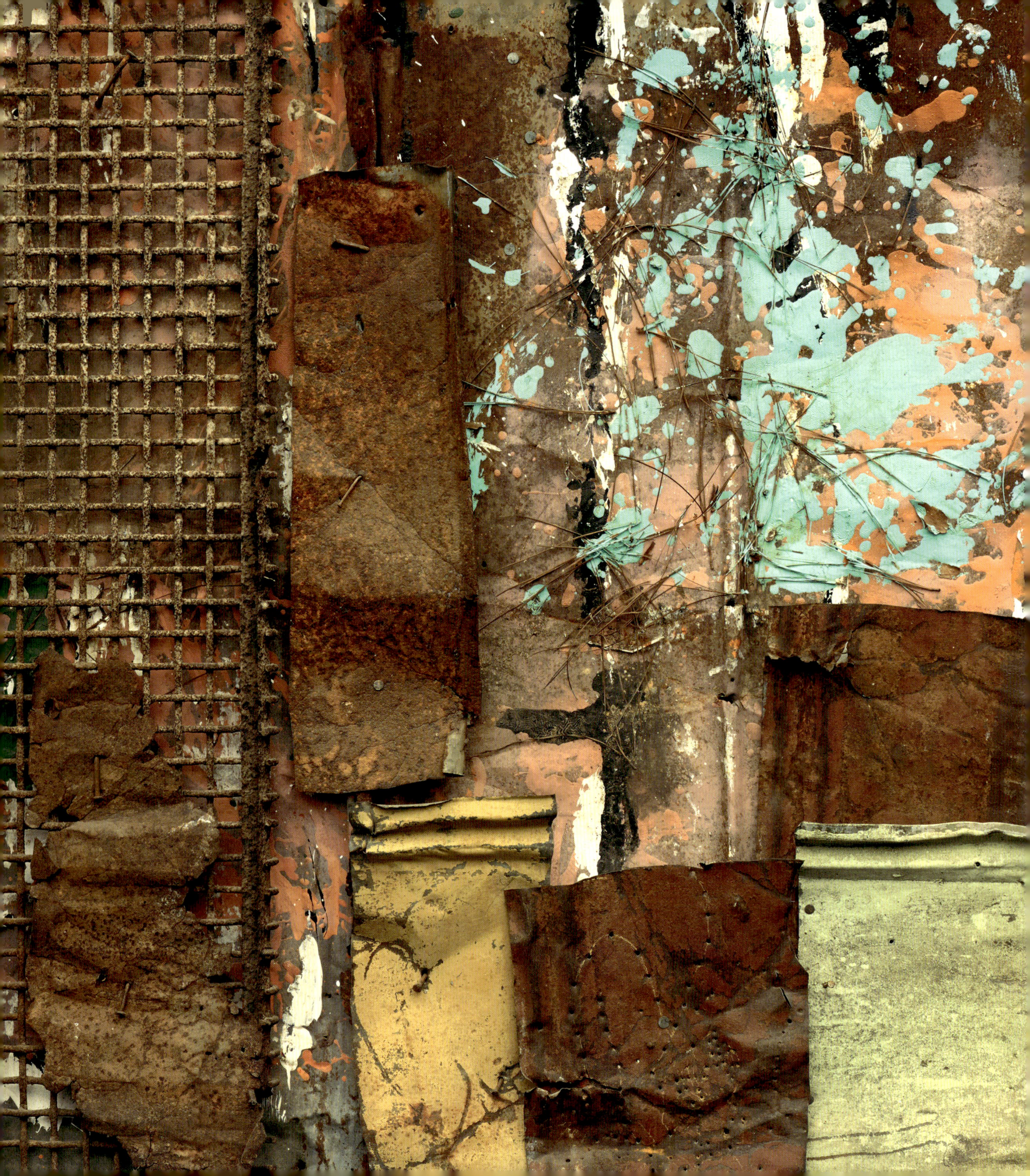

THE NEGRO SPEAKS OF RIVERS

I've known rivers:
I've known rivers ancient as the world and older than the
flow of human blood in human veins.

My soul has grown deep like the rivers.

I bathed in the Euphrates when dawns were young.
I built my hut near the Congo and it lulled me to sleep.
I looked upon the Nile and raised the pyramids above it.
I heard the singing of the Mississippi when Abe Lincoln
went down to New Orleans, and I've seen its muddy
bosom turn all golden in the sunset.

I've known rivers:
Ancient, dusky rivers.

My soul has grown deep like the rivers.

LANGSTON HUGHES

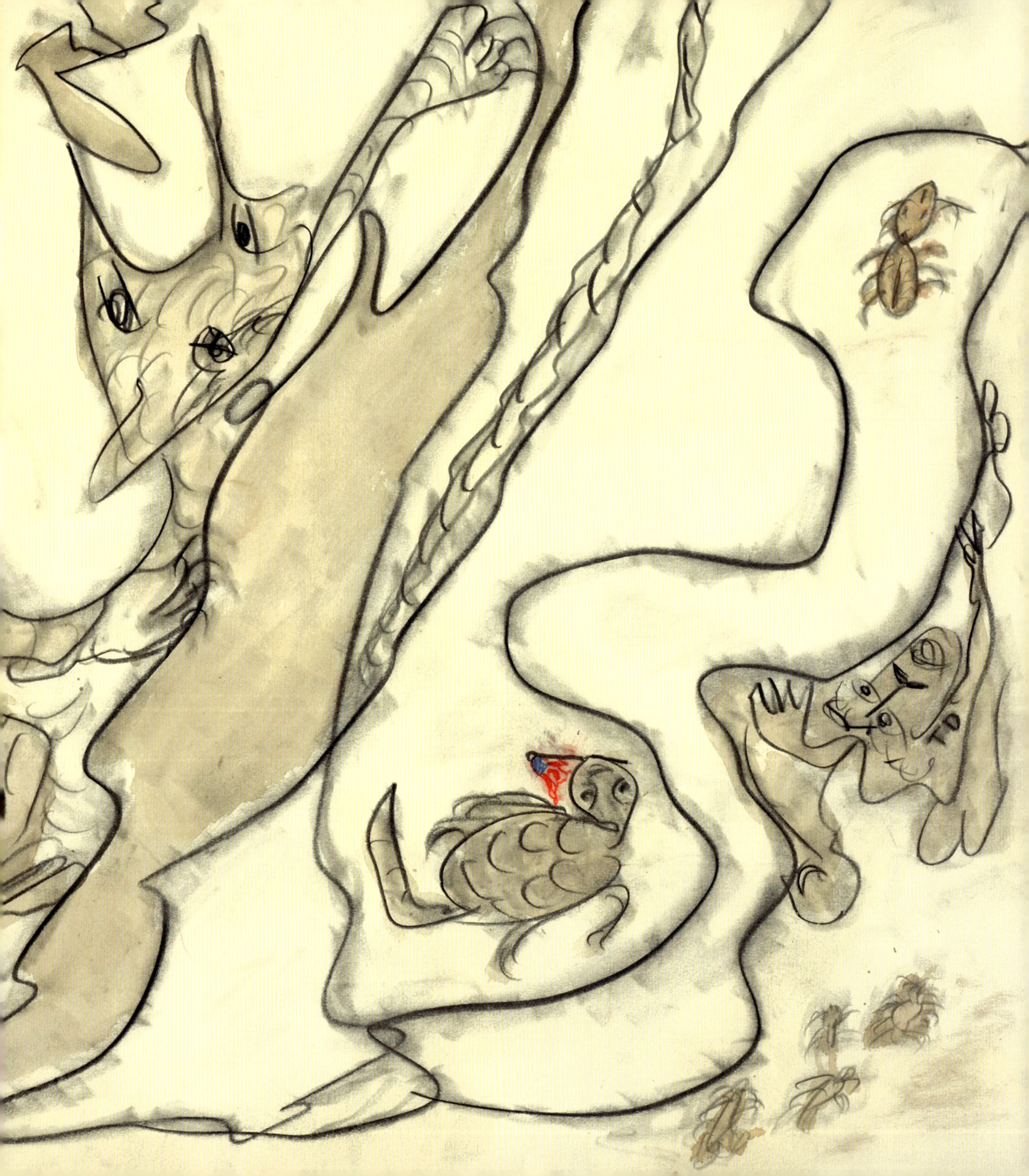

INTRODUCTION: TROUBLING THE WATERS

CHERYL FINLEY

Simply titled *January 20, 2009* (2009, pl. 12), an abstract drawing by Thornton Dial composed of graphite, pastel, and coffee quietly celebrates the inauguration of America's first black president, Barack Obama. In contrast, a sculpture of pitchforks and shovels welded out of found metal enshrines in gold the backbreaking tools of *Four Hundred Years of Free Labor* (1995, pl. 6), a monument to the legacies of slavery, by Joe Minter. These are just two of the fifty-seven works of art in this volume, celebrating the landmark 2014 gift from the Souls Grown Deep Foundation to The Metropolitan Museum of Art. Established in 2010 by the Atlanta-based collector William S. Arnett, the Souls Grown Deep Foundation was established to bring greater recognition to little-known black artists working in the southeastern United States through the production of new scholarship (documentation, exhibitions, and publications) and targeted institutional placement.[1] Consisting of fifty-seven works across various media—painting, drawing, and sculpture by Dial, Minter, Lonnie Holley, Mose Tolliver, and Purvis Young, among others, as well as twenty quilts from the female artist collective the Gee's Bend quilt makers—this is the largest single gift of art made by African Americans presented to The Met to date. The works were executed over a nearly eighty-five-year span, from 1930 to 2013, by artists living in primarily poor, rural parts of the American South, including Georgia, Alabama, Tennessee, Mississippi, and Florida, and thus bring to The Met and New York a distinct regional, economic, and racial perspective on American art that is both timely and worthy of further consideration. Part of a larger nationwide effort to raise institutional and public awareness for this important yet overlooked work, the Souls Grown Deep Foundation donation serves to broaden The Met's holdings of American art.[2]

Nearly thirty years prior to the establishment of the foundation, three exhibitions of note introduced the work of some of the same artists and produced pioneering scholarship that remains relevant today. "More than Land or Sky: Art from Appalachia" (1981–82), organized by the Smithsonian American Art Museum, Washington, D.C., included work by Holley.[3] Another traveling exhibition key to this genealogy, "Black Folk Art in America, 1930–1980" (1982–83), which began at the Corcoran Gallery of Art, also in Washington, featured work by William Edmondson (1874–1951), Tolliver, and Bill Traylor. The formative touring exhibition "Black Art, Ancestral Legacy: The African Impulse in African-American Art" (1989–91), organized by Alvia J. Wardlaw with Maureen McKenna at the Dallas Museum of Art, stressed the connections and continuities between African and African American art and practice.[4] The catalogue included, among others, art historian Robert Farris Thompson's influential essay, "The Song That Named the Land," which introduced the kind of environmental installations or "yard art" shows for which Holley and Emmer Sewell are well known.[5] Exhibitions such as these acknowledged the work of these African American artists from the South on the national stage for the first time and lay the groundwork for Arnett as he built a collection that would eventually become the Souls Grown Deep Foundation.

While nearly all of the artists in the collection are self-taught, with no apparent formal training from art schools, branded or otherwise, each has a sensibility, a certain style, and a keen awareness about whom and what to portray, when and how. Dial is the most recognized artist of the collection, with ten works at The Met.[6] A native of Emelle, Alabama, he was often inspired by historic and current events and composed drawings in response even as they unfolded. Drawings such as *January 20, 2009* and *9/11: Interrupting the Morning News* (2002, pl. 13) demonstrate the artist's agile hand at memorializing significant moments in American history using nontraditional materials such as coffee for pigment. These works drive home the fact that although he lived in Alabama, Dial was certainly neither shut off from (or naive about) national and world events—see his rigorous, multimedia assemblage *Victory in Iraq* (2004, pl. 14)—nor incapable of making bold statements about them. Other mixed-media works pay homage to the vestiges of African culture and the memory of slavery, such as *Shadows of the Field* (2008), an earth-toned composition made of wood, burlap, twine, and sheet metal, or *History Refused to Die* (2004, pl. 8), which uses okra stalks and roots to signal the crop's arrival in the Americas from West Africa with the transatlantic slave trade and its continuing presence in African American cuisine. Adept at sourcing other raw materials collected from his surroundings, including corrugated steel, tin, raw hewn wood, plant life, and discarded objects made of plastic and other nonbiodegradable materials, Dial's assemblages are massive, some as big as eight feet square. Yet his seasoned manipulation of these often-worn materials gives them new meaning and vibrant possibility.

Probably the most familiar works in this catalogue, twenty examples by sixteen different women, are the product of the Gee's Bend quilt makers. These multicolored, highly designed textiles have been the subject of critically and internationally acclaimed traveling exhibitions, such as "The Quilts of Gee's Bend" (2002–8) and "Gee's Bend: The Architecture of the Quilt" (2006–8).[7] The quilts were described as "eye-poppingly gorgeous" by *New York Times* art critic Michael Kimmelman, who called the seventy-two works in the former show "declarations of style, flags of independence hung to dry on wire lines for the neighbors or anyone else to see."[8] Their titles, such as *Nine-Block Quilt* (1930s, pl. 45) by Martha Pettway and *Housetop and Bricklayer with Bars* quilt (ca. 1955, pl. 34) by Lucy T. Pettway, describe the dominant visible patterns of the quilts and link them to a larger history of American quilt design. Additionally, works such as the denim and cotton twill *Blocks and Strips work-clothes quilt* (ca. 1950, pl. 36) by Emma Lee Pettway Campbell (1928–2002) and the denim and corduroy *Strip Medallion quilt* (1976, pl. 37) by Annie Mae Young evoke the strip-cloth construction and patterning of West African textiles found in The Met's collection and foreshadow the work of Ghanaian contemporary assemblage artist El Anatsui (fig. 1).[9]

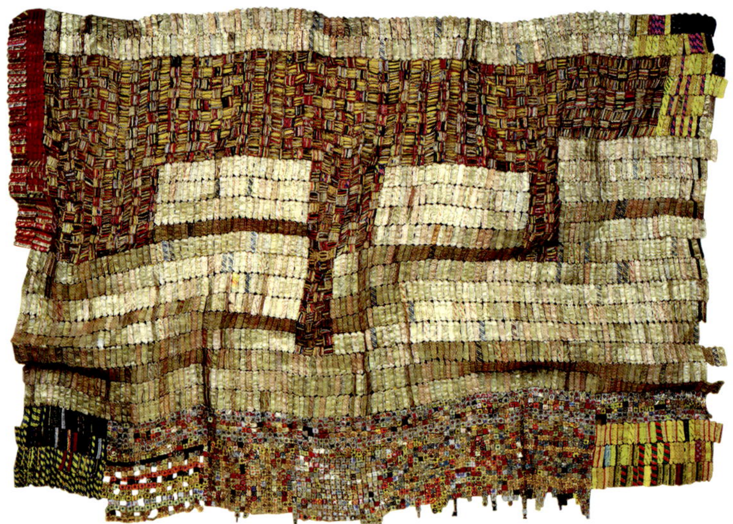

Fig. 1. **El Anatsui**, *Between Earth and Heaven*, 2006

ARTISTIC CONNECTIONS

Once again dismissing the claim that these artists lack formal training or knowledge of mainstream histories of art, one might instead consider the connections that some artists in the Souls Grown Deep gift had to *one another* as well as their familiarity with a larger coterie of artists and genres. Ronald Lockett, who died of AIDS at the young age of thirty-three, was a protégé of Dial's. Lockett's works using corrugated tin, a cheap and familiar housing material found in economically deprived areas of the rural South, came from a dilapidated structure on Dial's property. *The Enemy Amongst Us* (1995, pl. 3), Lockett's mixed-media assemblage, combines rusted and worn scraps of metal, pine needles, nails, and paint on wood in an emotional composition that might now carry the weight of his untimely demise.

Tolliver's *Bill Traylor People* (1987, pl. 1) is the artist's homage to the Montgomery-based illustrator born into slavery who completed the majority of his more than fifteen hundred drawings there (also Tolliver's hometown) between about 1935 and 1949.[10] Traylor's works were championed for their simple depictions of everyday people, animals, and scenes gleaned from his perch on lively Monroe Street in Montgomery. Tolliver emulates Traylor's recognizable stylistic tendencies in his painting of two men, notably their flattened geometric figures and relationship to the picture plane (fig. 2). Executed in house paint on wood, the work features an economy of materials that mirrors Traylor's own creative use of scant available resources—tempera, cardboard, charcoal, and pencil (which created a familiar, recurring color palette and texture associated with the artist based on the availability of materials)—and underscores how black artists have cleverly and successfully challenged economic adversity, turning what some might consider a hardship owing to scarce supplies into meaningful works of art.

Working together over several decades, the Gee's Bend quilt makers share familial connections as sisters, mothers, daughters, granddaughters, cousins, and aunties—representing four generations of women sharing a mnemonic aesthetic committed to textile artistry. That these quilts form a definitive corpus of black women's artistic practice reaching back to the pre-Emancipation era is echoed by artistic foremothers in geometric lines present in their abstract designs as well as legacies of shared patterns and styles dating back to quilts made by black women during slavery.[11] With formal ties to West African textile making, these ancestral and artistic connections have enabled the Gee's Bend quilt makers to thrive, even to this day, serving as unlikely, shining examples of an African American

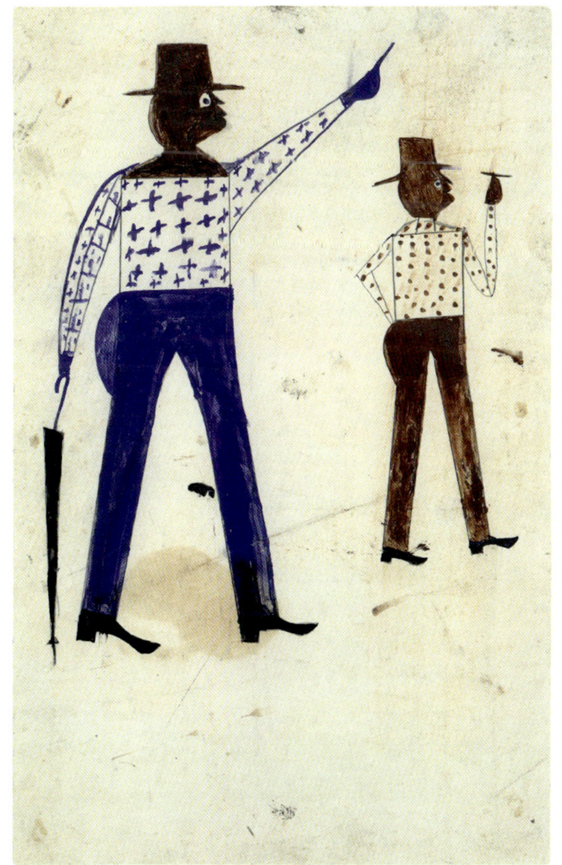

Fig. 2. **Bill Traylor**, *Two Men Walking*, ca. 1939–43

artistic tradition now taught in grade-school textbooks and traveling exhibitions and celebrated by special-issue postage stamps.[12] The first examples of this extraordinary collective's enduring handwork to be collected by The Met, they offer new pathways to interpreting other American and African textiles as well as modern works of art in the museum's collections.

CHALLENGING ADVERSITY

One defining factor identifying these artists, other than race or geographic location, is economic background. Nearly all were subject to generations of severe socioeconomic deprivation, poverty, and racism, little or no education, and a lack of basic mental and physical hygiene resources. Not to be discounted, the socioeconomic backgrounds of the artists helped shape their aesthetic choices, and they also offer another lens through which these and other works in The Met's holdings might be considered, possibly for the first time. That is, taking into account how poverty affected not only the formal qualities of the works but also the artists' lives, potential, and productivity presents a new criterion of value for a mainstream art institution whose collections overwhelmingly favor formally trained artists of some means, if not pedigree. This is something to consider in an age when institutions like The Met are leading the way in transforming and enhancing their collections, leadership, staff, exhibitions, programs, and curatorial choices to include a spectrum of diverse artists and thinkers, especially those who previously have been grossly underrepresented.

To be sure, a shared legacy of Jim Crow segregation, racial terror, and poverty affected the artists of the Souls Grown Deep gift, the subjects they portrayed, and the materials they used to execute their works. So too did the activism and struggle of the Civil Rights movement taking root there and in nearby urban centers such as Montgomery, Birmingham, Selma, Atlanta, Memphis, and Natchez, known for pivotal events and outspoken local and national leaders.[13] The women quilters of Gee's Bend were active in the movement, eager to march and register voters well before the winter 1965 visit of Dr. Martin Luther King Jr. to Gee's Bend, some sixty miles southwest of Montgomery, the state capital. They knew well of King, pastor of the Dexter Avenue Baptist Church in Montgomery from 1954 to 1960. Recall that Montgomery is the site of the 1955 bus boycott organized by King shortly after Rosa Parks's refusal to give up her seat on a city bus to a white man earlier that year. It is also the victorious culminating point of the bloody Selma to Montgomery March, a pivotal voting-rights protest held in March 1965 along the fifty-four-mile stretch of US 80, a highway named for Jefferson Davis, President of the Confederate States of America.

Contemporary tragedies and mounting racial violence in America also became subjects of the artists in this exhibition. Take Nellie Mae Rowe's *Atlanta's Missing Children* (1981, pl. 10), which treats the case of the mysterious murders of eighteen children and six adults that terrorized the city and the nation between 1979 and 1981. That painting and collage, executed in commercial paint, crayon, pastel, graphite, and ink, offers a visual meditation in a series of vignettes with indeterminate meaning during a period of pain and bewilderment in African American households nationwide. A tempera and graphite illustration by Georgia Speller, *Head of the Penitentiary*, depicts a buff, pink-skinned figure with beady eyes wearing blue uniform trousers. Adopting a power stance, he asserts his supremacy with arms akimbo before a boldly painted green-and-yellow wall. With obvious reference to the racialized brutality of prison life—unwarranted violence in the name of so-called reform often meted out by predominantly white prison guards along racial lines—this work also foreshadows the pervasive problems of today's prison industrial complex, which disproportionately and unfairly affects black Americans.[14]

FORMAL DOCUMENTS

The Souls Grown Deep Foundation's vast archives of documentary photographs lend another perspective on how the works on view in the Museum were experienced in the rural environments in which they initially were conceived and displayed. Images such as these play a crucial role in defining the specific place value of each work and the artist's particular regional working methodology. Take, for example, the site-specific photographs of Holley's assemblages surrounded by lush green trees and tangled vines (fig. 3). These documentary images fix a sense of the work in a certain time and place, referencing the landscape's power to provide malleable source material. Thompson and fellow art historian Lizzetta LeFalle-Collins both assert the power of place

Fig. 3. **Lonnie Holley**, *Dish of the Receiver*, 1983 (destroyed 1997)

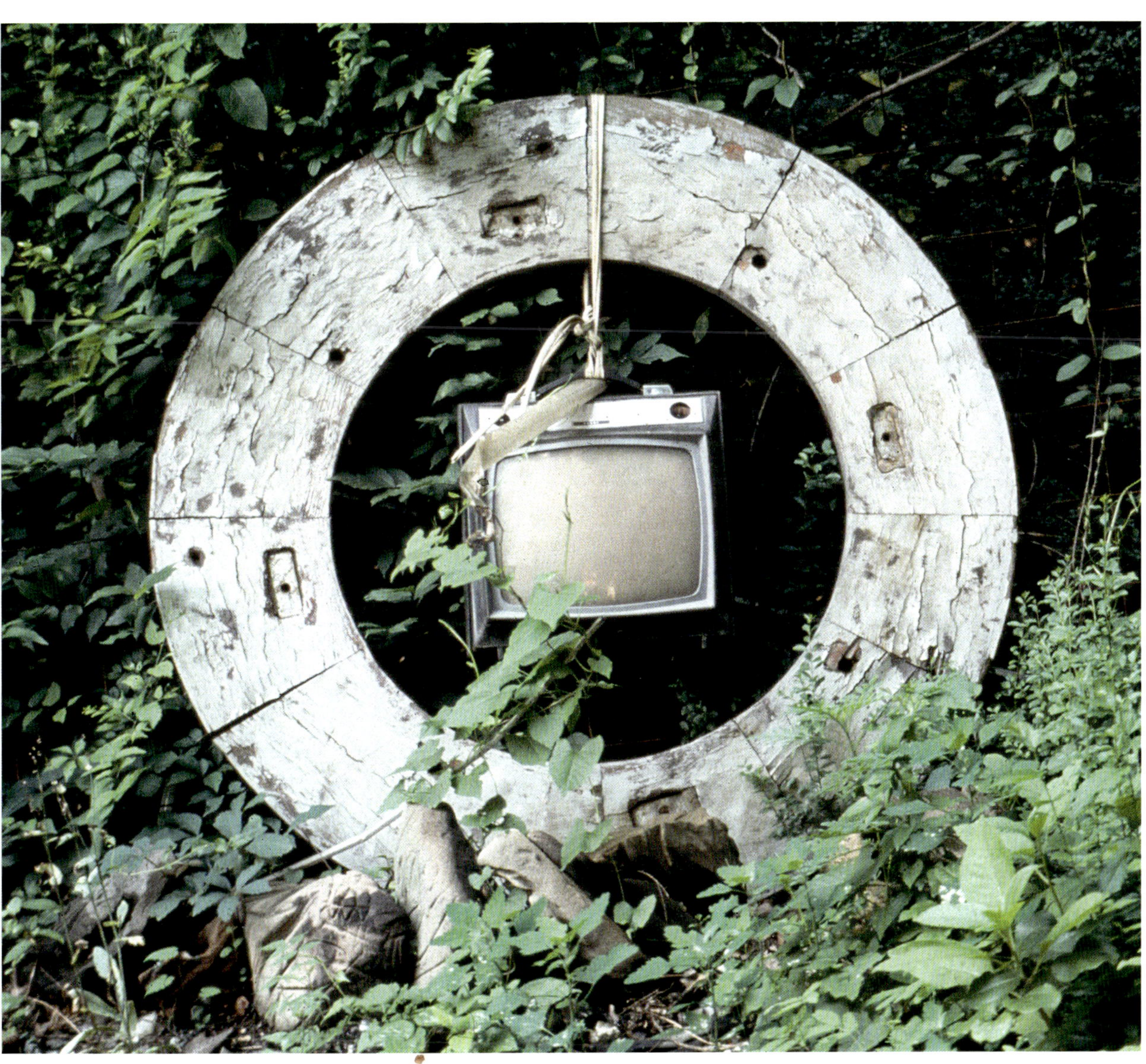

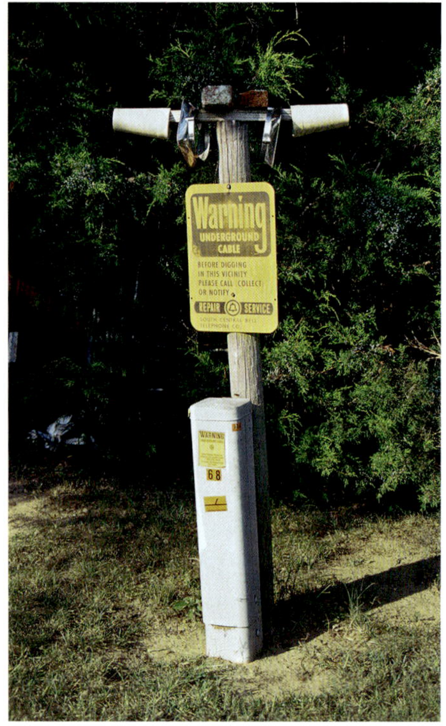

Fig. 4. **Emmer Sewell**, *Untitled*, 1998

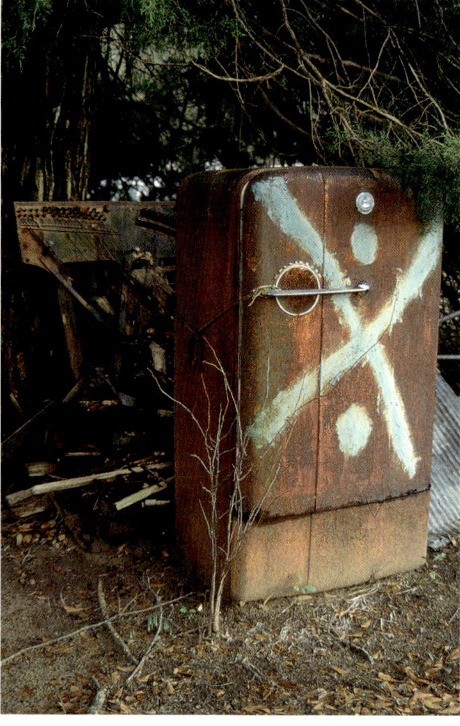

Fig. 5. **Emmer Sewell**, *Untitled (X Symbol)*, before 1997

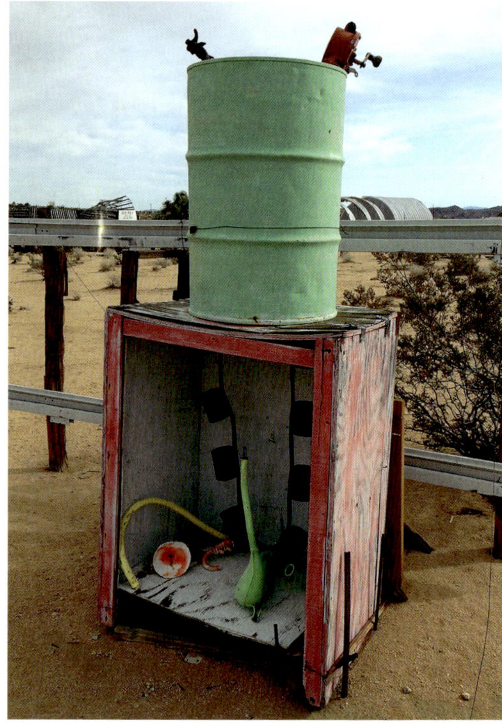

Fig. 6. **Noah Purifoy**, *Crank Pump*

inherent in works made by artists such as Holley and Sewell in the yard, if not *for* the yard, displayed in situ for the enjoyment of all. According to Thompson, "Many of the most famous traditional African-American artists of our time—Lonnie Holley, Mary T. Smith, Hawkins Bolden, Joe Light, Mose Tolliver, Henry Dorsey, Ralph Griffin, Nellie Mae Rowe, Sam Doyle, David Butler, and many more—caught the attention of art historians with their public yard-shows."[15] Sewell's sculptural and assemblage pieces provide several intriguing examples. A tightly cropped photograph of a signpost decorated by the artist with a wood bar, bricks, cups, and metal rings lends the appearance of bicycle handsles to an otherwise benign utility marker (fig. 4). An old, abandoned refrigerator the color of burnt orange rust emerges as a totem amid the pine brush adorned by Sewell's simple yet symbolic white spray paint markings (fig. 5). Together, some of these documentary images convey the artists' aesthetic choices literally emerging from the landscape that defines them, whether natural or riddled by discarded, man-made objects. In the case of Sewell, whose environmental assemblages were conceived in her yard, carefully arranged plastic chairs or abandoned objects reveal the photograph's role as document or evidence of a performance. Shown outdoors instead of in a white cube, these environmental works also reference the late assemblages of Noah Purifoy, the Chouinard Art Institute–trained sculptor and arts educator who spent the last fifteen years of his life working on sculptures of found objects in the California desert (fig. 6).[16] Now part of the Noah Purifoy Foundation's permanent site-specific installation of the late artist's assemblages, these prescient works were ahead of their time in

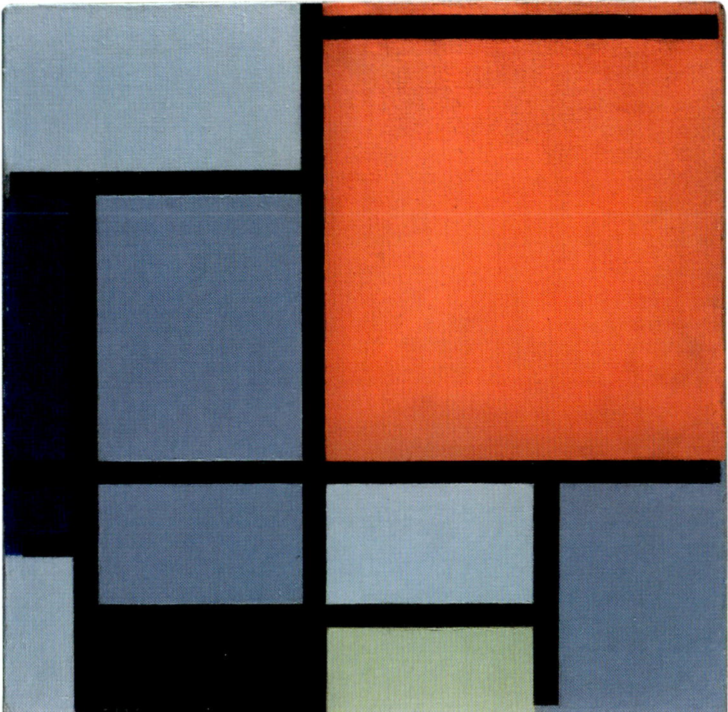

Fig. 7. **Piet Mondrian**, *Composition*, 1921

more ways than one: methodologically, formally, and site-specifically. For Sewell, Holley, and Purifoy, the relationship of their man-made work to the natural environment was paramount.

From a formal point of view, some of the artworks from the Souls Grown Deep gift might be compared to works by European and European American artists. For example, Sewell's *Untitled* (1990, pl. 2), composed of an automobile tire, plastic chair, and cinder block fragment, in its architectural simplicity and symmetry echoes the readymades of Marcel Duchamp (1887–1968), while a handful of Dial's works heavily loaded with found objects have a sensibility that recalls that of Robert Rauschenberg. Even the quilts of the Gee's Bend collective, notably Louisiana P. Bendolph's *Housetop quilt* (2003, pl. 27) seem to conjure the recurring color palette and geometric patterns of *Composition* (1921, fig. 7), an early example of the Dutch artist Piet Mondrian's increasingly abstract paintings, one which was noted for its reference to jazz rhythms and patterns in West African strip cloth.[17] But other works in the gift also engender stylistic comparisons with the works of black, Los Angeles–based artists working in the late 1960s and early 1970s, who relied on found objects to create poignant works of sculpture, often in conversation with the turbulent times of the Civil Rights and Black Liberation movements. Of note, the assemblage works of Purifoy and David Hammons (born 1943), such as the mixed-media *Bird* (1973), formally resonate with those of Minter and Holley, such as *Four Hundred Years of Free Labor* (1995, pl. 6) and *Grown Together in the Midst of the Foundation* (1994, pl. 9), respectively. These cross-currents of formal observations lend particular weight to the works in the Souls Grown Deep gift, highlighting their potential in the able hands of Met curators and educators to trouble the waters of the art world in years to come.

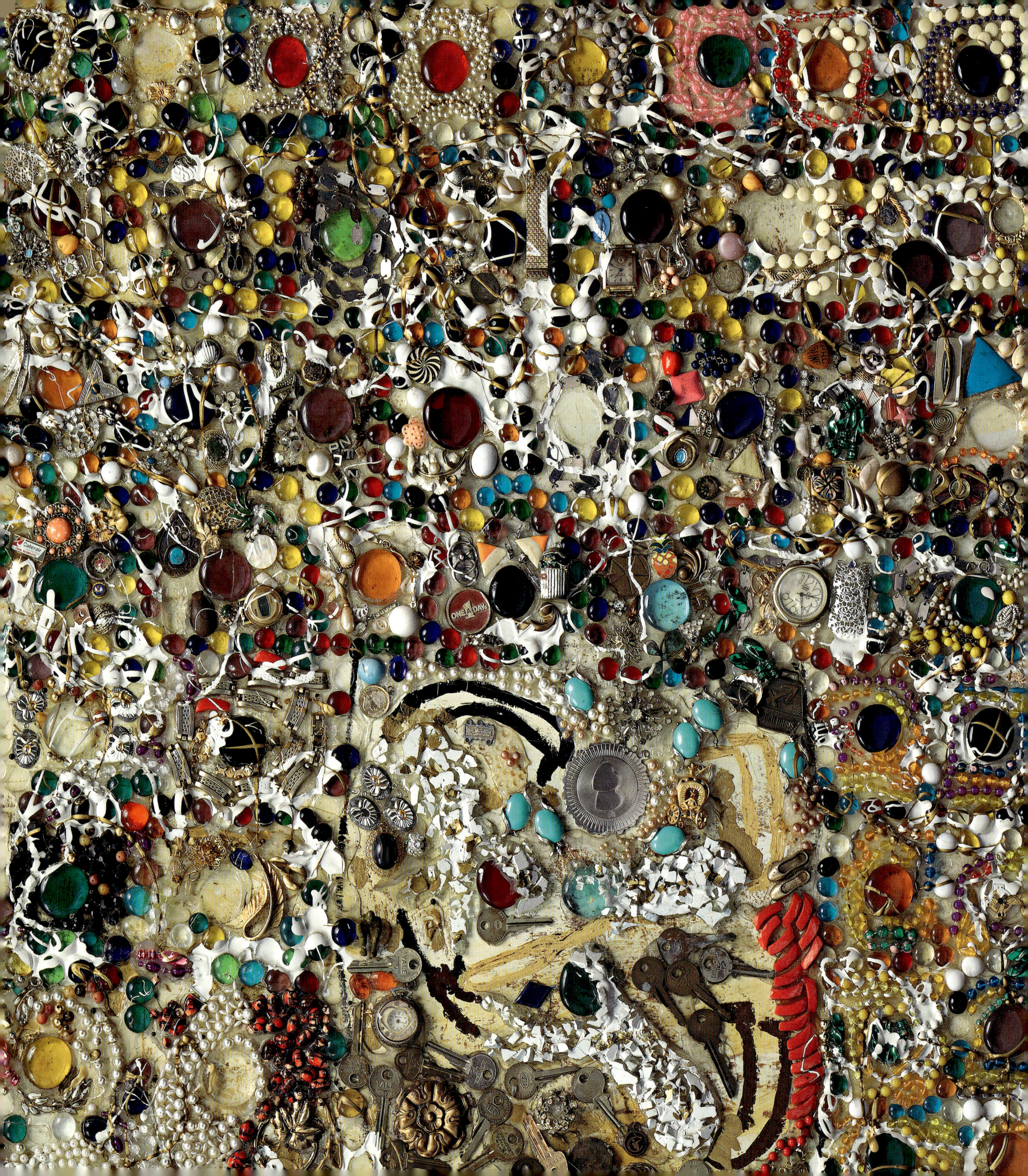
ONE A DAY

SELF-TAUGHT AND MODERN

RANDALL R. GRIFFEY

The arrival of a group of fifty-seven works by self-trained contemporary artists from the American South into the collection of The Metropolitan Museum of Art, a gift from the Souls Grown Deep Foundation, complicates the already-complex notion of so-called outsider art. For years, art historians have struggled to identify the most accurate and appropriate means of describing work produced by painters and sculptors working outside urban art capitals and without traditional academic artistic training. They have debated a range of nuanced adjectives and categories—"outsider," "folk," "self-taught," "vernacular"—each fraught with similar assumptions about the relationship between "high" and "low" culture and, in different ways, each exposing the power of authority to define the center and the margins of society.[1] This essay uses "self-taught" and "self-trained," as they grant agency to the artist.

Amid what historian Didi Barrett and others have described as "term warfare," many museums have expanded their programs to include work by contemporary self-trained artists.[2] In this regard, The Met's presentation of the gift from the Souls Grown Deep Foundation exists on a trajectory of exhibitions and related activities over the past thirty or so years. Critical to this history was a groundbreaking show, "Black Folk Art in America, 1930–1980," which toured seven venues across the country in 1982 and 1983.[3] Among the twenty artists whose work the exhibition brought to widespread public attention for the first time were Nellie Mae Rowe and Mose Tolliver (pl. 1), two artists included in the

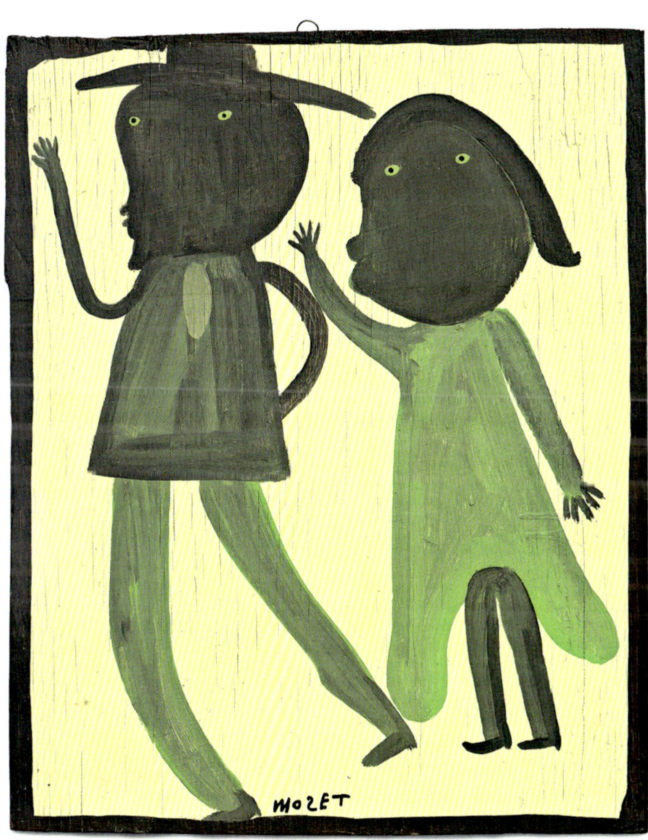

Pl. 1. **Mose Tolliver**, *Bill Traylor People*, 1987

Souls Grown Deep gift. Writing in the accompanying catalogue, exhibition curator Jane Livingston testified to the aesthetic merit and cultural significance of Southern folk art, claiming that, distinct from mere "craft," it represented a "truly formed American style which requires analysis and authentication as such."[4] An institutional watershed followed about a decade later, when, in 1994, the High Museum of Art in Atlanta founded its Folk Art Department, the first such department in a general art museum in the United States. The dedication of an endowed curatorial position for this area in 2014 deepened the High's commitment to self-taught art. Also critical to this history has been the advocacy of art historian and patron William S. Arnett, who began collecting work by Southern artists in the 1970s. In 2010, Arnett founded the Souls Grown Deep Foundation, which has supported and promoted dozens of exhibitions and publications dedicated to such artists as Thornton Dial, Ronald Lockett, and the quilters of Gee's Bend, Alabama, whose works are represented in the foundation's gift to The Met. Particularly now that works by these artists reside in the Museum's collection, among others included in the gift, the term "outsider" seems especially inadequate to describe them.

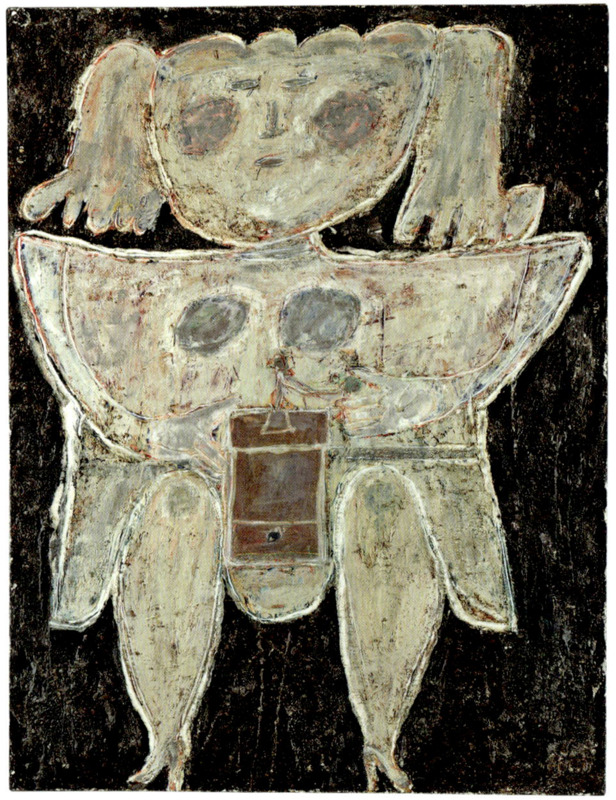

Fig. 8. **Jean Dubuffet**, *Woman Grinding Coffee*, 1945

As a new collection area within The Met, contemporary self-taught art extends the Museum's substantial historical holdings of works by untrained artists, both European and American, from the nineteenth and early twentieth centuries. In this context, Dial, Lockett, and others take their places alongside French artists Henri Rousseau (1844–1910), perhaps the most renowned European self-taught painter, and Jean Dubuffet (fig. 8), who coined the term "Art Brut," or "raw art," to describe and celebrate artistic creations that fall outside conventional academic traditions, including the art of children and the mentally ill. The reception among museums and galleries of self-taught artists associated with Souls Grown Deep has been predicated in part on the widespread institutional embrace and endorsement of Art Brut and its aesthetic and cultural merits.[5] Additionally, The Met's acquisition of work by this group of self-taught artists puts their art into dialogue with many nineteenth- and twentieth-century self-taught American painters. These include Baltimore portraitist Joshua Johnson (fig. 9); Edward Hicks (fig. 10), remembered for his variations on the theme of the messianic prophecy, the Peaceable Kingdom; Horace Pippin (fig. 11), likely the most famous modern American "folk" artist; and John Kane (fig. 12), who, during his lifetime critics dubbed the "American Rousseau" for his scenes painted in and around his adopted hometown of Pittsburgh. Throughout the early twentieth century, art historians, gallery owners, and museums often promoted these artists as uniquely American because their work appeared free from European influences and traditions.

Many works in the Souls Grown Deep gift are striking for the degree to which they seem conversant with practices and ideas associated with canonical—and decidedly blue-chip—modern and contemporary art.

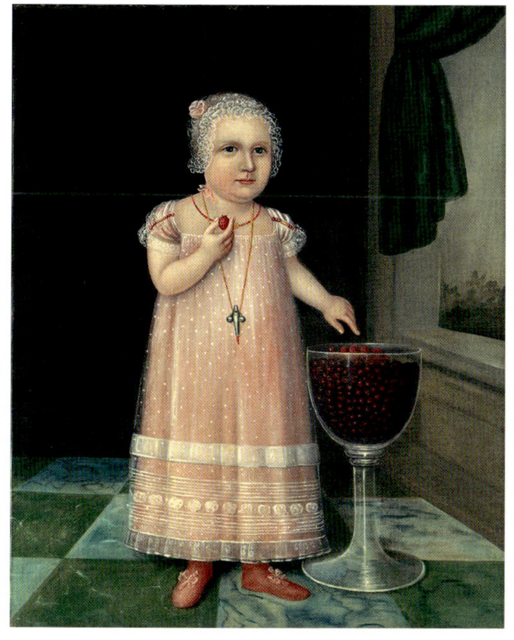

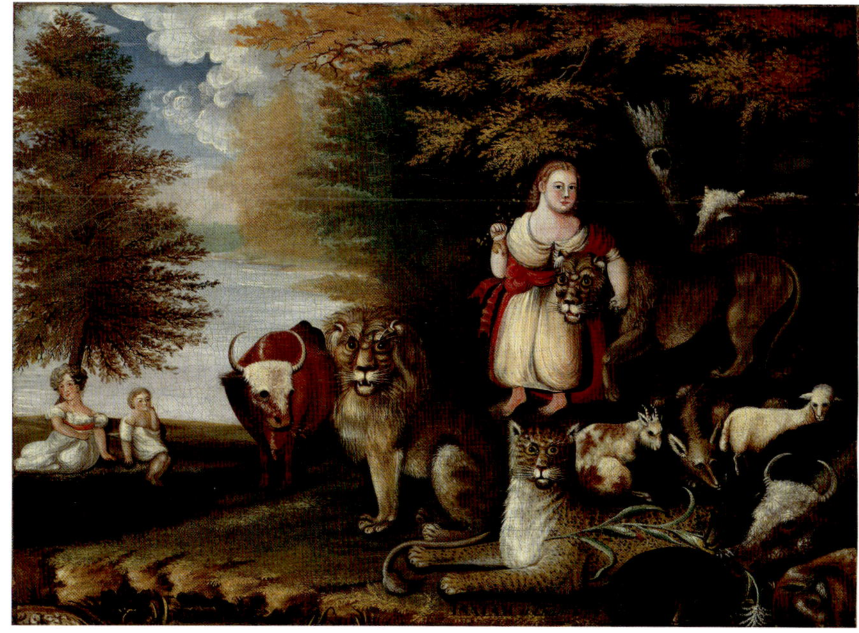

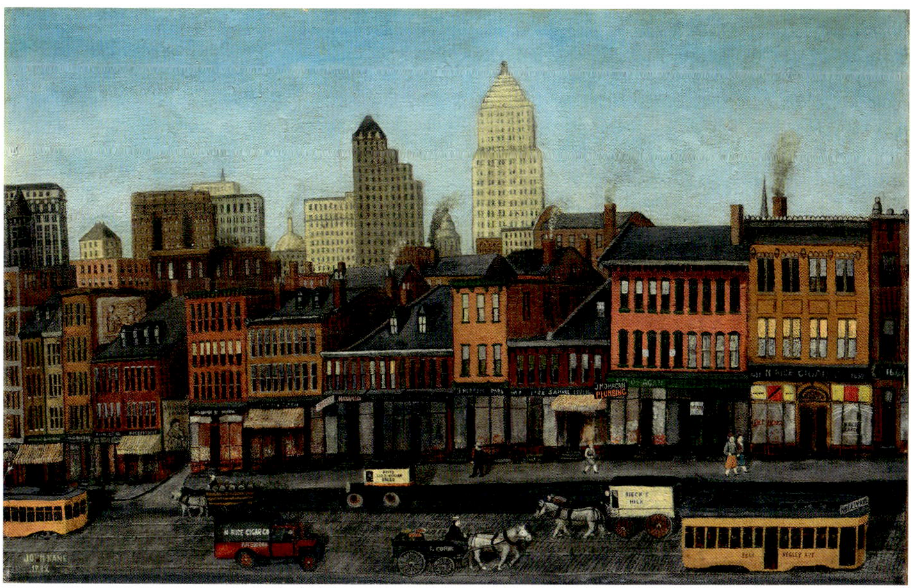

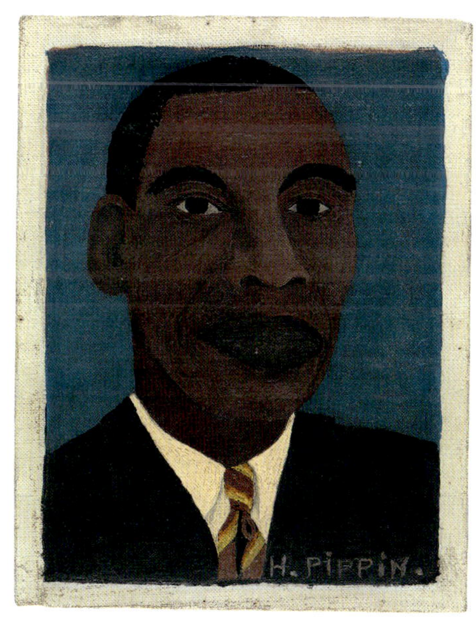

(clockwise from top left)

Fig. 9. **Joshua Johnson**, *Emma Van Name*, ca. 1805

Fig. 10. **Edward Hicks**, *Peaceable Kingdom*, ca. 1830–32

Fig. 11. **Horace Pippin**, *Self-Portrait II*, 1944

Fig. 12. **John Kane**, *From My Studio Window*, 1932

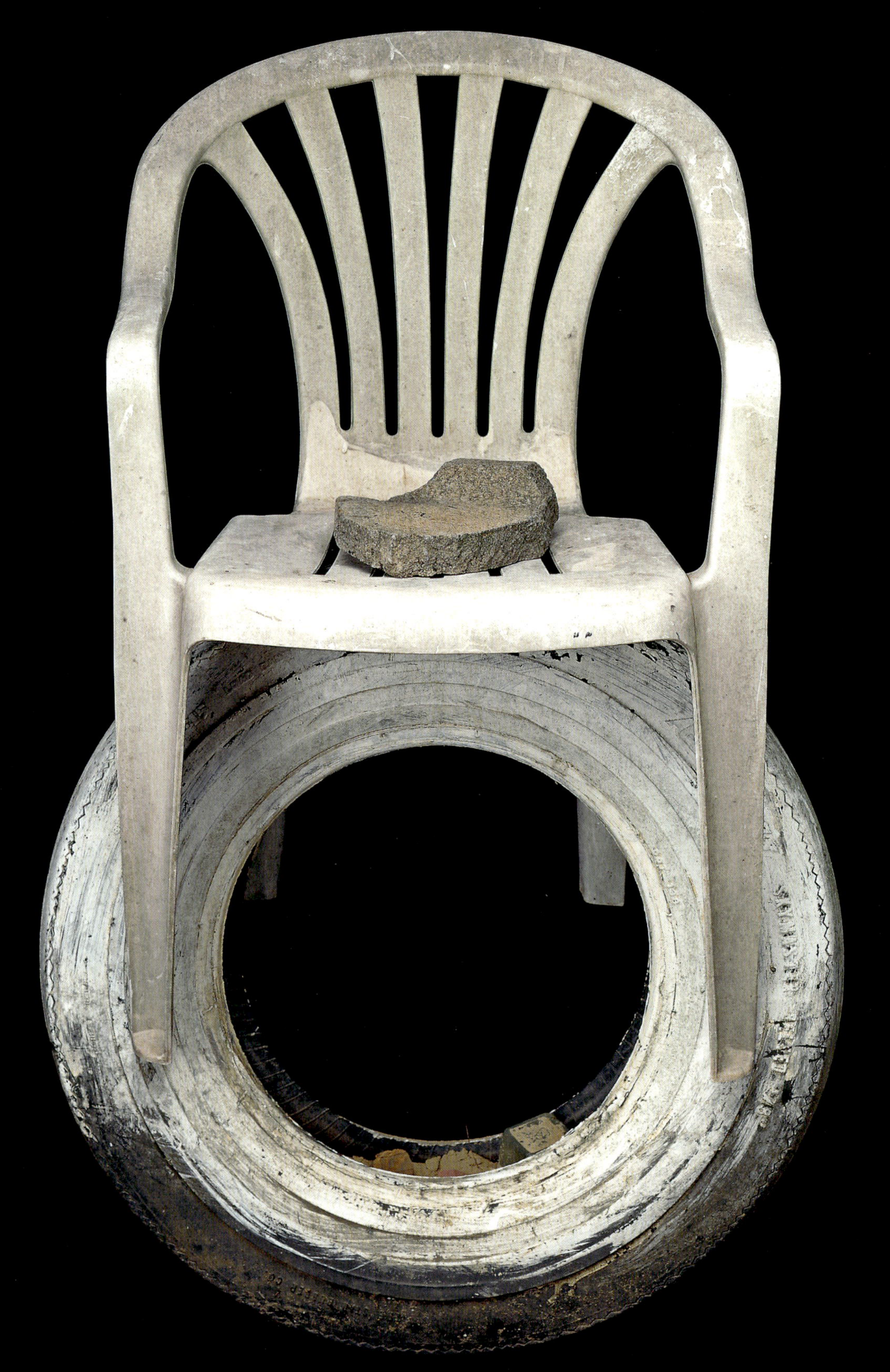

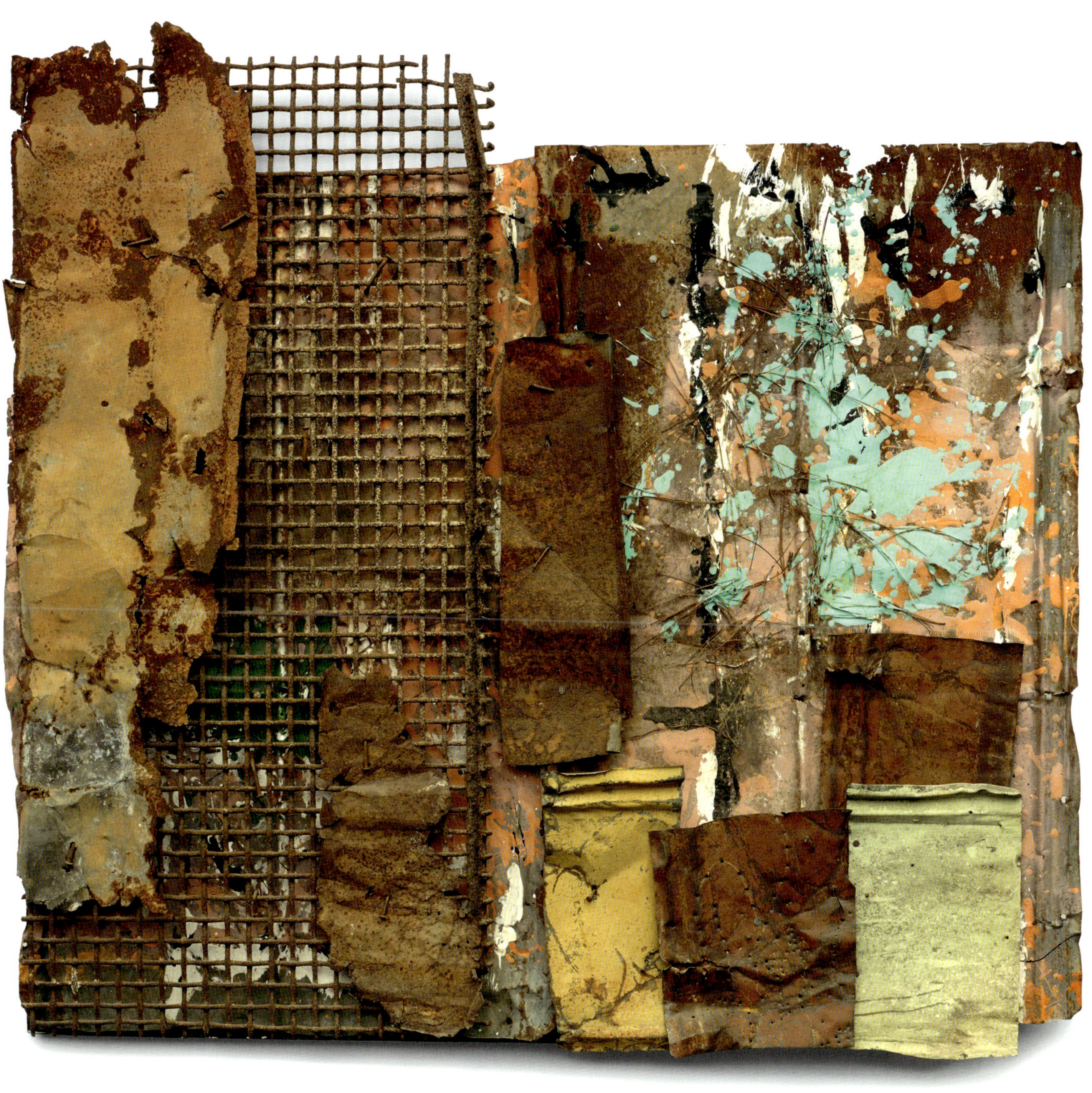

(opposite) Pl. 2. **Emmer Sewell**, *Untitled*, early 1990s

Pl. 3. **Ronald Lockett**, *The Enemy Amongst Us*, 1995

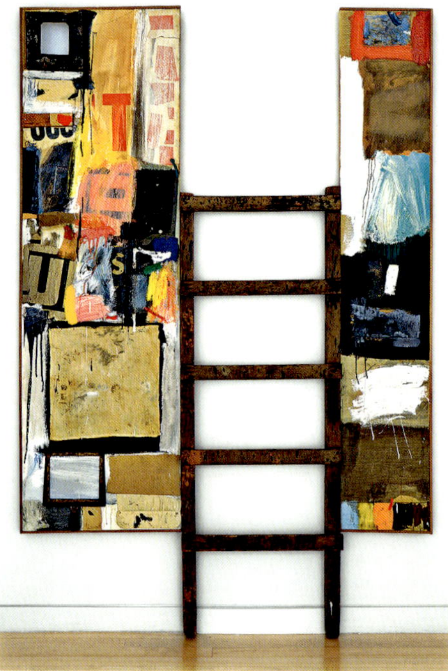

Fig. 13. **Robert Rauschenberg**, *Winter Pool*, 1959

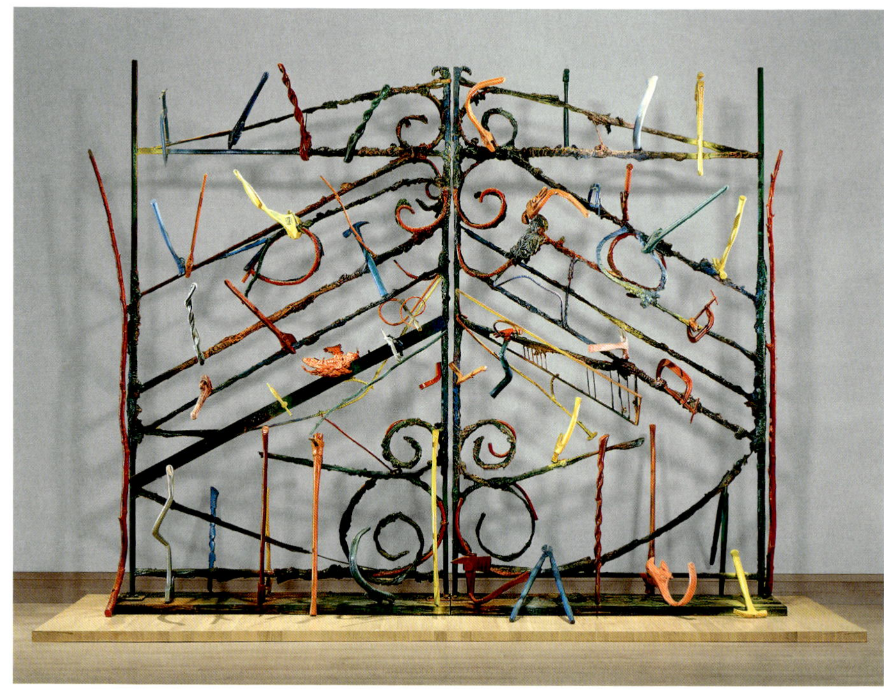

Fig. 14. **Jim Dine**, *The Crommelynck Gate with Tools*, 1983

The prevalence of found objects and strategies of appropriation resonates remarkably with Dada, the radical movement that emerged during World War I, embraced elements of chance, and challenged artistic standards of beauty and originality by using common objects and materials, adapting them (sometimes subtly, sometimes radically) to subvert expectations and activate new meanings. French Dada artist Marcel Duchamp (1887–1968)—who infamously incorporated a urinal, a bottle rack, and a bicycle wheel, among other objects, into various works he produced—called such creations "readymades." On first inspection, works like Emmer Sewell's sculpture *Untitled* (early 1990s, pl. 2), consisting merely of a painted tire, plastic chair, and piece of cinder block, seem to exhibit a Dadaist sensibility. Moreover, Lockett's wood and metal construction *The Enemy Amongst Us* (1995, pl. 3) calls to mind the mixed-media work of Robert Rauschenberg, particularly the latter's Combines, such as *Winter Pool* (1959, fig. 13). Speaking to this visual lineage, Rauschenberg's work is often called "neo-Dada," though he resisted that characterization. Suggesting the poetic use of inanimate objects by Félix Gonzáles-Torres (1957–1996), Joe Minter's assembled and anthropomorphized tools (pl. 6) evoke themes of mortality and personal loss and are also reminiscent of the sculpture of Jim Dine (fig. 14). As several scholars have observed, Dial's large, ambitious, and sometimes seemingly apocalyptic creations, such as *History Refused to Die* (2004, pl. 8), recall the work of Anselm Kiefer, which likewise reflects on tragedy at an epic scale and takes a long view of history (fig. 15). The striking stylistic, technical, and conceptual parallels linking these predominantly rural Southern artists to their more famous art-world contemporaries underscore the considerable imagination and ingenuity of their work.

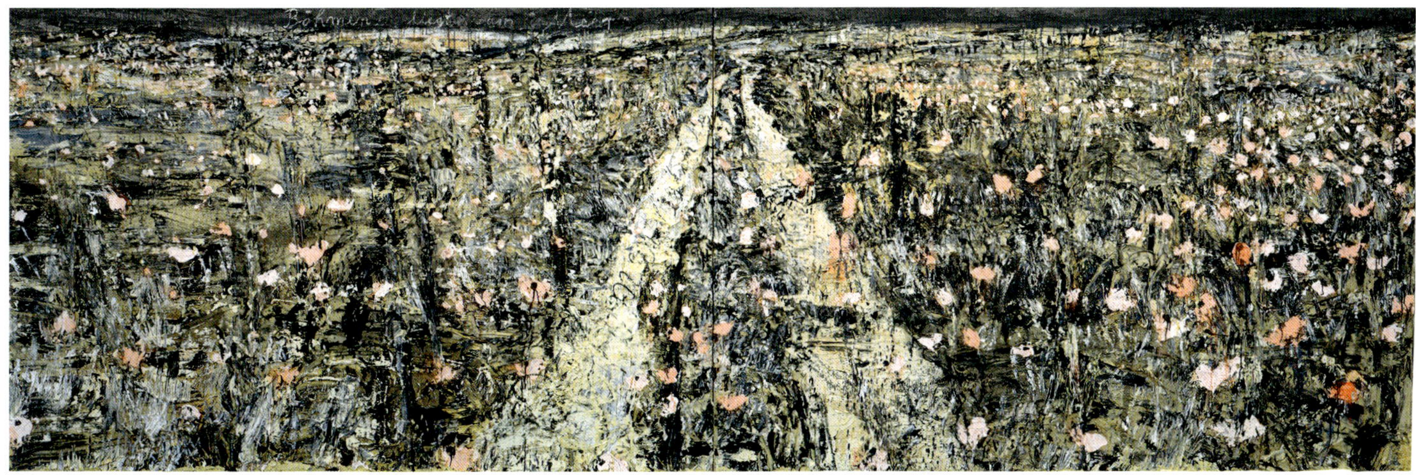

Fig. 15. **Anselm Kiefer**, *Bohemia Lies by the Sea*, 1996

However, because the artists included in this gift were largely unfamiliar with contemporary art outside their communities, such similarities are mostly coincidental and, if accepted uncritically, minimize the degree to which their socioeconomic circumstances predetermined their art making. Indeed, unlike Duchamp and other artists in the modern and contemporary canon, Dial, Sewell, and their Southern counterparts were drawn to common materials and found objects less out of a self-conscious spirit of artistic rebellion—unlike, say, artists associated with Arte Povera—and more owing to necessity brought on by their shared conditions of poverty. Signs of real poverty appear most undeniably in the material form and sheer volume of cheap, discarded, and reclaimed materials—house paint, torn fabrics, scrap metal, trash—the artists used to make their work. In this regard, too, material becomes metaphor, surreptitiously symbolic in the aggregate of an economically disadvantaged culture of creative scavenging, reuse, and repurpose.

These shared difficult conditions precipitated the production of art that is remarkable for, among other qualities, its pronounced eclecticism, seeming randomness, and diversity in size, style, technique, media, and subject matter. The large assemblages of Dial and Lockett starkly contrast with the intimate delicacy of John B. Murray's mixed-media designs (pls. 23–25). Mary Proctor's spiritually infused and decoratively encrusted construction *The Keys* (1996, pl. 26) differs markedly from the bold sensuality of Georgia Speller's and Henry Speller's nude imagery (pls. 4–5). The cultural and historical potency of Minter's powerful sculpture *Four Hundred Years of Free Labor* (1995, pl. 6) serves as a foil to Joe Light's comparatively whimsical painting *Pony* (1988, pl. 19). Some scholars argue that its eclecticism is its most defining trait.[6]

This great range of expression speaks to myriad particular sensibilities, experiences, and perspectives that coexist within a tightly shared group of historical, cultural, and socioeconomic circumstances. This relationship sets in motion a dynamic push and pull between individual and group identity, between the particle and the wave of which it is a part. As art historian Roger Cardinal has written:

> The folk art of the African American South has a hyperdynamic cogency, a characteristic richness and profundity, full of lilt and savor, which, just like

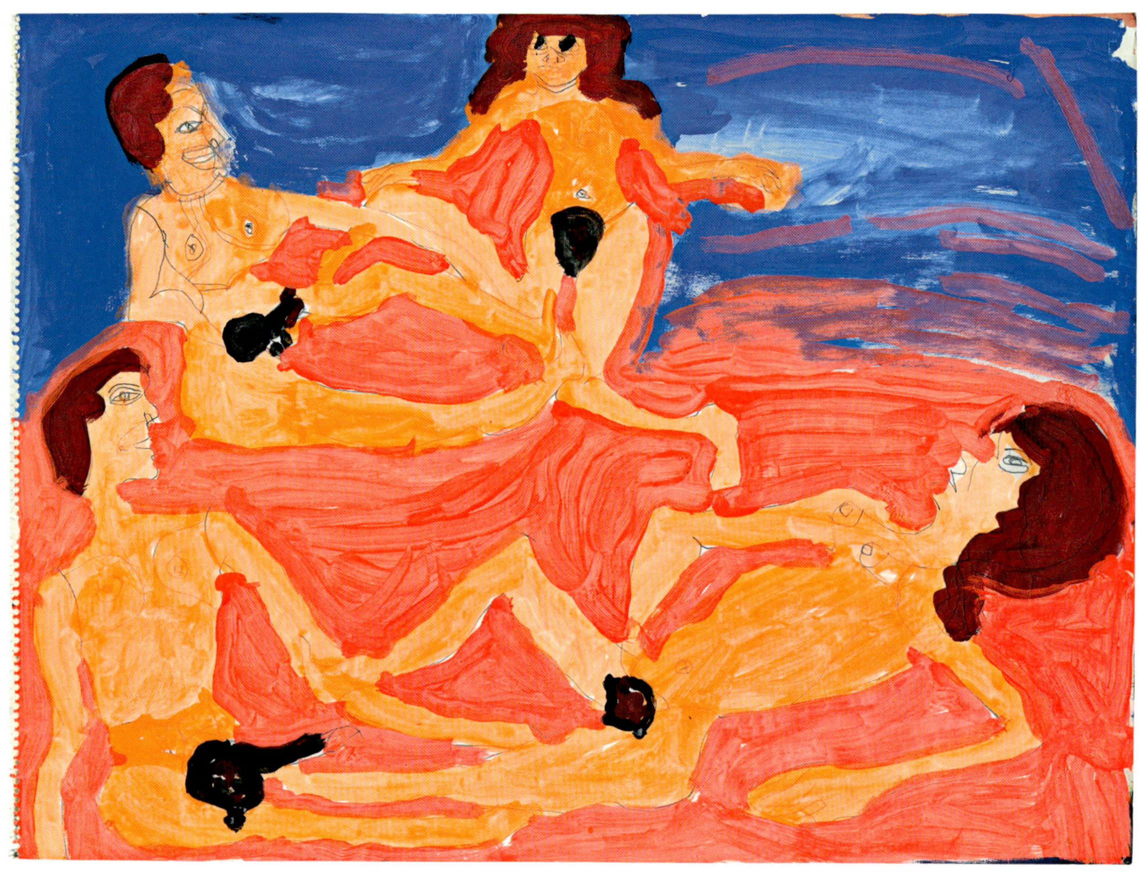

Pl. 4. **Georgia Speller**, *Minnie and Her Friends*, 1987

a regional dialect, inflects the visual figures of southern artists, making them persuasive insofar as they channel yet never submerge the expressive impulses of the individual subject. Indeed, time and time again one is forced to rethink the *idée reçue* that folk art is synonymous with an impersonal tradition, and to recognize instead that contemporary southern African American folk art positively thrives on uninhibited improvisation.[7]

However, in his promotion of the "uninhibited improvisation" of work by contemporary self-taught artists, Cardinal encroaches on a kind of romanticism of which, however alluring in its suggestion of a freedom of expression, one might better steer clear, as it invokes a level of personal liberation and artistic license that in many respects these artists did not experience. Indeed, the remarkable demonstration of commitment to their art making in spite of the challenging circumstances they endured calls to mind the ode to artistic fortitude that critic Robert Hughes offered during the heated congressional debates regarding federal support of the arts in the 1990s: "Painters, dancers, actors are tough as weeds," Hughes asserted, "and can grow in cracks in the concrete."[8] His point was that artists (and art) can flourish even where and when the odds are stacked heavily against them.

Among the most powerful works in the gift are those incorporating found objects, such as Minter's *Four Hundred Years of Free Labor*. One of the largest pieces in the group, the sculpture is composed of old rusted metal shovels, pitchforks, pickax heads, and a

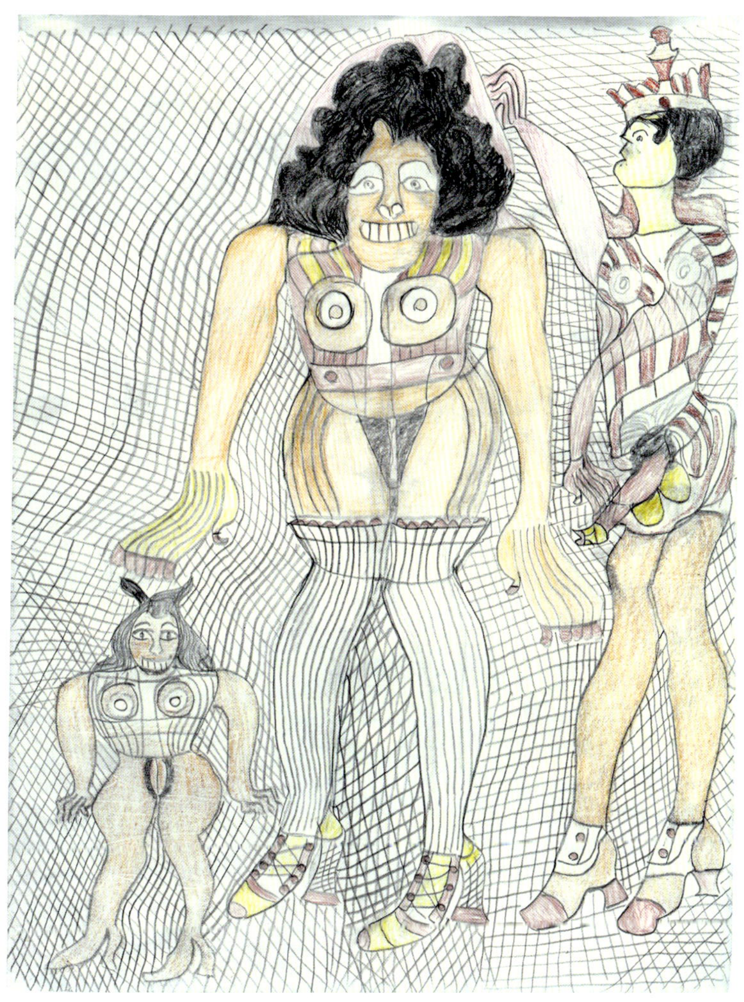

Pl. 5. **Henry Speller**, *Untitled*, 1985

hoe held together by welded pipes, all bound together by chains. Shown upright, these tools collectively assume a human presence. As a group, they confront the viewer like spectral surrogates of their former users, evoking multiple groups of African Americans subjected to forced labor over time, from slaves harvesting cotton before the Civil War to chain gangs digging ditches and building roads in the twentieth century. The prevalence of chain-gang labor throughout the South appears in more explicit form in the *Deep South* panel of the *America Today* mural (1930–31, fig. 16) by Thomas Hart Benton. But, whereas Benton's relatively small figures convey the artist's sympathy for his downtrodden subjects, Minter's assembled tools stand as iconic testaments to the nobility of the lives of the anonymous laborers who once wielded them, not least of which were the prisoners in chain gangs that played a substantial role in building Birmingham.

The intertwined subjects of African American identity, history, and labor recur in Lonnie Holley's hauntingly provocative and historically resonant *African Mask* (2004, pl. 7). Showing a welder's mask mounted onto and encircled by a shredded radial tire and various plastic objects (including an electrical socket), Holley's

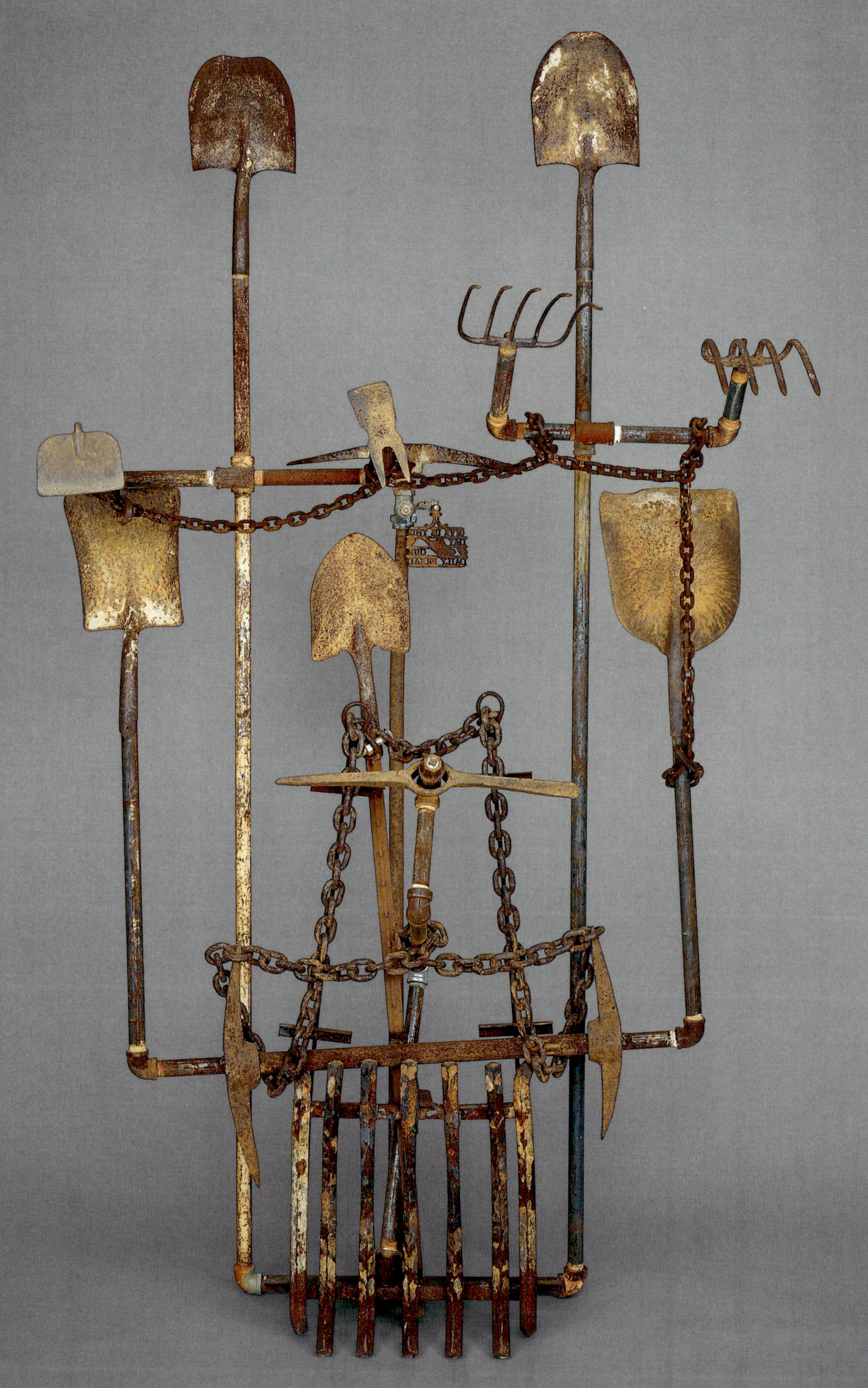

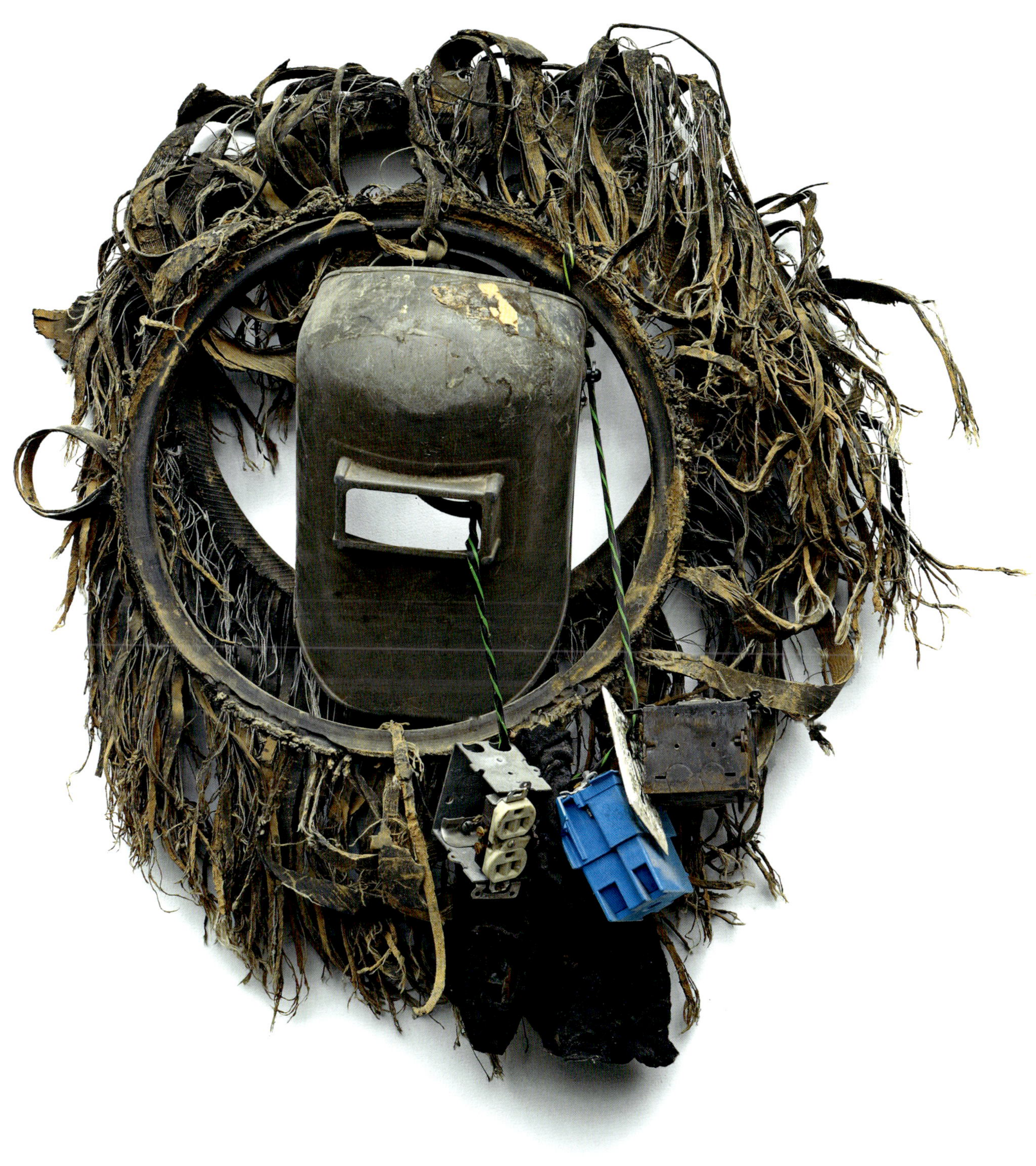

(opposite) Pl. 6. **Joe Minter**, *Four Hundred Years of Free Labor*, 1995

Pl. 7. **Lonnie Holley**, *African Mask*, 2004

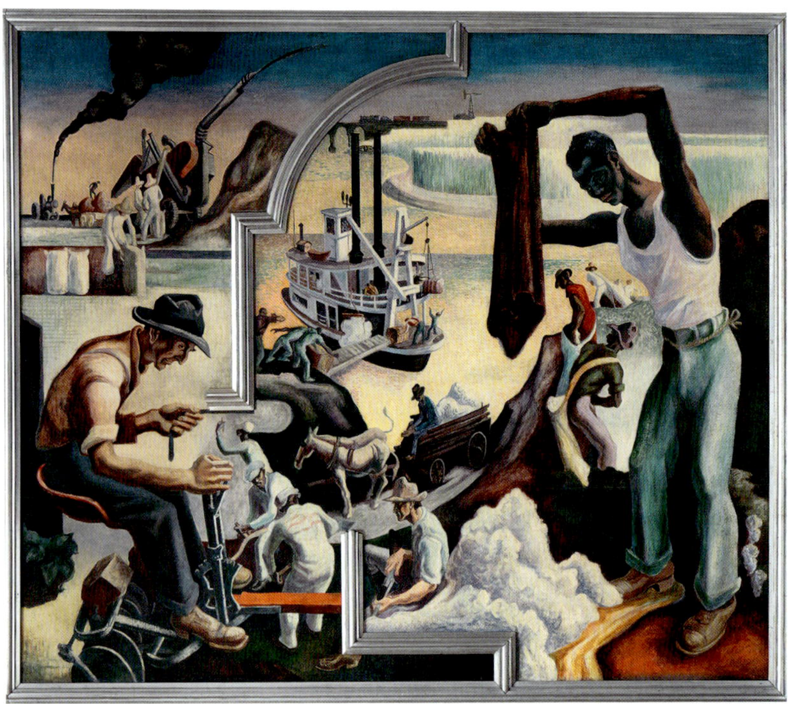

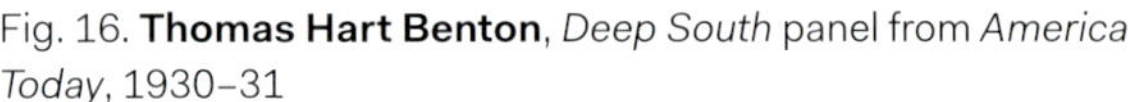

Fig. 16. **Thomas Hart Benton**, *Deep South* panel from *America Today*, 1930–31

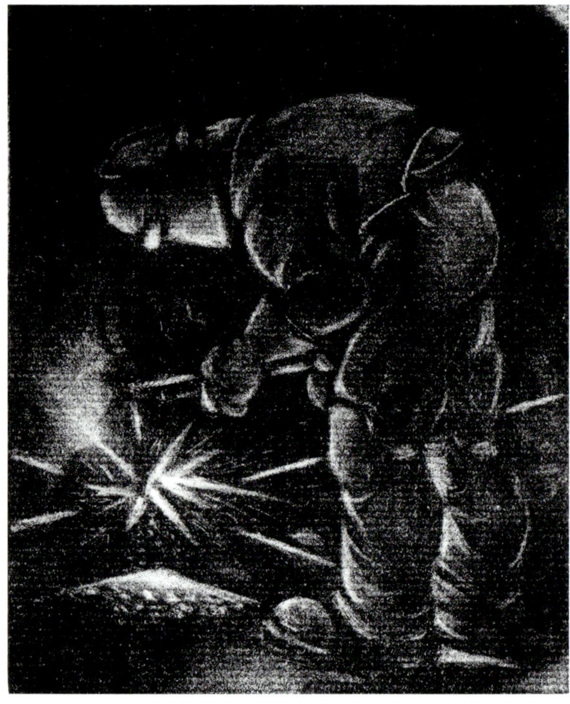

Fig. 17. **Dox Thrash**, *The Welder*, ca. 1936–41

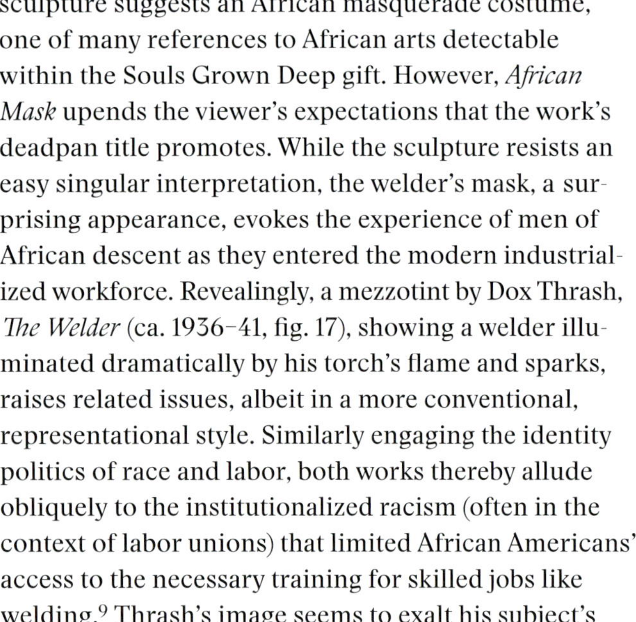

sculpture suggests an African masquerade costume, one of many references to African arts detectable within the Souls Grown Deep gift. However, *African Mask* upends the viewer's expectations that the work's deadpan title promotes. While the sculpture resists an easy singular interpretation, the welder's mask, a surprising appearance, evokes the experience of men of African descent as they entered the modern industrialized workforce. Revealingly, a mezzotint by Dox Thrash, *The Welder* (ca. 1936–41, fig. 17), showing a welder illuminated dramatically by his torch's flame and sparks, raises related issues, albeit in a more conventional, representational style. Similarly engaging the identity politics of race and labor, both works thereby allude obliquely to the institutionalized racism (often in the context of labor unions) that limited African Americans' access to the necessary training for skilled jobs like welding.[9] Thrash's image seems to exalt his subject's occupation and, by extension, celebrate his triumph over obstacles that no doubt impeded his path to middle-class stability and respectability. By contrast, Holley's *African Mask* is more ambivalent, a stark evocation of the postindustrial South.[10]

Key works in the Souls Grown Deep collection incorporate not only inanimate, mass-produced objects but also organic materials, which likewise function symbolically. One of the most striking and ambitious gifts, Dial's impressive two-sided multimedia construction *History Refused to Die* consists of torn and stained clothing and wire, among other common materials in addition to okra stalks and roots. Interwoven throughout *History Refused to Die*, the plant serves as an organic metaphor for the shared genealogy—the roots—of those whose personal genealogies tie back to Africa. Widely associated with Southern cuisine, okra is indigenous to Africa and, like kidney and lima beans, came

(opposite) Pl. 8. **Thornton Dial**, *History Refused to Die*, 2004

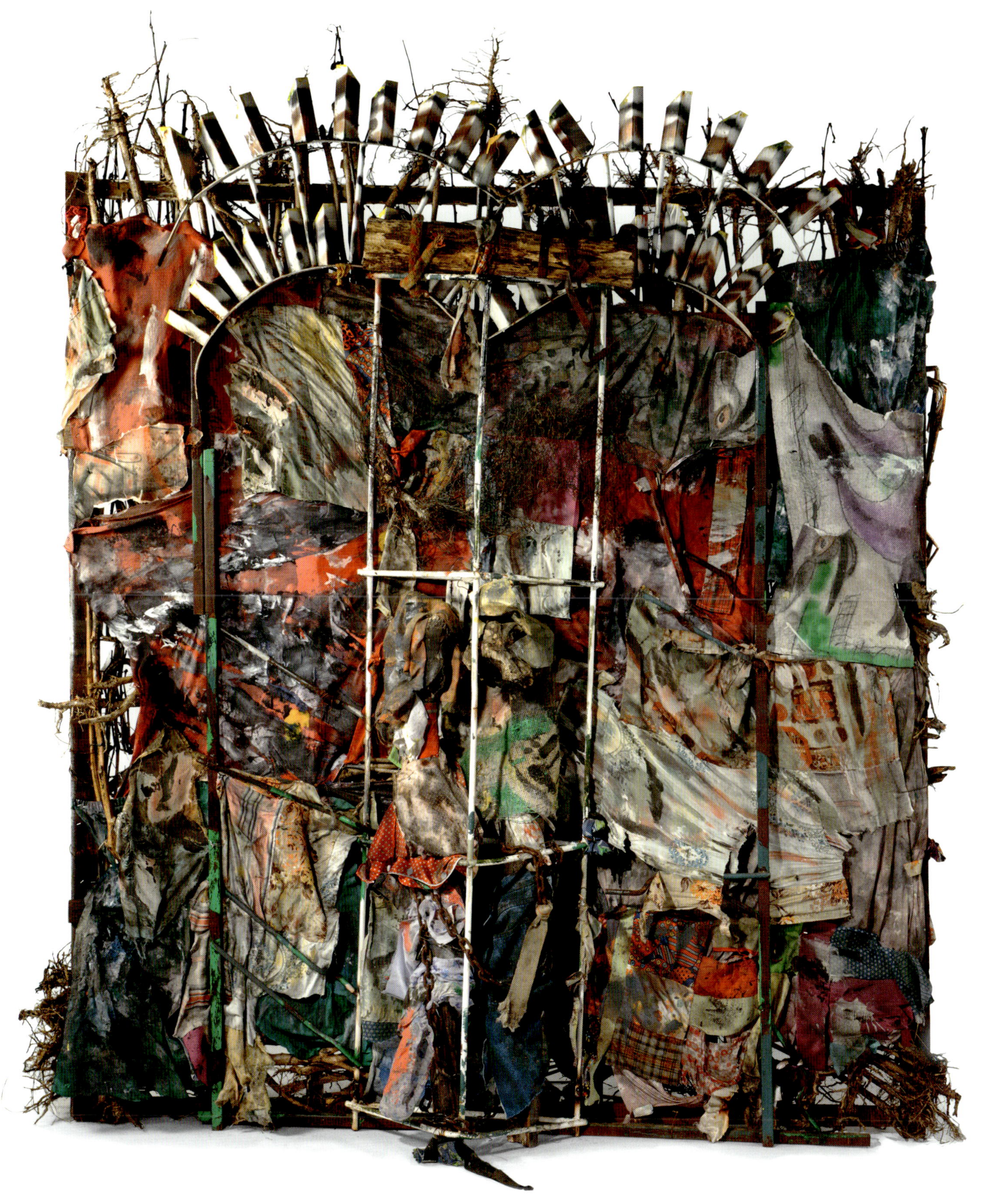

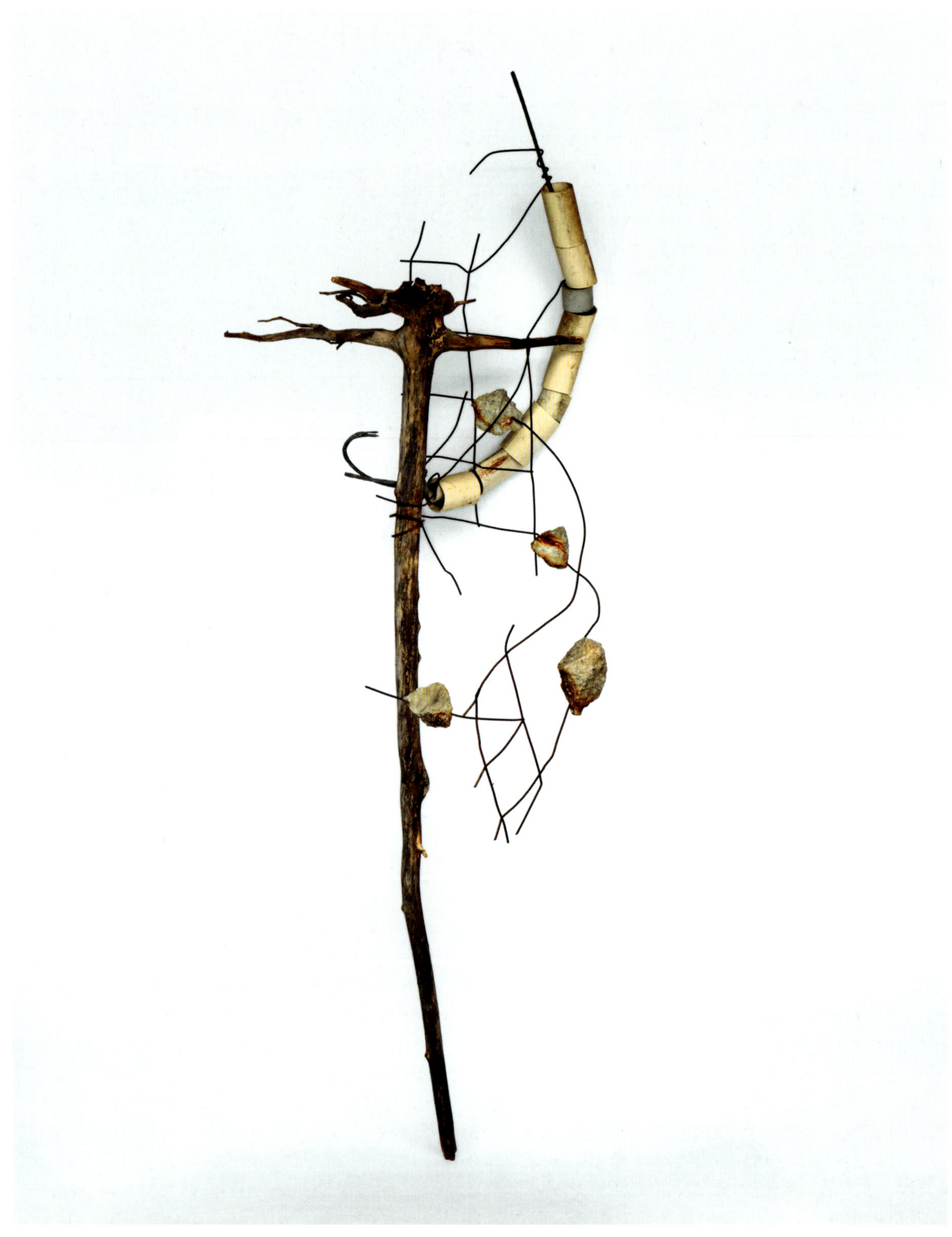

Pl. 9. **Lonnie Holley**, *Grown Together in the Midst of the Foundation*, 1994

to the Americas via the international slave trade.[11] The plant's presence in Dial's sculpture recalls this ecological transplantation that paralleled the forced displacement and enslavement of millions of Africans throughout the New World. Adorned across the top by okra roots turned upside down, *History Refused to Die* evokes, among other sensations, a precarious, overwhelming, and inescapable state of geographical and cultural uprootedness.

Also incorporating roots, Holley's *Grown Together in the Midst of the Foundation* (1994, pl. 9) evokes the tangled histories of labor in the artist's home of Birmingham: slavery and steel manufacturing. Like most Southern African Americans, Holley traces his ancestry back to slavery, symbolized here by the cotton tree root. Birmingham was a city that grew from modern industry, when rural freemen came to work in dangerous iron blast furnaces and coal mines. The steel and wire emblematize the African American labor force that established the city as the industrial center of the Southeast. "Grown together" in the title refers to how these forms of labor laid Birmingham's "foundation."

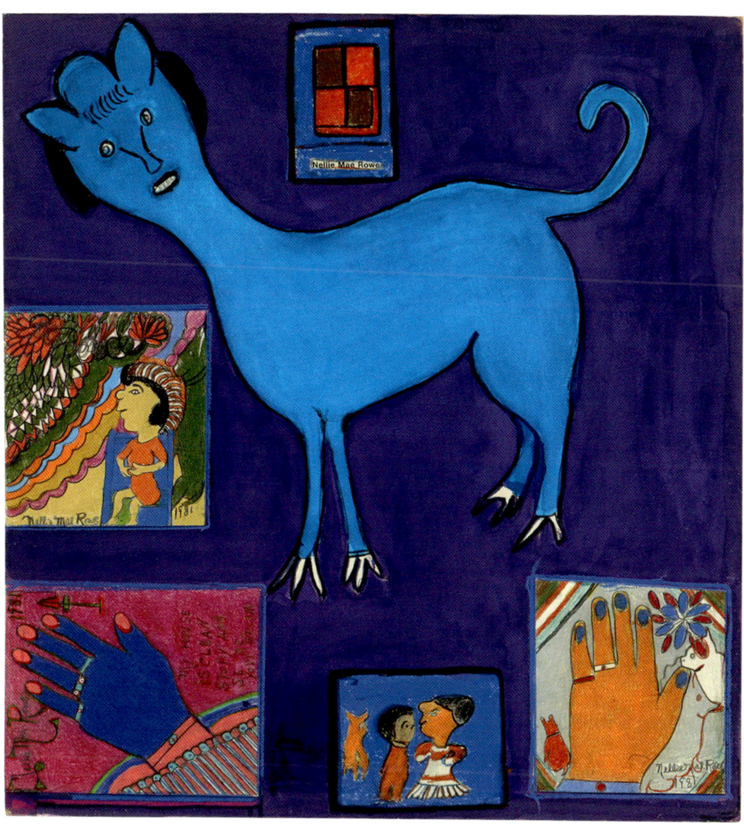

Pl. 10. **Nellie Mae Rowe**, *Atlanta's Missing Children*, 1981

While several works wrestle with the tangled histories of slavery and labor, a few others appear to take on current topical events or the news. Rowe's fantastical and densely coded *Atlanta's Missing Children* (1981, pl. 10) responds to a series of murders between summer 1979 and spring 1981 of at least eighteen children (and six adults) attributed to Wayne Williams.[12] Dial often commemorated newsworthy events with particular resonance among African Americans in his drawings. The surprising death of Olympic track-and-field star Florence Griffith Joyner (Flo-Jo) in 1998 prompted Dial to pay tribute to her life and accomplishments in *African Athlete* (1998, pl. 11), a languidly energetic nude figure drawing that features the athlete's signature brightly colored fingernails. Like many of Dial's drawings, *African Athlete* distorts the figure and perspective, providing the viewer a vantage point seemingly from above. A similar effect appears in *January 20, 2009* (2009, pl. 12), which, featuring a procession of figures and animal-like forms (including a flag-waving turtle), commemorates the inauguration of President Barack Obama. A striped creature with claws occupies the lower-left corner and stretches into the center of the composition. Its markings identify it as a tiger, an animal that Dial adopted in his art as a recurring symbol of various minorities' struggles for survival and social justice.[13] The artist's initials appear near a man's face with a mustache, suggesting a self-portrait and his imaginary presence at this celebration.

Dial created a substantial body of work in response to the terrorist attacks on September 11, 2001, and the subsequent U.S. invasion of Iraq. The Met's group includes a poignant, semiabstract drawing, *9/11: Interrupting the Morning News* (2002, pl. 13). Composed of a pile of tangled lines, some of which whip about like flames, while others, harder and more angular, suggest

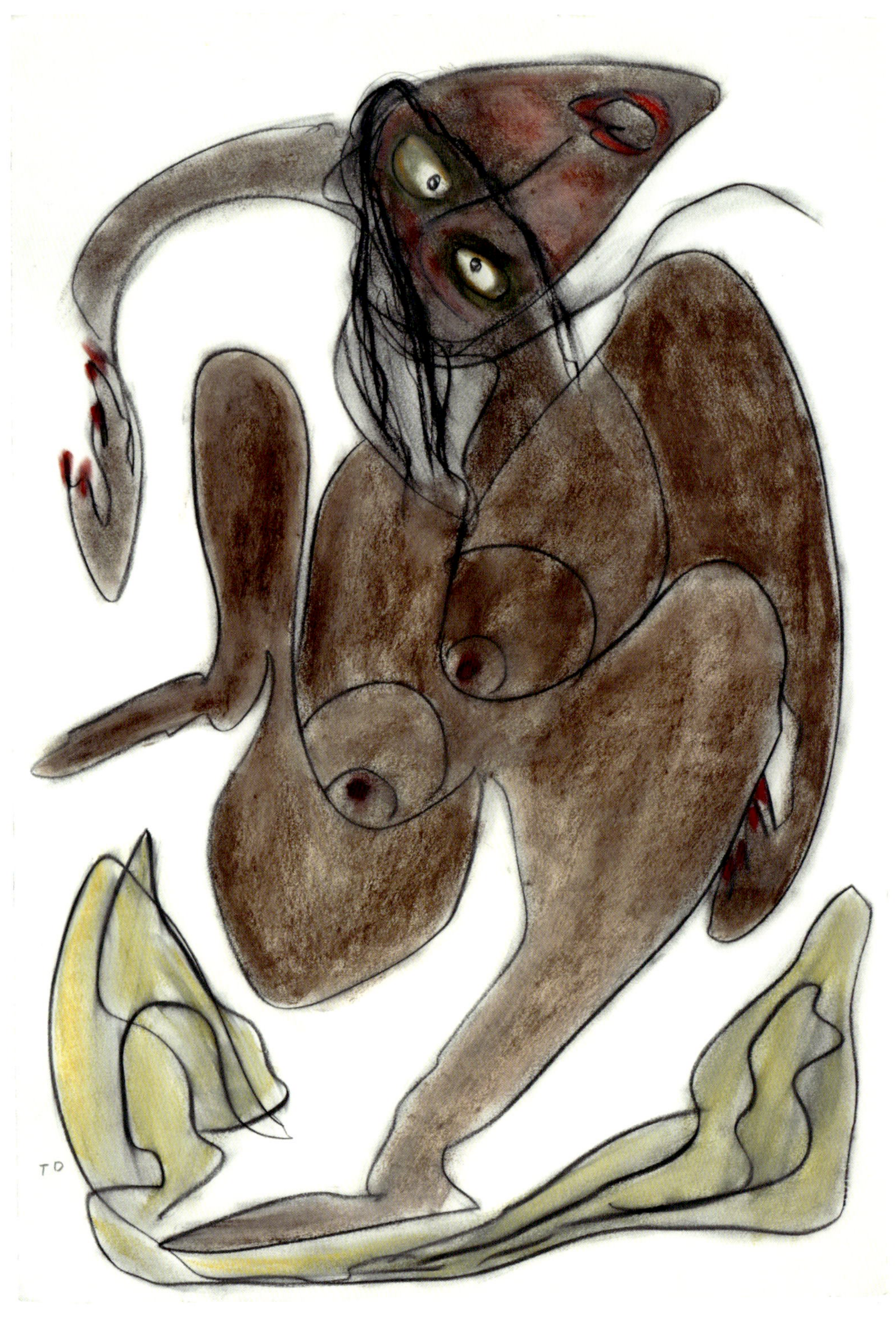

Pl. 11. **Thornton Dial**, *African Athlete*, 1998

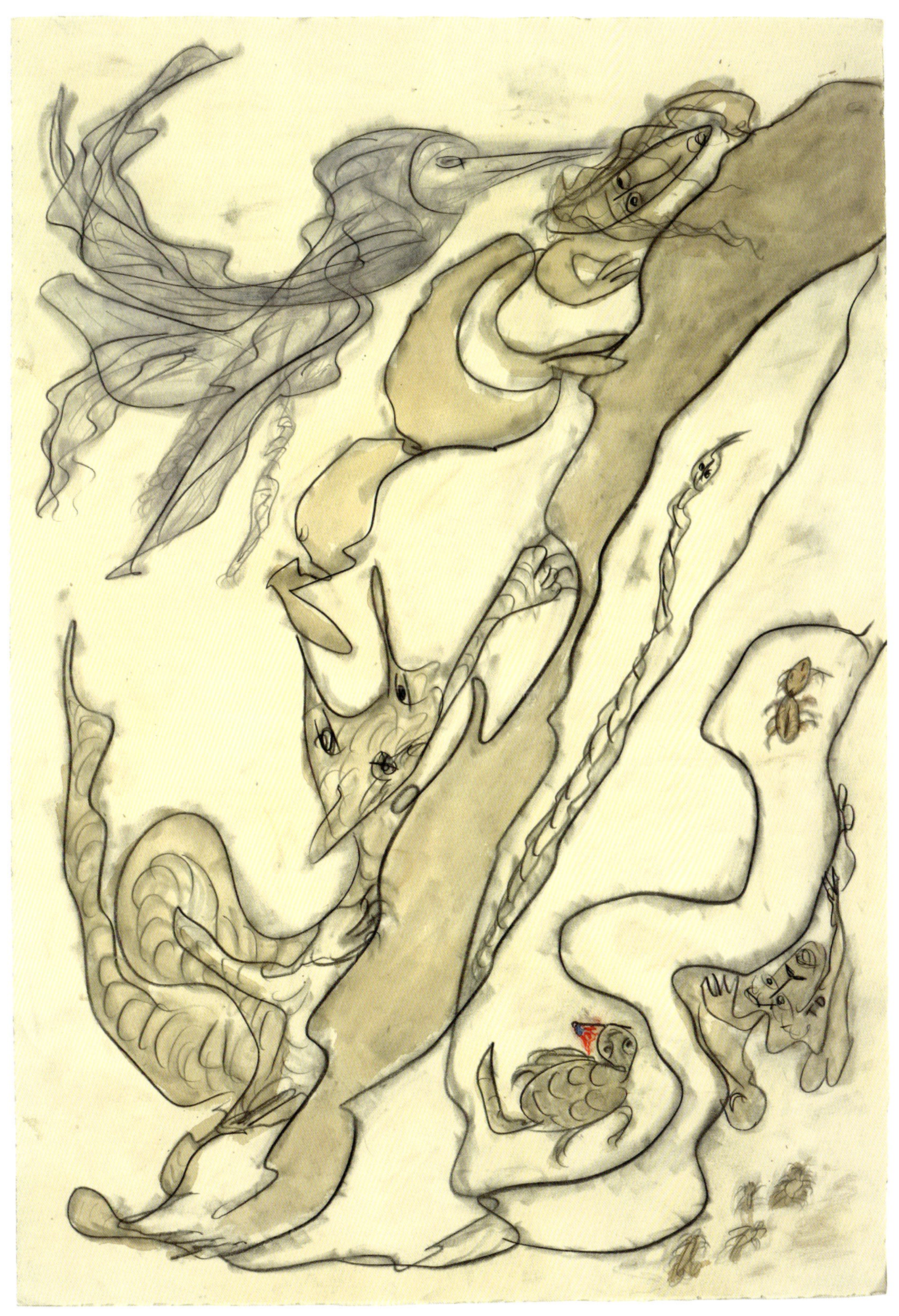

Pl. 12. **Thornton Dial**, *January 20, 2009*, 2009

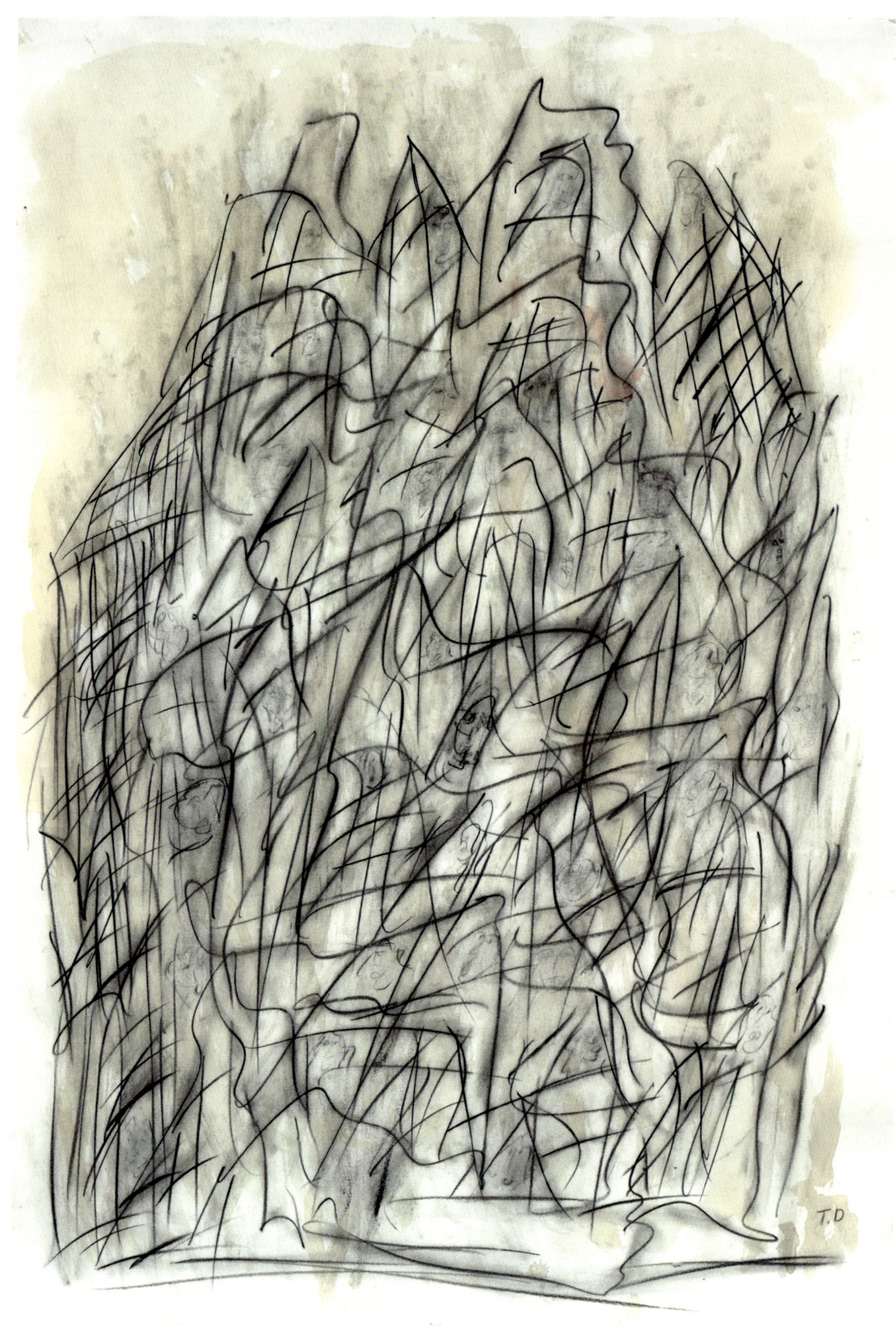

Pl. 13. **Thornton Dial**, *9/11: Interrupting the Morning News*, 2002

a fragmented structure, *9/11: Interrupting the Morning News* reflects on the artist's watching the aftermath of the terrorist attack on the World Trade Center on television, the means by which Dial derived several of his subjects. Featuring faint faces scattered throughout a thicket of lines, the drawing is an imaginative re-creation of the tower's collapse and an evocation of lives lost in the tragedy.

Modest in size and seemingly spontaneous in execution, Dial's drawing stands apart in many interesting ways from another artist's interpretation of the same subject in The Met's collection, *jpeg ny02* (fig. 18) by Thomas Ruff, a monumental photograph that depicts the conflagration in a more recognizable fashion. While Dial created *9/11: Interrupting the Morning News* from memory, using washes of coffee to suggest the personal morning ritual the tragedy disrupted, Ruff based his composition of an image of the tower's collapse he had found and appropriated from the internet and then expanded like a great history painting. Ruff's enlargement enhances the blurring effect of the image's pixilation, causing the apocalyptic scene to appear strangely distant, like a memory shrouded by the passage of time. Dial's drawing, too, memorializes the 9/11 tragedy, but, unlike Ruff's photograph and aside from its title, it does not call attention to the critical role that mass media played in the public's consumption of images and information about the attack.

The full extent of Dial's artistic response to pressing and contentious contemporary events manifests powerfully in *Victory in Iraq* (2004, pl. 14). Encountering this dark, messy, and rather threatening assemblage, one is struck by a distinct disconnect from its confident, declarative title, which recalls President George W. Bush's infamous pronouncement of victory in Iraq—"Mission Accomplished"—on May 1, 2003. Indeed, juxtaposed with the threatening morass to which it is connected, the work's title teems with irony, suggesting perhaps the artist's skepticism or even cynicism regarding his government's activities in the Middle East. With twisted, tangled, and broken forms and a seemingly random

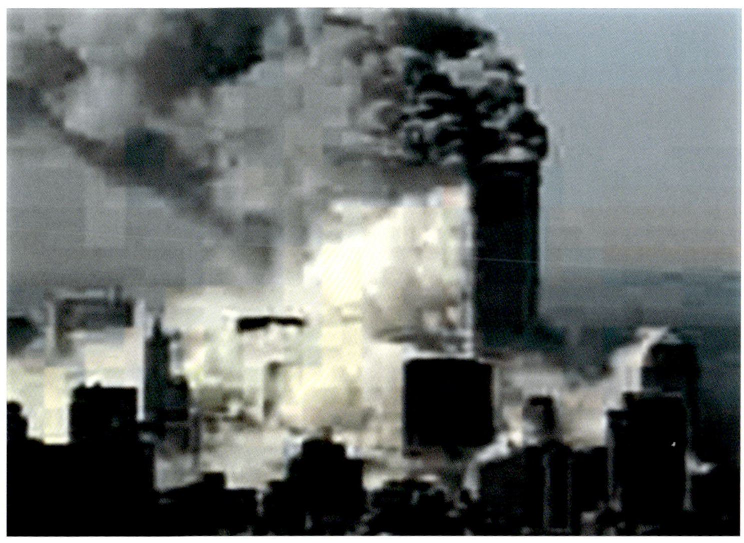

Fig. 18. **Thomas Ruff**, *jpeg ny02*, 2004

array of objects—barbed wire, a mannequin head, stuffed animals—Dial's daunting construction evokes a chaotic, dangerous war zone. Embedded within this web of destruction, two wood poles form an asymmetrical "v," a reference to the word "victory," while the work's large size suggests the enormity of the international conflict and its consequences. The presence of toy cars and action figures amid the panoply of materials and objects suggests that war is a kind of game played by the powerful, while others pay a fateful price.

Although compositions by Minter and Dial tackle difficult historical and social issues, other works in the Souls Grown Deep gift appear more detached from worldly concerns in what might be and has been considered "visionary." This description has been applied often to the art of Rowe, whose fanciful and exuberant imagery, filled with bright patterns, verdant vegetation (the Tree of Life is a recurring motif), stylized figures, and somewhat indistinct, somewhat hybridized animals, offers a view into a seemingly private pictorial universe.[14] *Nellie's Birthday* (1981, pl. 15), for example, exemplifies the artist's unique conflation of fantasy and autobiography. As Souls Grown Deep founder Arnett has explained, Rowe executed this drawing to commemorate her

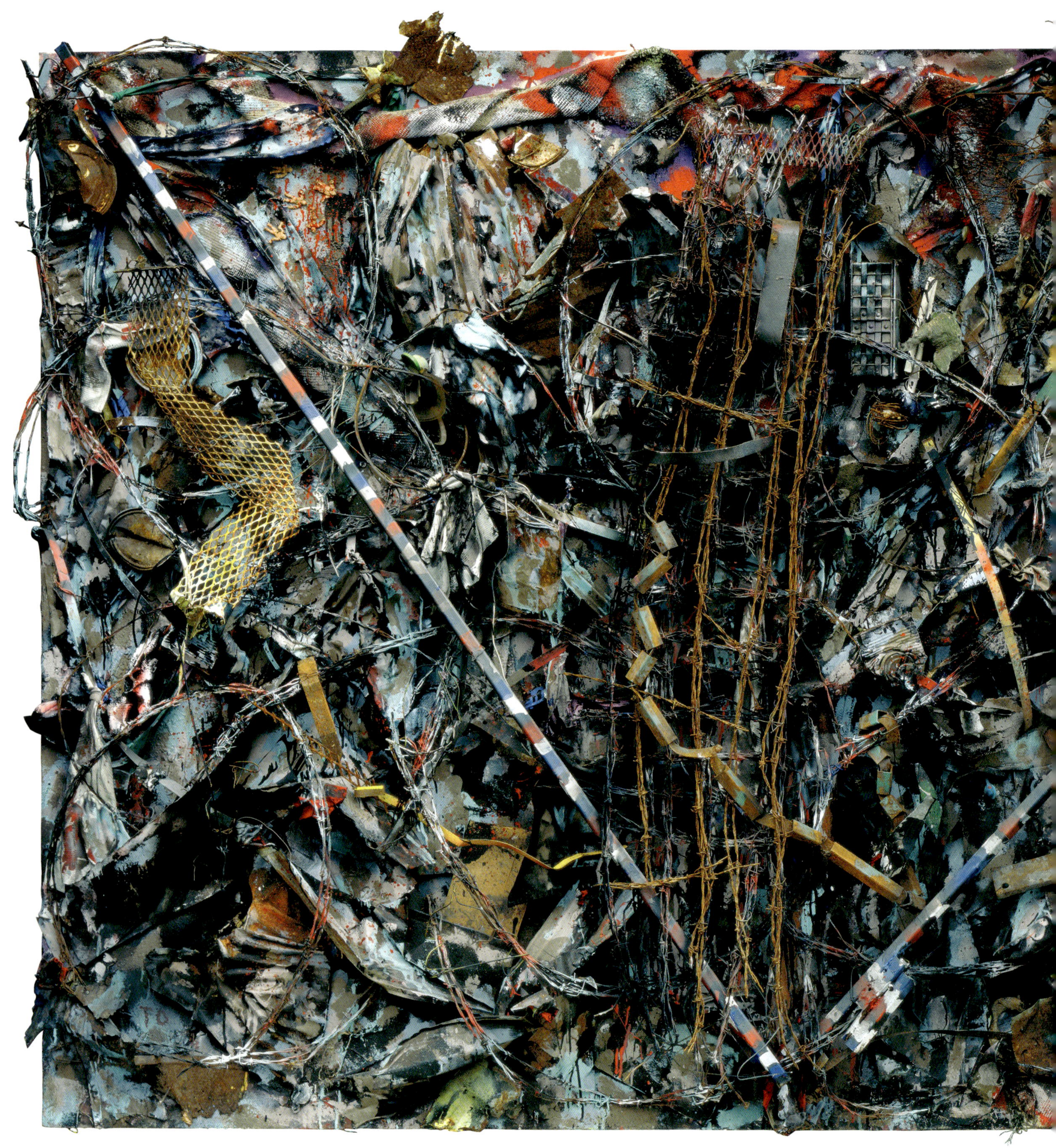

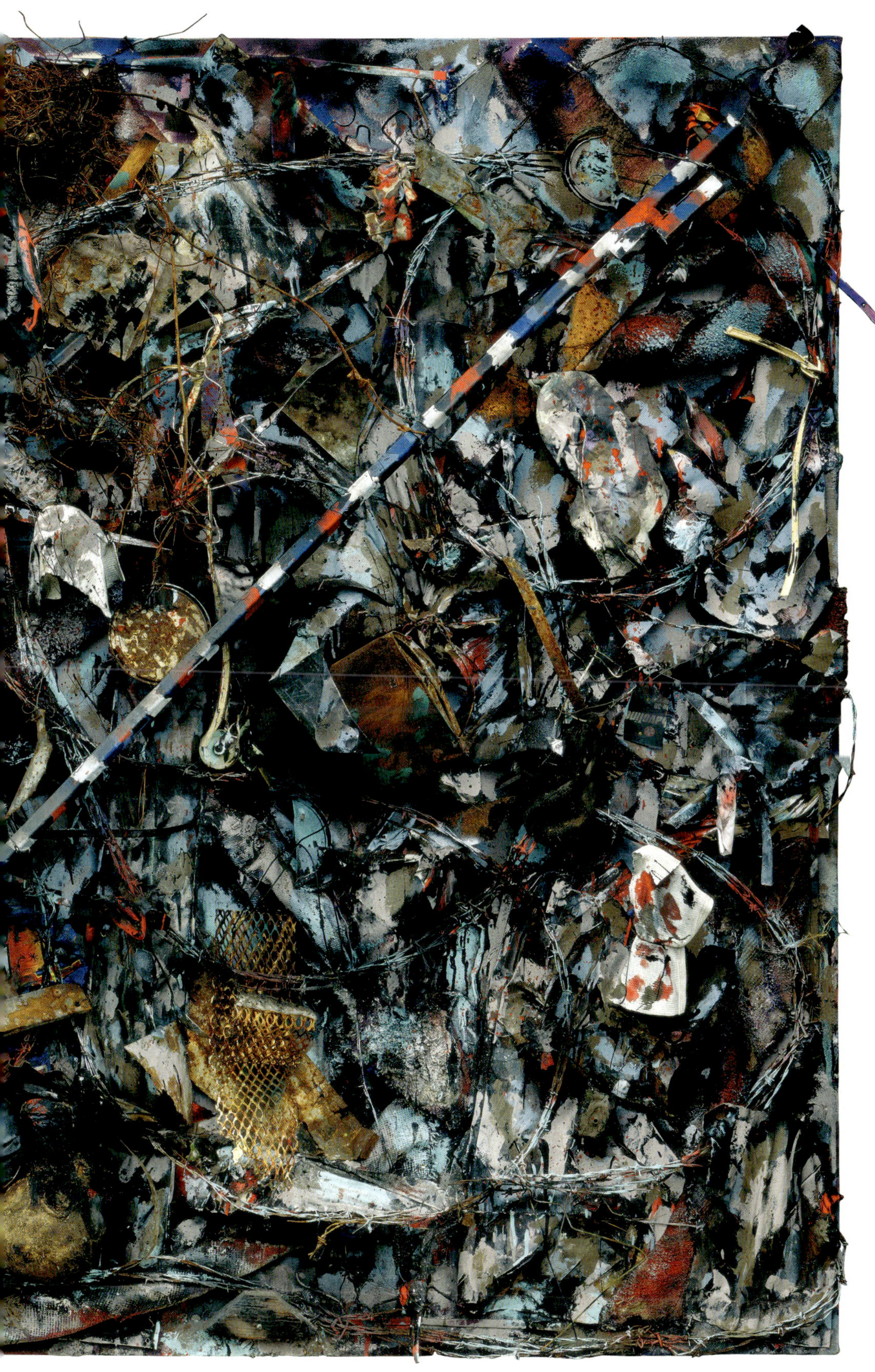

Pl. 14. **Thornton Dial**, *Victory in Iraq*, 2004

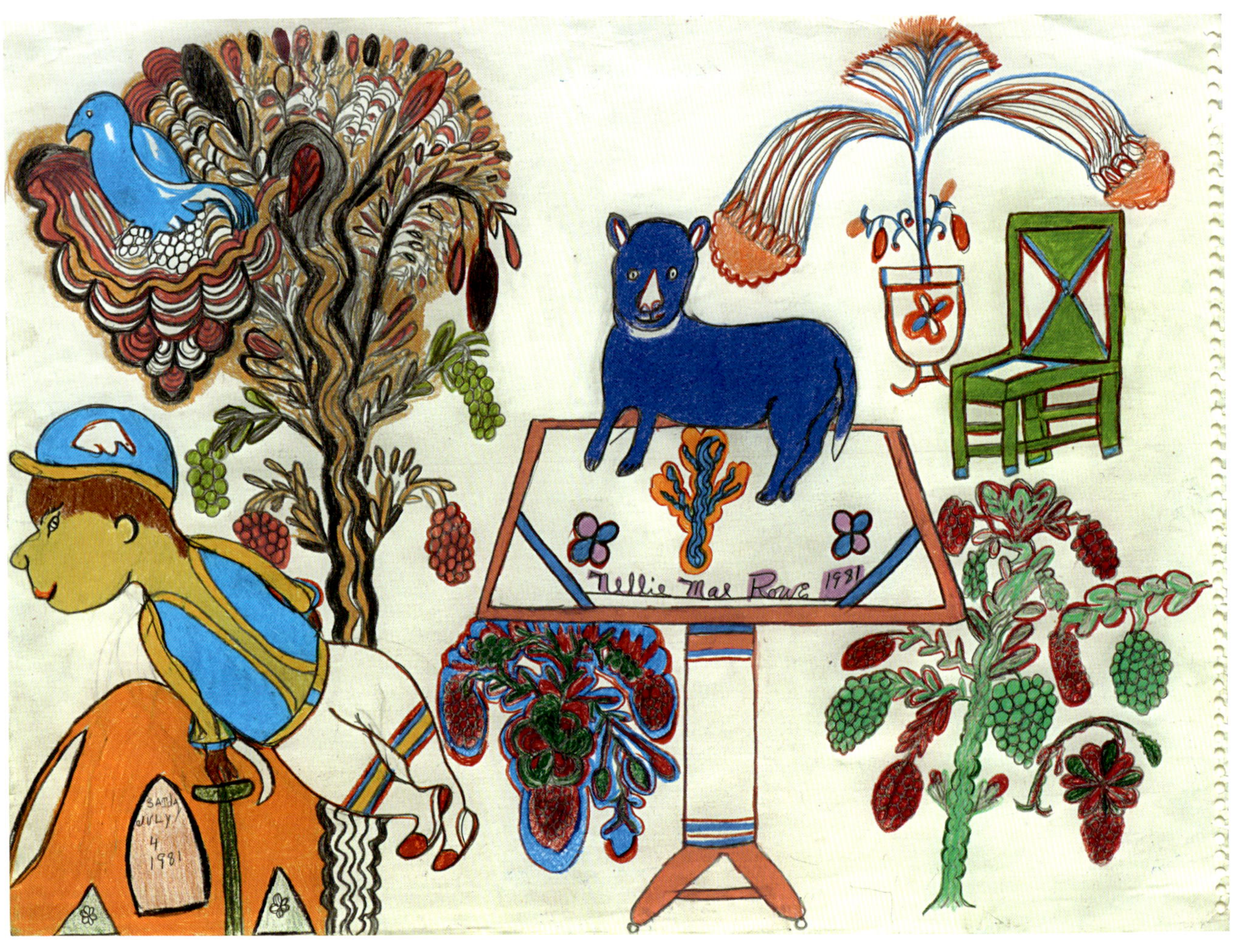

Pl. 15. **Nellie Mae Rowe**, *Nellie's Birthday*, 1981

eighty-first birthday in 1981, which, owing to her cancer diagnosis earlier that year, she thought would be her last.[15] This potent emotional content is concentrated on the left side of the composition, where a Tree of Life appears near a figure looking over a grave marker bearing Rowe's name. The artist reflects on her own mortality again in *Empty Chair* (1981, pl. 16), in which a female figure in a matching red hat and shirt, a surrogate for the painter, gazes upon a younger version of herself that hovers over an empty chair, likewise suggesting absence and loss. The subject of *Woman Scolding Her Companion* (1981, pl. 17) appears less dire but remains even more cryptic, focused on a mysterious conflict between the drawing's two main protagonists,a figure in profile wearing a flamboyant hat and a cartoonish zoomorphic creature that looks away, perhaps in shame or regret.

A similarly cartoonish, if not always explicitly comical, artistic sensibility can be seen in paintings by Light (pls. 18–19). Like Rowe, Light explored in his art a menagerie of rather indistinct creatures. But, whereas Rowe's figures are woven into densely decorative

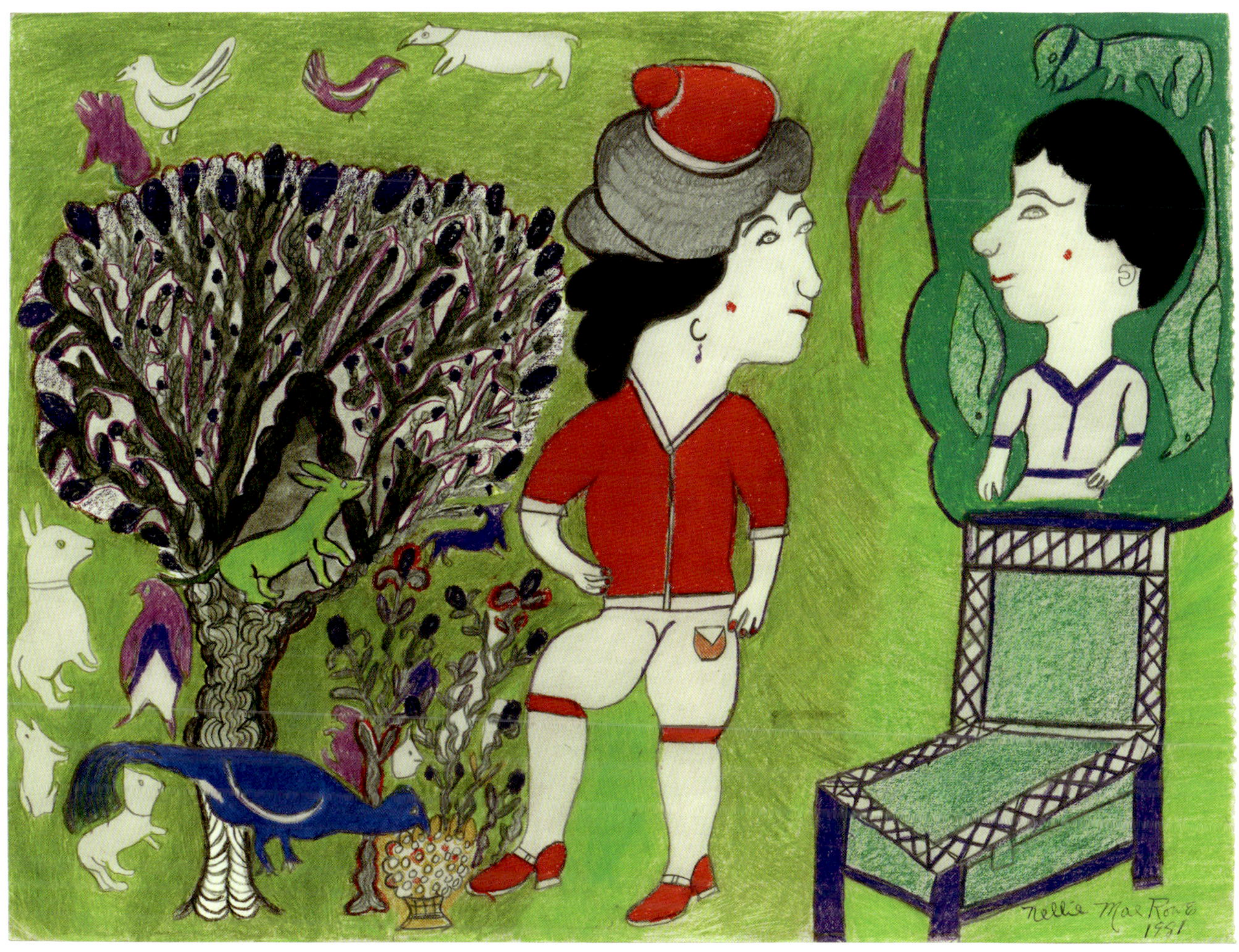

Pl. 16. **Nellie Mae Rowe**, *Empty Chair*, 1981

compositions suggesting a degree of horror vacui, Light's funky characters tend to occupy flat, open passages of bright, unusually nonnaturalistic color, evoking an almost Disneyesque world of wonder and imagination. *Hobo # Birdman* (1988, Pl. 18) unites two motifs integral to the artist's private iconography and personal philosophy, which combined Christian, Native American, and Islamic sources. In an interview, Light explained that the hobo symbolizes an existential journey to enlightenment, while the birdman exemplifies a more conscious state.[16] Here they appear together on a journey before a hilly brown landscape. Two popular images occupy the space between them, items Light may have acquired at one of the flea markets he frequented. A photograph showing the Capitol Building injects a whiff of politics into this otherwise otherworldly scene, while the adjacent Currier and Ives print, *Winter in the Country*, after an 1862 painting of rural ice harvesting in New England by George Henry Durrie (1820–1863), imparts a bit of sentimental nostalgia. Whatever the artist meant these images to signify, both places depicted exist at great distances from the artist's native Tennessee.

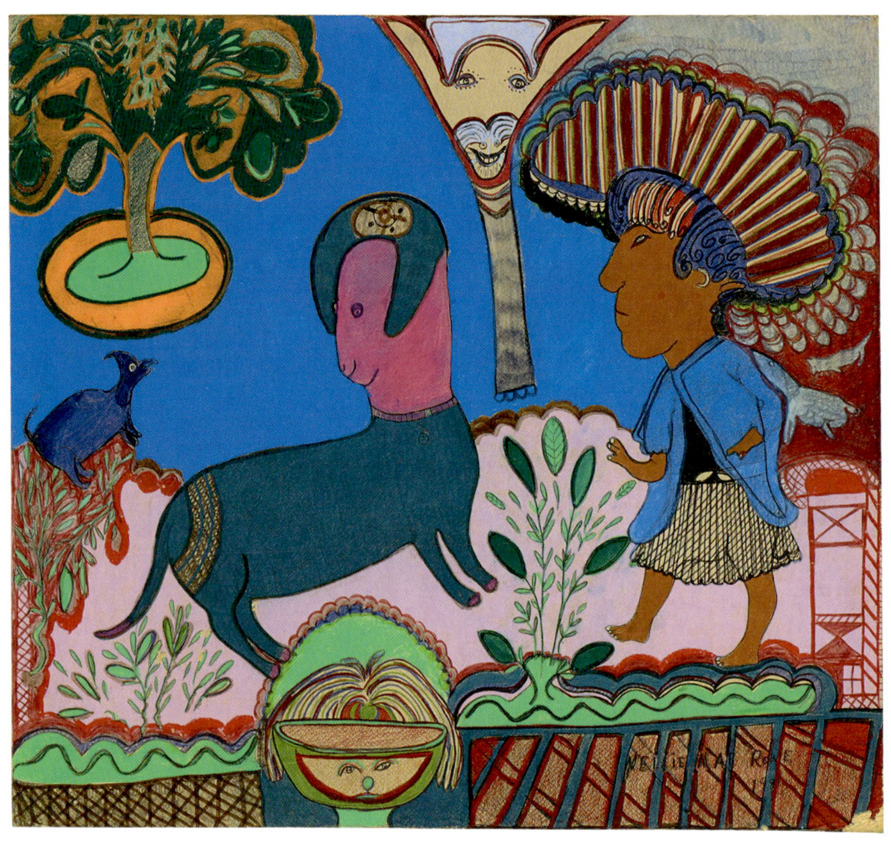

Pl. 17. **Nellie Mae Rowe**, *Woman Scolding Her Companion*, 1981

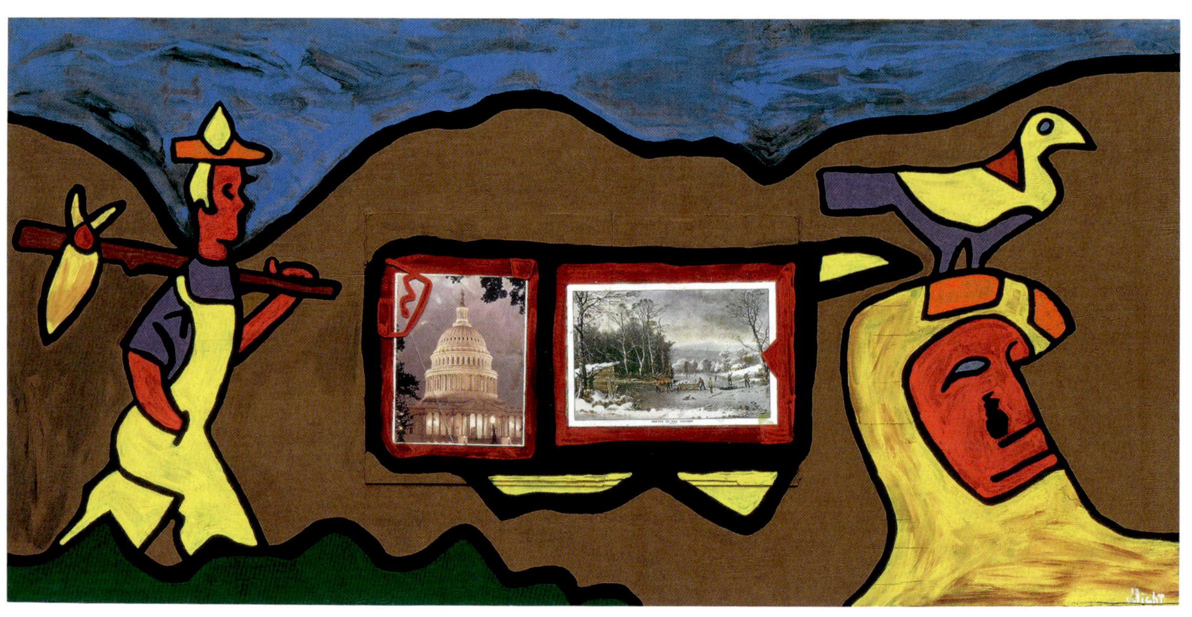

Pl. 18. **Joe Light**, *Hobo # Birdman*, 1988

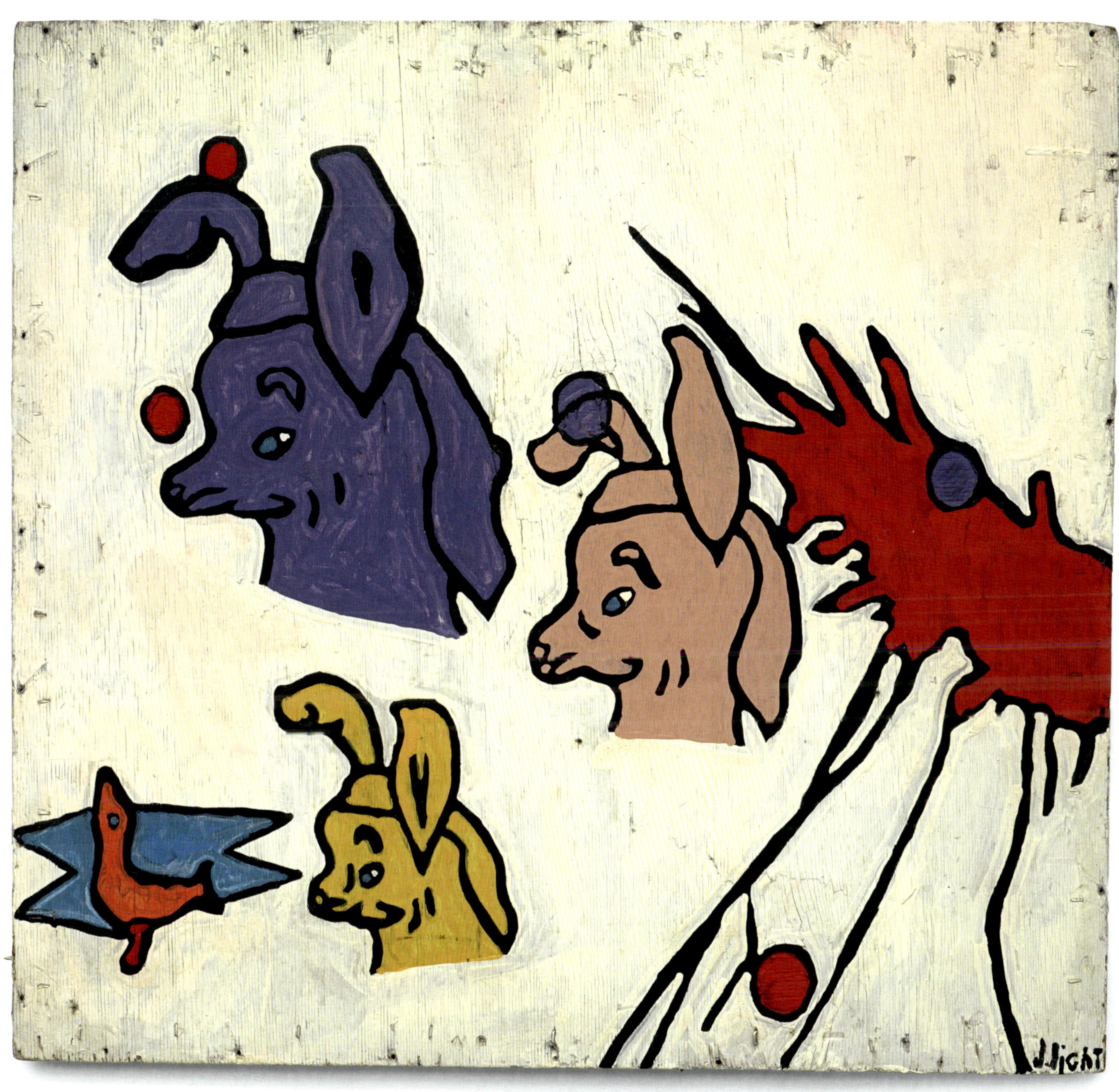

Pl. 19. **Joe Light**, *Pony*, 1988

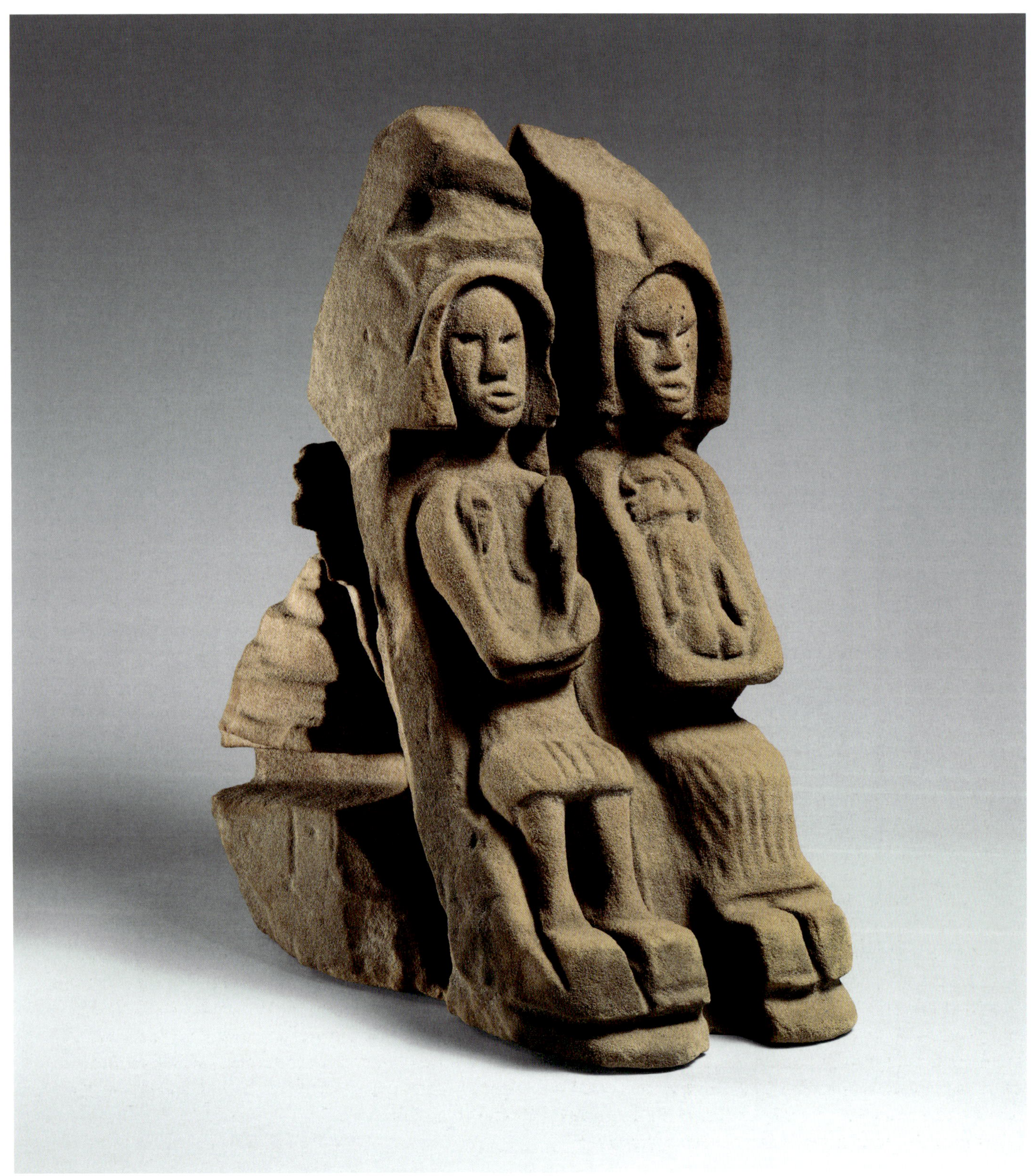

Pl. 20. **Lonnie Holley**, *Ruling for the Child*, 1982

The consequences of Holley's boldly titled sculpture *Ruling for the Child* (1982, pl. 20) appear even more charged than Light's vibrant painting. Carved from a waste mold, composed of sand bound by resin, that Holley scavenged from a nearby industrial foundry, a resource from which the artist drew raw materials for several sculptures, *Ruling for the Child* is superficially reminiscent of royal Egyptian sculpture. Its static, frontal composition and invocation of power and lineage are qualities that conjure the ancient arts of Africa that the artist seemingly aspired to channel. By the sculptor's own account, the work depicts a king and queen seated side by side, their arms crossed tightly in front of their bodies.[17] Wearing a long dress, the queen holds near her breast their child, who, carved in rather shallow relief, appears almost integral to the mother's body. Protected and nurtured, the child will, one assumes, grow up to ascend the throne and all that comes with it.

A pronounced spiritualism often permeates art by the Souls Grown Deep painters and sculptors, many of whom were raised in the evangelical Protestant tradition.[18] Even so, expressions of religious faith vary widely and sometimes take unconventional forms. The intended spiritual content of Dial's abstract mixed-media composition *Out of the Darkness, the Lord Gave Us Light* (2003, pl. 21) is evoked by its commanding title. Composed of shard-like fragmented shapes in black, dark purple, and light green, the construction suggests a contest between darkness and light, between the absence and the presence of God. Murray's smaller, more subtle work likewise conflates spiritualism and abstraction. Three untitled mixed-media drawings (pls. 23–25), all from the 1980s, represent examples of what Murray called "spirit works" or "spirit drawings" that he executed while in a heightened state of communion with God. As art historian Sharon Patton has explained, "composing extemporaneously, he considered himself the conduit for God's divine message."[19] Thus, like a medieval monk illuminating a manuscript, Murray understood himself as a scribe producing a kind of spiritual stenography, even if its abstract vocabulary makes it effectively indecipherable to others.

Mary Proctor's *The Keys* (pl. 26) is far more explicitly religious and features a crucifixion just below the center of the composition, accompanied by two biblical inscriptions, one from Revelation 1:18 ("He have [*sic*] the keys to hell and of death") and another from the book of Matthew 16:19 ("I will give thee the keys to heaven"). These dual references are reinforced by the presence of actual keys among the wide range of materials—including coins, jewelry, and buttons—that decorate the work's surface, a door panel that extends the key concept. Following traditional Christian iconography, *The Keys* presents the crucified Christ as the means to salvation, but, according to the artist's account, the work also testifies to the generosity of a wealthy motel owner and philanthropist, Ruby Pearl Diamond, a doyenne of Tallahassee society who, Proctor emphasized, "opened a lot of doors for people."[20] In fact, the eclectic and commonplace tesserae with which Proctor composed her quotidian mosaic are derived from Diamond's various personal effects, which the artist had acquired from Diamond's chauffeur, "Smiley" Bruce, who had inherited them after her death.

The Met's acquisition of this gift from the Souls Grown Deep Foundation attests to the place that self-taught art has earned within larger narratives of contemporary art practice. For decades, focused institutions like the American Folk Art Museum in New York and the Museum of International Folk Art in Santa Fe promoted "outsider" artists whom encyclopedic museums tended to neglect. However, as traditional, mostly Eurocentric narratives of modern art have given way to more expansive and inclusive alternatives, art museums have become more open to representing cultures that exist beyond academic systems of training and learning and bicoastal centers of production, exchange, and consumption. What was (or seemed to be) outside no longer remains so.

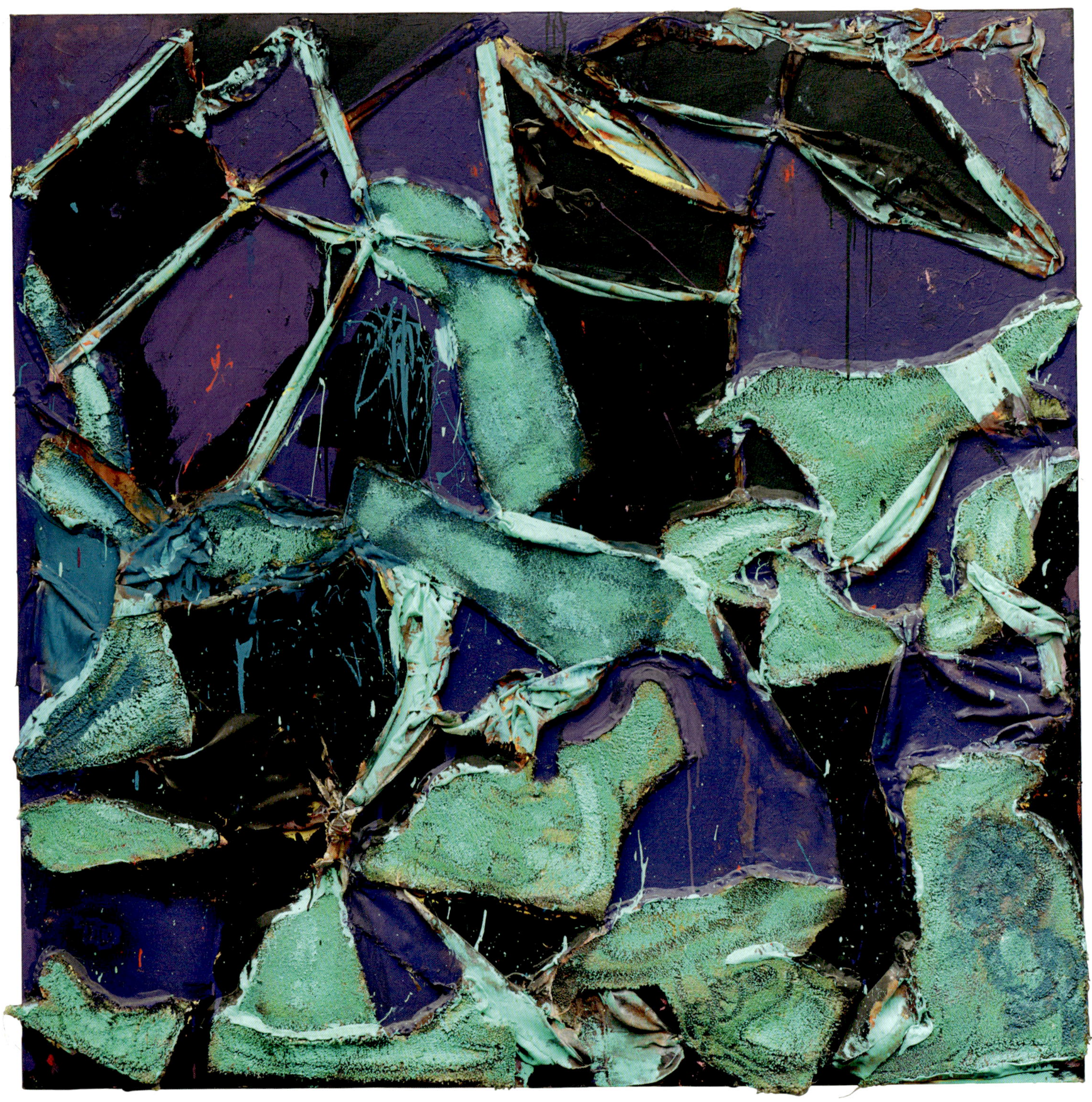

Pl. 21. **Thornton Dial**, *Out of the Darkness, the Lord Gave Us Light*, 2003

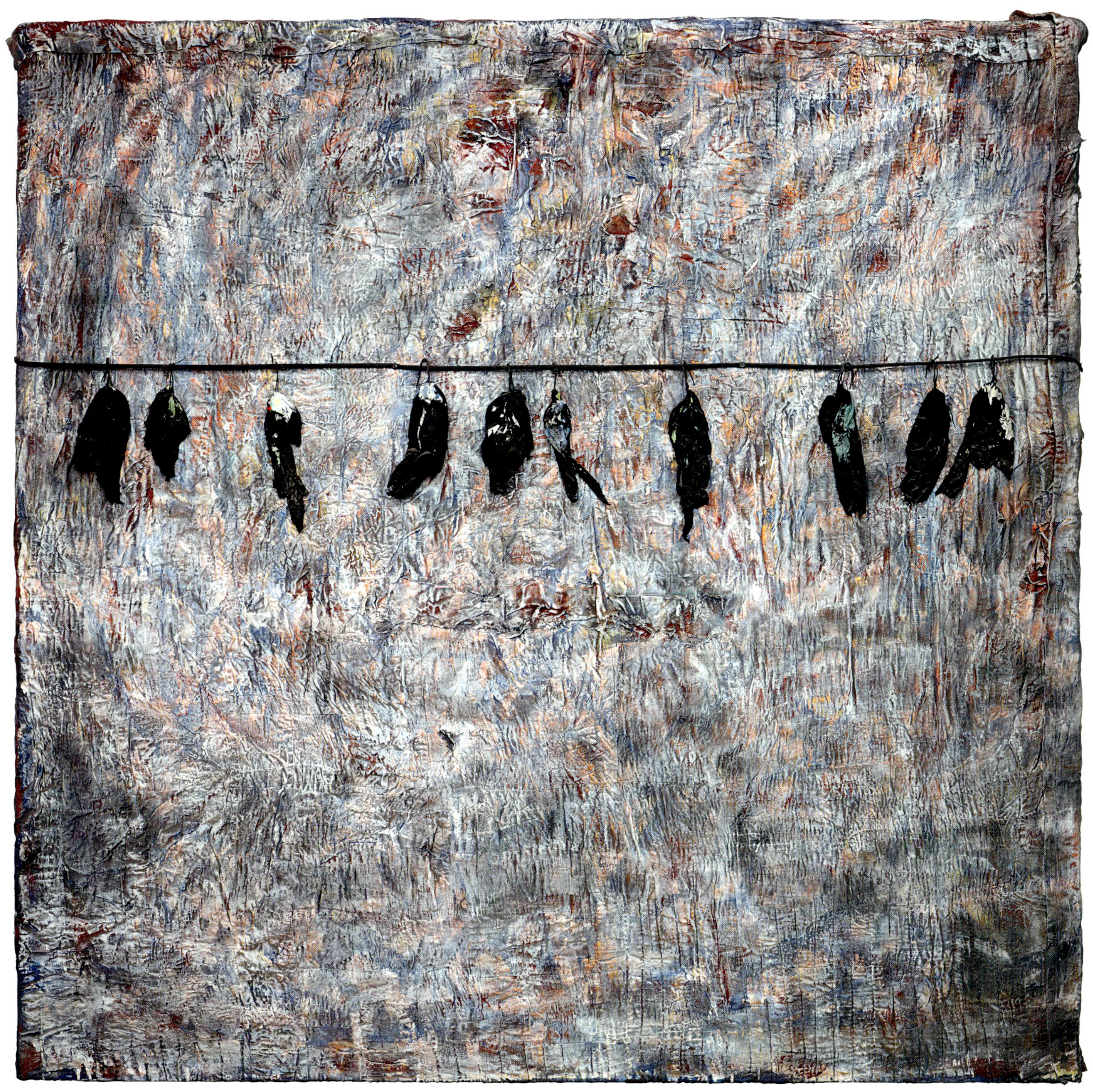

Pl. 22. **Thornton Dial**, *The End of November: The Birds That Didn't Learn How to Fly*, 2007

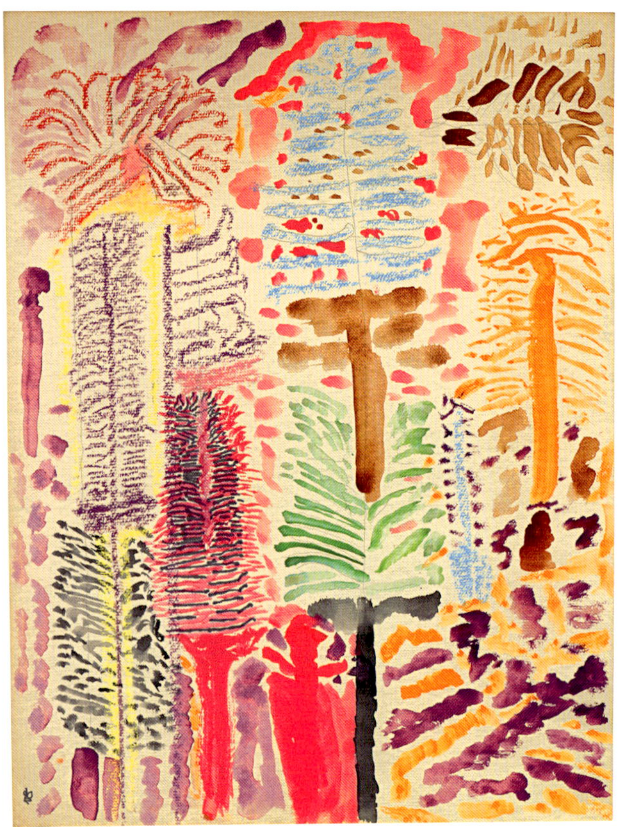

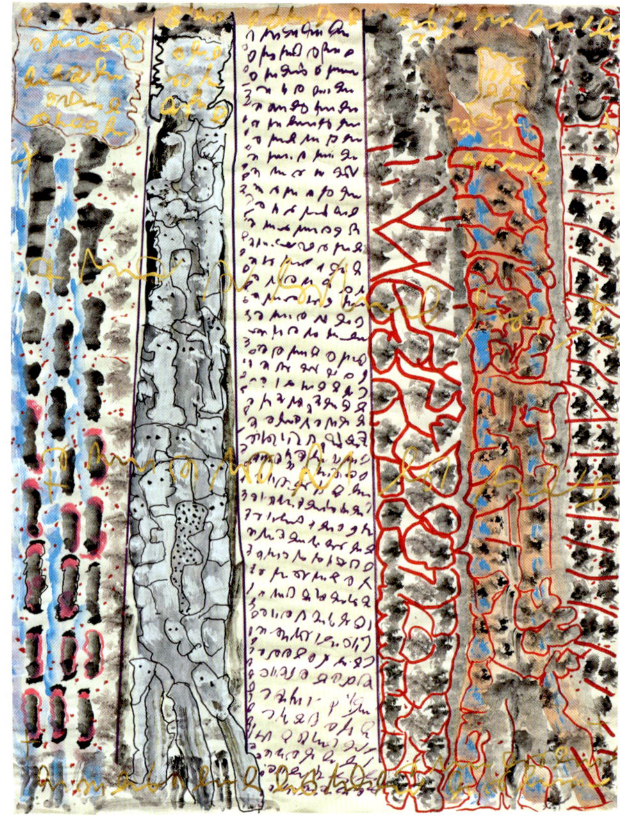

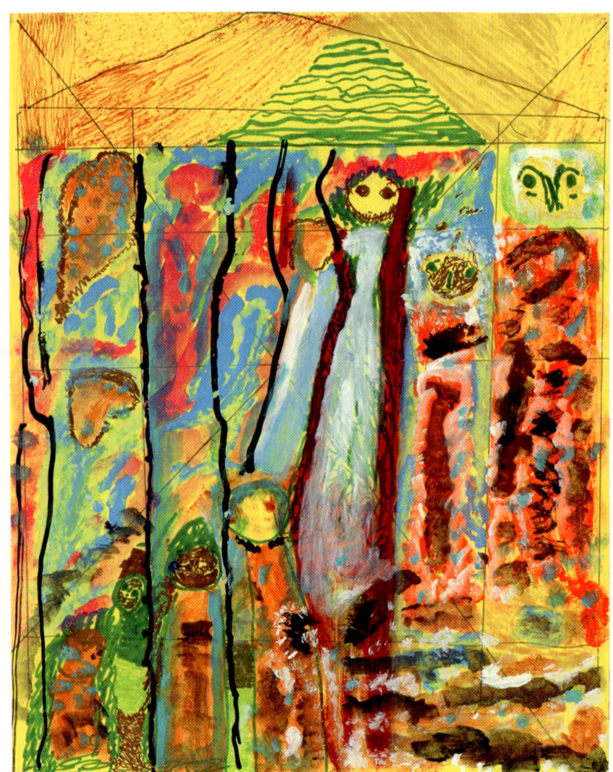

(clockwise from top left)
Pl. 23. **John B. Murray**, *Untitled*, early 1980s

Pl. 24. **John B. Murray**, *Untitled*, 1987

Pl. 25. **John B. Murray**, *Untitled*, early 1980s

(opposite)
Pl. 26. **Mary Proctor**, *The Keys*, 1996

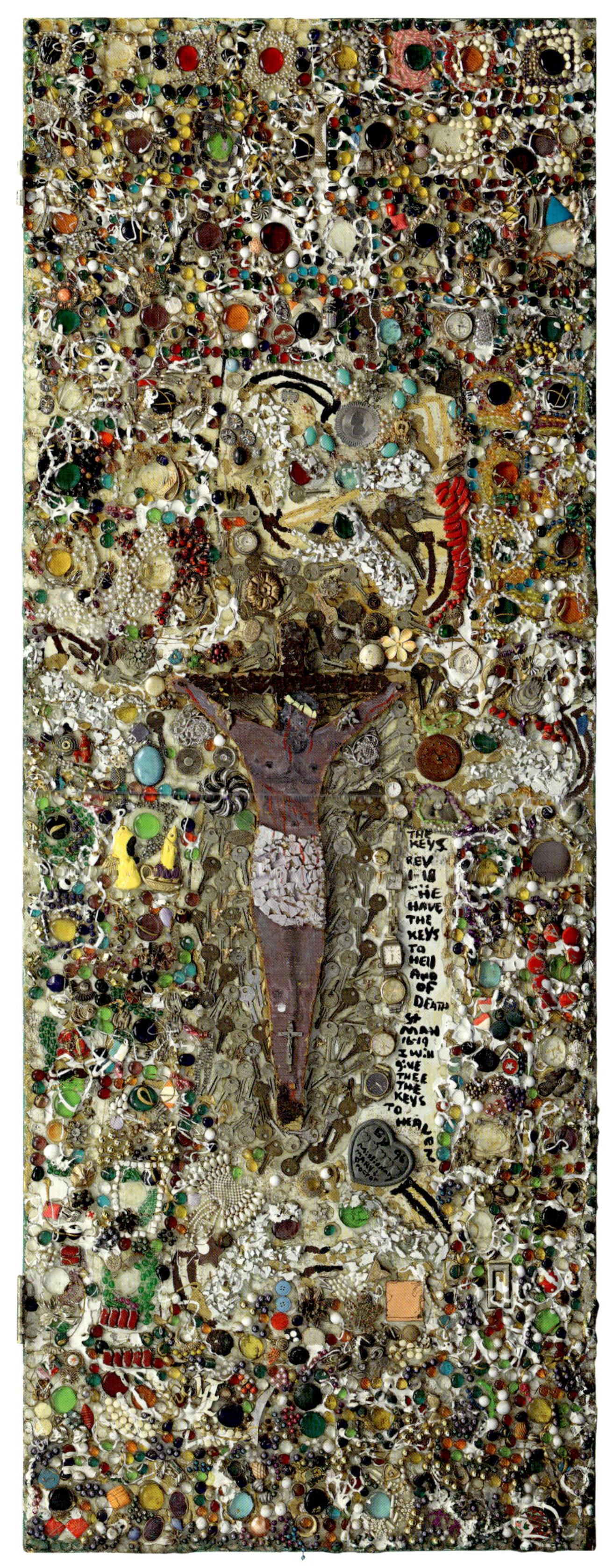
THE KEYS
REV 1-18
HE HAVE THE KEYS TO HELL AND OF DEATH
ST MATT 16-19
I WILL GIVE THEE THE KEYS TO HEAVEN

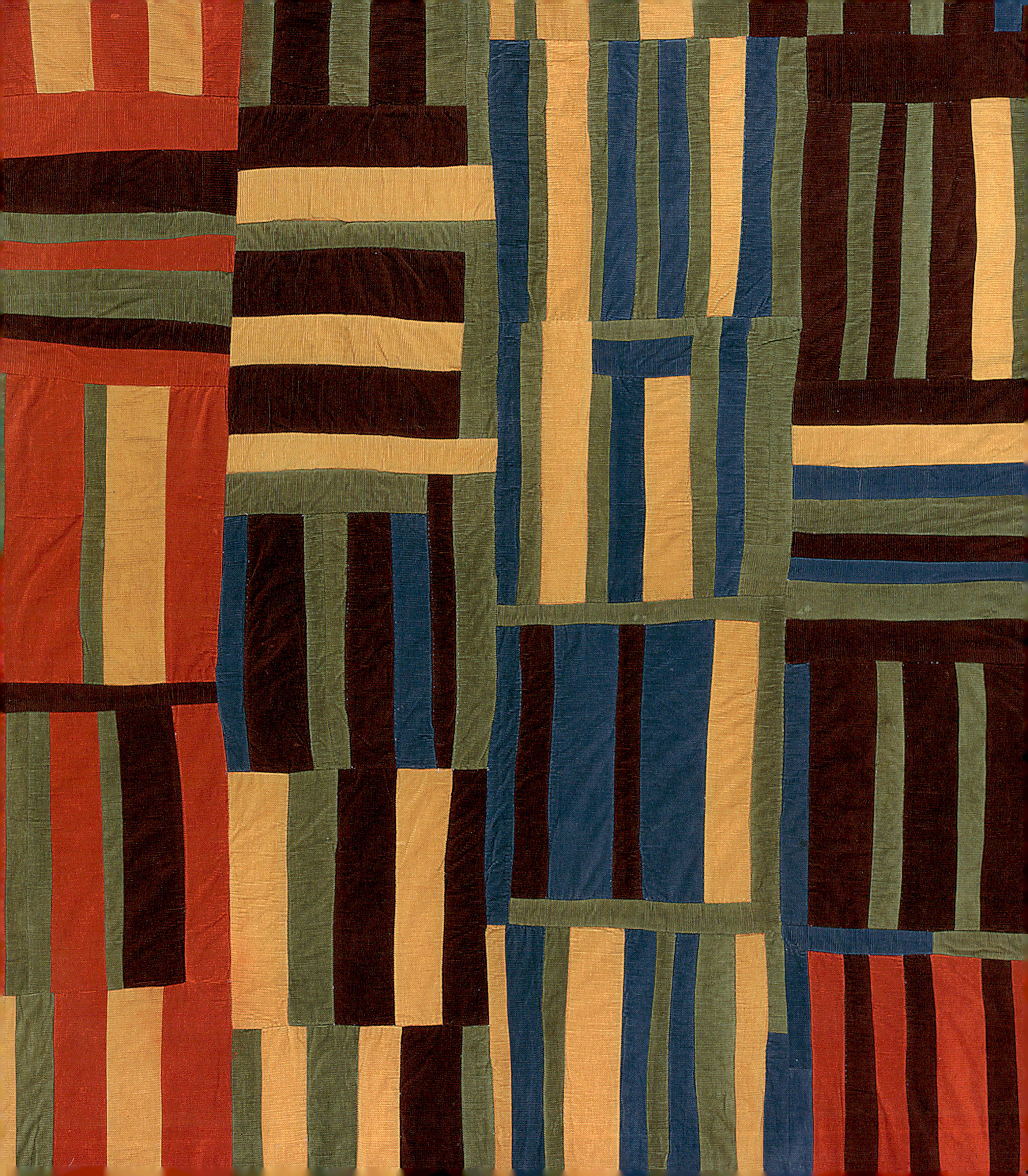

QUILT/ART
DECONSTRUCTING THE GEE'S BEND QUILT PHENOMENON

AMELIA PECK

When the Gee's Bend quilts were first displayed in museums in 2002, they were widely hailed as beautiful and powerful works of art. The path these originally humble textiles took on their way to being appreciated in exhibitions at the Museum of Fine Arts (MFA), Houston; the Whitney Museum of American Art, New York; and many other museum venues was praised by some and viewed with deep suspicion by others. The stories in the oral histories that accompanied these works made by extremely poor African American women were celebratory, heartbreaking, and indicative of the deep issues of race relations that still exist in this country. The original team that presented these quilts to the public consisted of collectors William (Bill) S. Arnett and Paul Arnett and curators John Beardsley, Jane Livingston, and Alvia J. Wardlaw, all of whom clearly believed that they had the best interests of the quilters at heart.[1] For the quilters, who often traveled to the openings at the various venues, this exhibition validated more than their quilts—it was a validation of their selves and of the struggles they had endured for most of the days of their lives.[2]

At the time of the show and in ensuing years, certain attitudes and actions on the part of collectors and commercial ventures have made the stories around the Gee's Bend quilts less positive and more problematic. There have been lawsuits about licensing agreements and questions of whether the quilters were fairly paid for their works, which were later sold to museums and collectors for high sums.[3] The exhibition's premise of the exceptionalism of the quilts has been challenged, since there are and have always been other great black quilters in this country. In some museums, the unfortunate result has been that a museum with a Gee's Bend quilt in its collection is thought to adequately represent *all* African American quilters. Responding to this essentializing notion, scholars have challenged the idea that there is even a specific recognizable African American style. For example, the *Star of Bethlehem quilt* (fig. 19), a formal and regimented star quilt made by two African American enslaved women for their owners in the mid-nineteenth century, is the only other quilt in The Met's collection known to have been made by African Americans. Without its documented history, it would not be recognized as an African American quilt.[4]

For better or worse, after the 2002 exhibition, the Gee's Bend quilts became something of an industry, and those made after the show are quite different in their intention than the first group of mid-twentieth-century quilts. Today's quilts by such makers as Louisiana P. Bendolph and Mary Lee Bendolph and other items based on the quilts' designs, are sophisticated works of art (pl. 27).[5] They were designed to respond to the way that these quilts were first judged by the art world—that

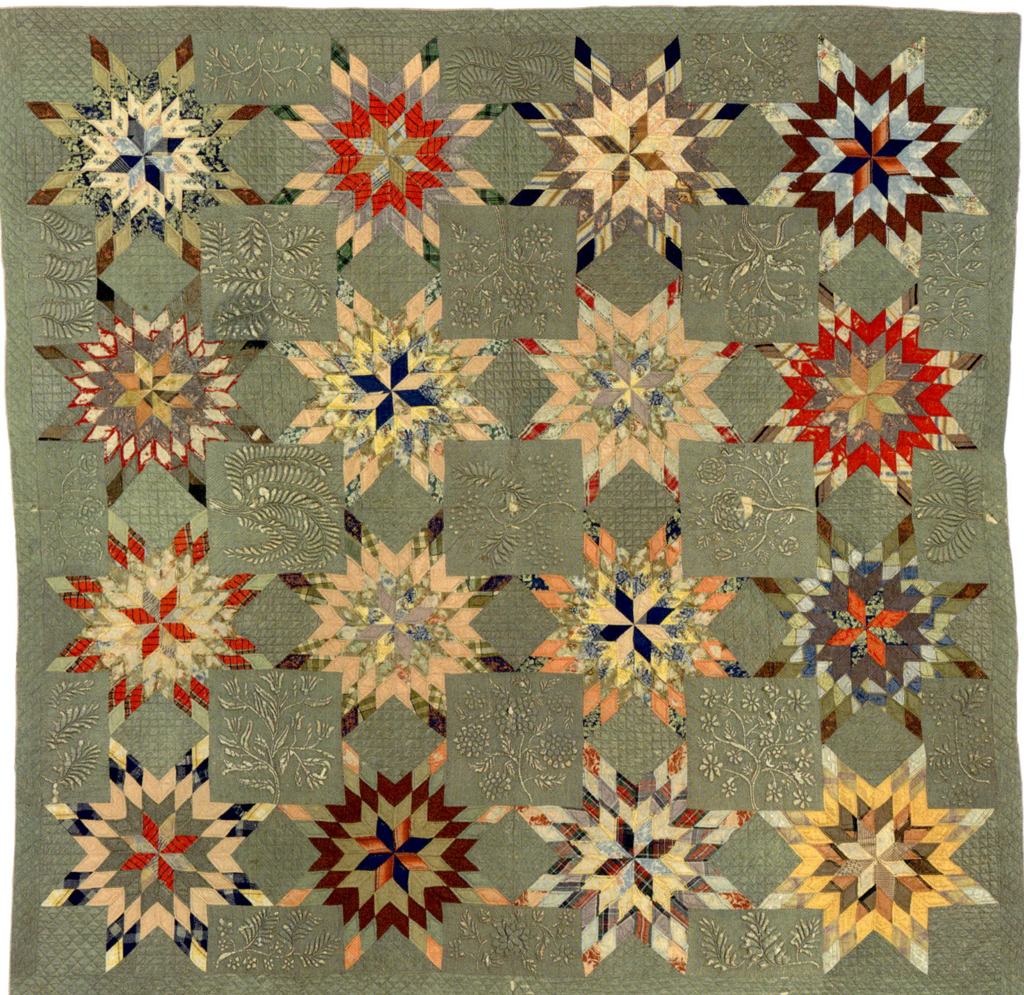

Fig. 19. **Ellen Morton Littlejohn** and **Margaret Morton Bibb**, *Star of Bethlehem quilt*, The Knob, near Russellville, Kentucky, ca. 1837–50

they were works of abstract art akin to the paintings of the popular Abstract Expressionist painters of the 1950s to 1970s, such as Barnett Newman and Mark Rothko (fig. 20, pl. 28). Because the earlier quilts in the exhibition, made by African American women living in an almost forgotten corner of Alabama, were created at the same time as the work of painters who were mostly white, urban males, they were judged as extraordinary expressions of the same aesthetic goals and ideas.

As a longtime textile historian, I find this correlation between abstract painting and quilt making an extremely false and frustrating way to understand quilts. In this essay, I mostly put aside issues of race and economics in the Gee's Bend quilts, since many writers have discussed them in great depth.[6] Instead, I intend to wade into the fray of whether these quilts can or should be labeled art, folk art, or craft. The literature around the Gee's Bend quilts made no bones about the fact that the curatorial team behind the show firmly asserted that the quilts were works of art and that the quilters were artists, not craftspeople. However, there are other ways of determining that quilts are art without trying to judge them by the same criteria as one would a painting. Quilts that are works of art have always existed, even if they served several purposes,

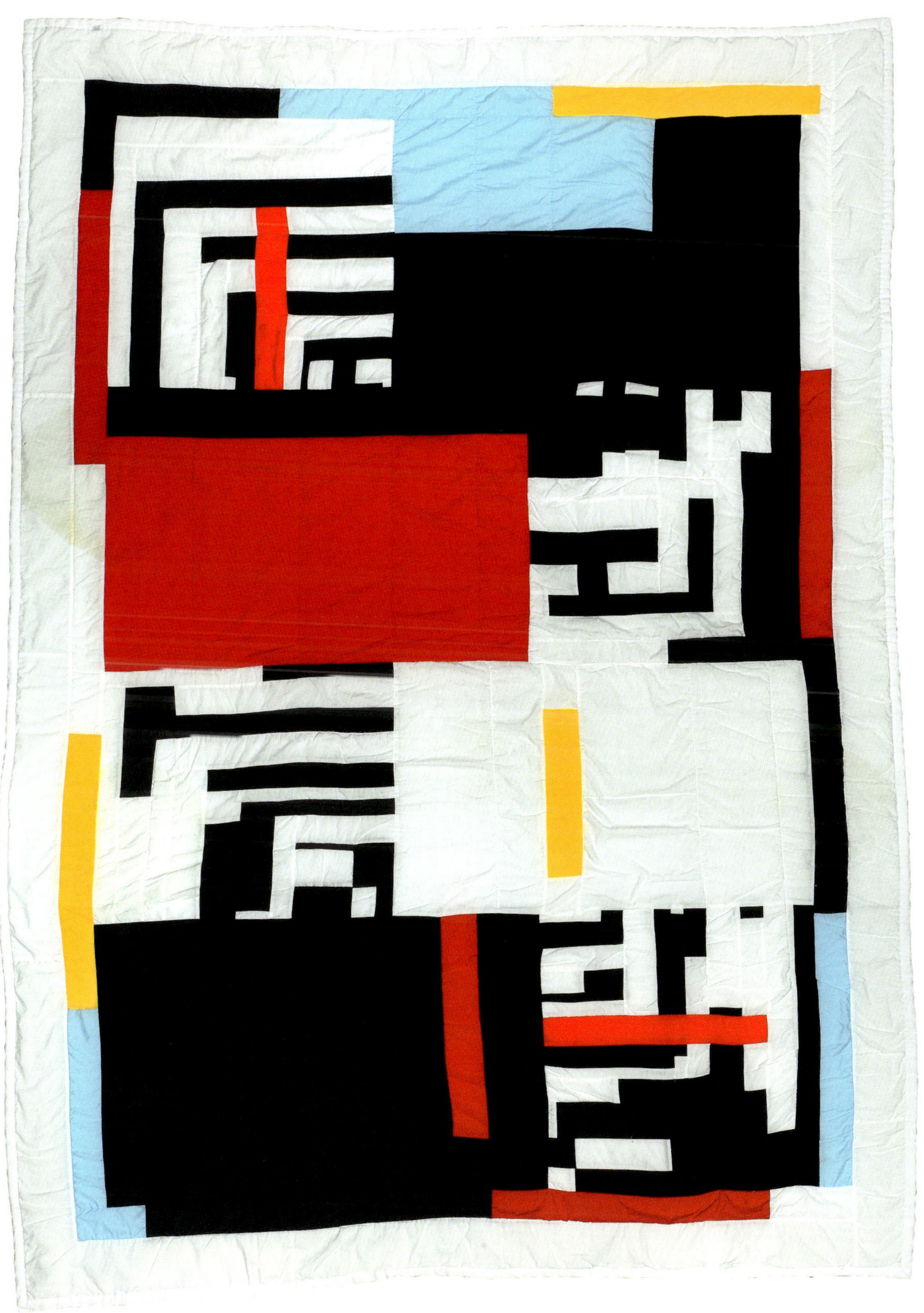

Pl. 27. **Louisiana P. Bendolph**, *Housetop quilt*, 2003

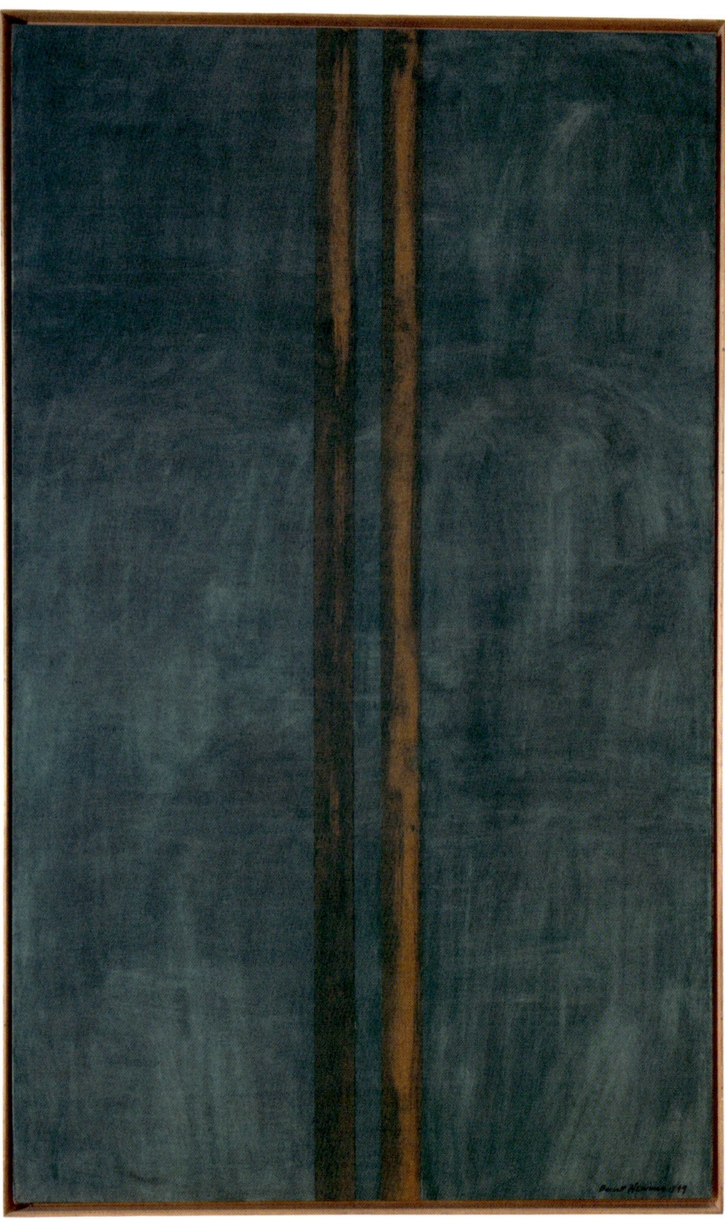

Fig. 20. **Barnett Newman**, *Concord*, 1949

including the most basic function of keeping a person warm. But in order to appreciate quilts, whether or not they were intentionally made as works of art, the last place a comparison should be made is to a modernist painting.

How did this phenomenon of the quilt = abstract painting first gain traction? In one way, it started with quilts very much like those celebrated in this catalogue. In October 1965, at the height of the Civil Rights movement, white Episcopal priest and native Alabaman Father Francis X. Walter felt called to move from an inner-city church in Jersey City back down to the state to become the executive director of the Selma Interreligious Project, a civil-rights group formed to help the rural African American poor of the Alabama Black Belt.[7] In an episode that would be repeated in the late 1990s when Bill Arnett "discovered" the Gee's Bend quilts, in the mid-1960s Walter saw some highly original, boldly patterned quilts hanging on a clothesline in rural Wilcox County (fig. 21). Wilcox County is the home of Boykin, the town formerly known as Gee's Bend, which was named after both a former white landowner and the deep bend in the Alabama River where the town is located. Because many of the quilts Walter saw depended on combinations of black and white or red and white fabrics for their design, he made the visual connection with both folk art and the popular Op art of the time (fig. 22) and, after discussing the quilts with some of the local women who made them, was convinced that they would be salable up north.[8] He and an Alabama friend, Tom Screven, who had moved to New York and was working for V'Soske, a custom carpet company, came up with the idea of auctioning them in Manhattan to benefit both the Wilcox County branch of the Southern Christian Leadership Conference and the quilters themselves. Father Walter purchased quilts for $10 each, which was at least twice the going rate.[9] After going from house to house, buying old quilts as well as new ones made specifically for the auction, Walter became convinced that all of the proceeds after expenses should go directly to the quilters, who would also benefit from forming a cooperative through which they could sell their handiwork. On March 26, 1966, the Freedom Quilting Bee cooperative was officially inaugurated in Rehoboth, a town about twelve miles north of Boykin.

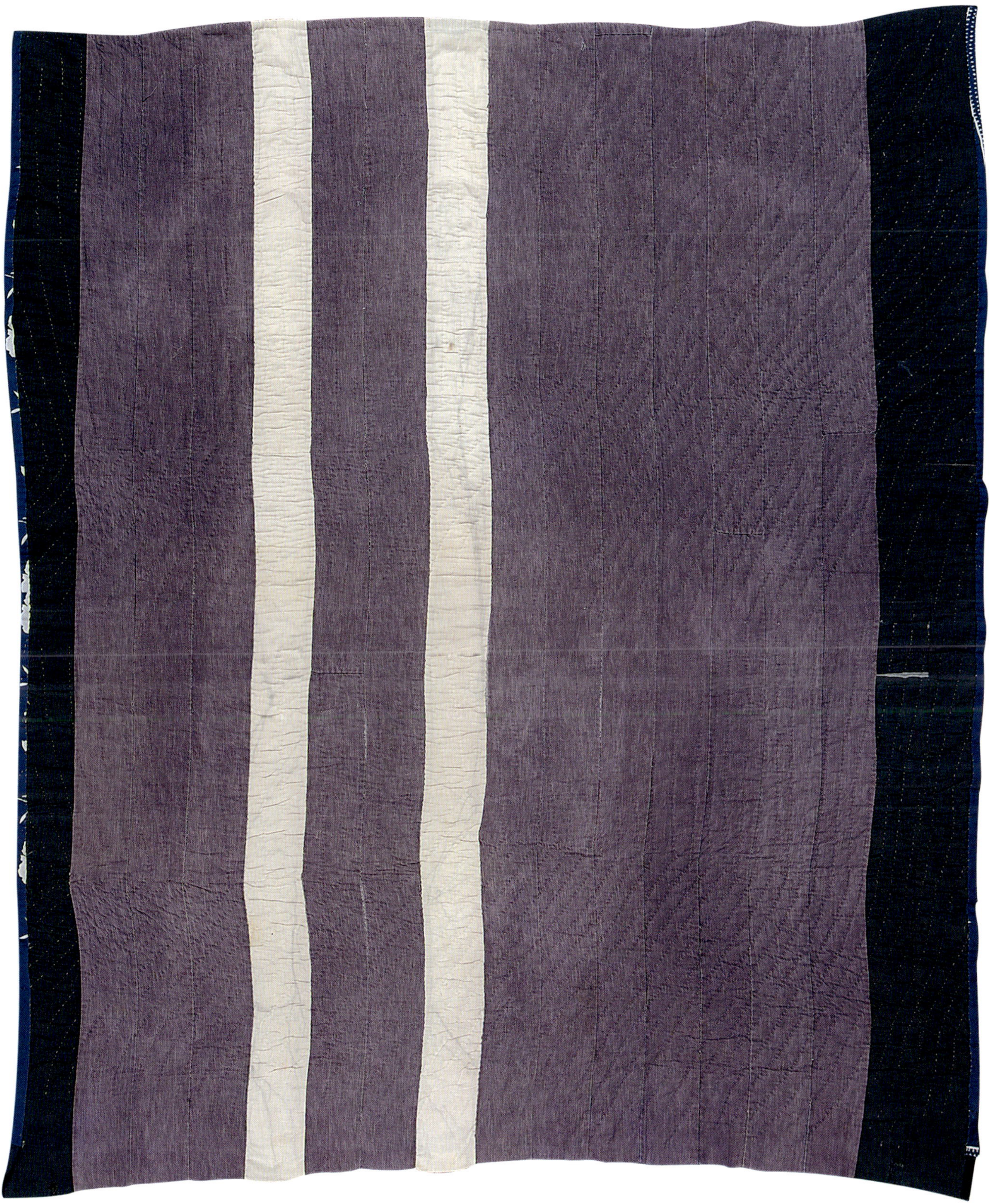

Pl. 28. **Loretta Pettway**, *Lazy Gal Bars quilt*, ca. 1965

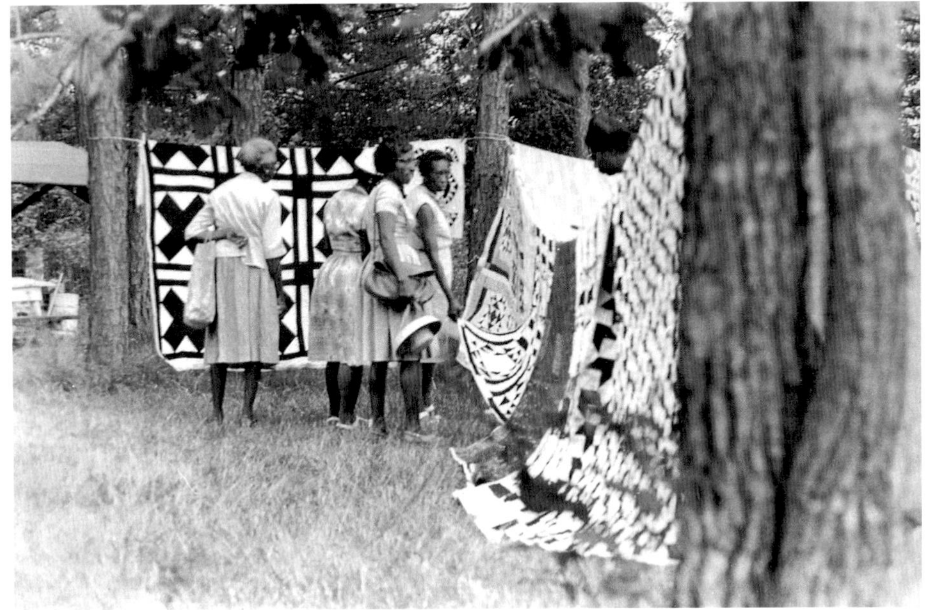

Fig. 21. Boldly patterned quilts on a clothesline, Wilcox County, Alabama, ca. 1960s

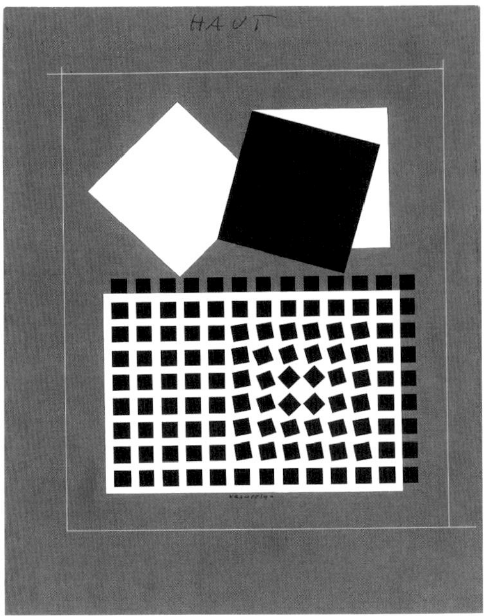

Fig. 22. **Victor Vasarely**, *Eridan III*, mid-1950s

The first auction of the quilts, organized by Screven, was held the day after, on March 27, 1966. Forty-seven quilts were offered for sale at Peter Basch's photography studio at 33 West Sixty-Seventh Street. Promotional literature urged people to "HAVE A TILT AT A QUILT" and explained, "Here is a unique opportunity for you to lend support to a worthy and urgent cause, and, in the process, acquire a totally handmade QUILT that is a genuine example of folk art." It went on to say:

> Probably, you have never heard of Wilcox County in Alabama, whose population is 80 percent Negro sharecroppers with an average *family* income of less than *$1,000 yearly*. The good ladies of these families have traditionally made quilts simply to keep their families warm, and they are currently amazed at the possibility that "outsiders" might actually pay money for their handiwork. Each quilt represents the individual maker's variation on one of the traditional folk patterns, the variations determined mostly by the materials at hand.[10]

About forty people, most of whom were more concerned with supporting equal rights than collecting quilts, came to bid on them, of which forty-two sold at an average price of $27. The auction was considered a success, and another was planned for May 24 at the Community Church of New York, on East Thirty-Fifth Street. With help from others enthusiastic about the cause, the May auction received a lot more advance publicity, and Screven designed a poster based on the quilt designs, of which he later said, "The whole op art phenomenon had been in flower. I hoped a poster of that style would capture attention of those likely to be attracted to the quilts."[11] Indeed, the first exhibition of Op art had opened at the Museum of Modern Art, New York, the previous year and had been a huge success with the public.[12] Two hundred copies of the auction poster were placed around Manhattan's East Side, and more than one hundred people attended, many of whom, perhaps attracted by the poster, were in the arts or home-furnishing business. One notable bidder was designer Ray Eames. The top bid was $70.

The auctions reintroduced traditional pieced quilts to a group of New York trendsetters. While quilts, the prevailing form of bedcovers in the eighteenth and nineteenth centuries, had enjoyed a revival in the Depression era, by the mid-1960s this art form had once again been mostly forgotten. One of the important steps in their eventual return to widespread popularity was directly related to the quilters of Wilcox County. Soon after the two auctions, in late 1966, Parish-Hadley, a premier interior-decorating firm in New York, contracted the Freedom Quilting Bee to make quilts that could be used in their interiors, often as upholstery fabric. The stylish Parish-Hadley interiors, in sync with the interest in handicrafts that were a hallmark of the 1960s, were featured in national magazines such as *Vogue* and *House & Garden*.[13] Both Sister Parish, the principal of Parish-Hadley, and Diana Vreeland, the editor of *Vogue*, were so enamored by the bold patterns that they bought Freedom Quilting Bee quilts for their own homes (fig. 23).

Another early collector was Abstract Expressionist Lee Krasner (1908–1984), who visited Tuscaloosa when an exhibition of her work was shown at the University of Alabama in 1967. The head of the art department, who was interested in the quilters' work, showed Krasner slides. Excited by the images, Krasner asked to go see the quilters. Father Walter accompanied her, and she was able to watch a group of women quilting in a Gee's Bend home. Krasner ordered three quilts and, on her return to New York, told many of her art-world contacts about her experience, and urged them to purchase a quilt (fig. 24). Of the quilts, she exclaimed, "They were a craft of the highest order. They were magnificent."[14]

Krasner was perhaps prescient. One of the people she raved to about the quilts was Henry Geldzahler, then-Curator of Contemporary Arts at The Metropolitan Museum of Art. He ordered some quilts for himself and apparently met with Father Walter to discuss the co-op and see samples of their work. According to Krasner, she even suggested that a show of the Freedom Quilting Bee's works be mounted at the Metropolitan Museum.[15] But Geldzahler thought of the quilts in terms of craft and design, rather than art, and in the 1960s, the Department of Contemporary Arts was more focused on paintings and sculpture. Geldzahler's evaluation of the quilts, from an interview in the mid-1980s, is interesting to note:

> I was touched by the quality of the work. I'm a curator of museums so I'm very involved with quality, but helping the Freedom Quilting Bee was not a question strictly of quality. There was a human question, of people making something with their own hands and having the possibility of making money out of their own aesthetics. Their aesthetic values didn't have to be mine for me to honor what they were doing. I'm not a crafts expert but I can tell strong, bold and controlled design when I see it and those qualities in the quilts were very good.[16]

The Freedom Quilting Bee, which lasted until 2012, was a financial boon to the quilters, but perhaps it hindered their creativity. While the first quilts sold at auction in New York were freer, though based on traditional patterns, and more purely the products of the women's imaginations and hands, the Bee began to receive specific commissions, thus requiring consistency in their product.[17] Soon, only certain patterns were offered (fig. 25), ones that could be produced quickly and with a high degree of uniformity.

Some of the more creative quilters drifted away from the group, like Annie Mae Young, who later said, "When they open up the quilting bee up there, they didn't want the type of sewing and piecing I do, and I didn't like what they was doing. They had to do things too particular, too careful, too many little blocks."[18] However, one unforeseen benefit of these commissions was the fabrics that were sent down with particular jobs. In the earliest days, as acts of charity, random lots of fabric remnants were sent to the quilters by textile houses in New York such as Scalamandré and Schumacher, some of which, such as heavy upholstery fabrics, were

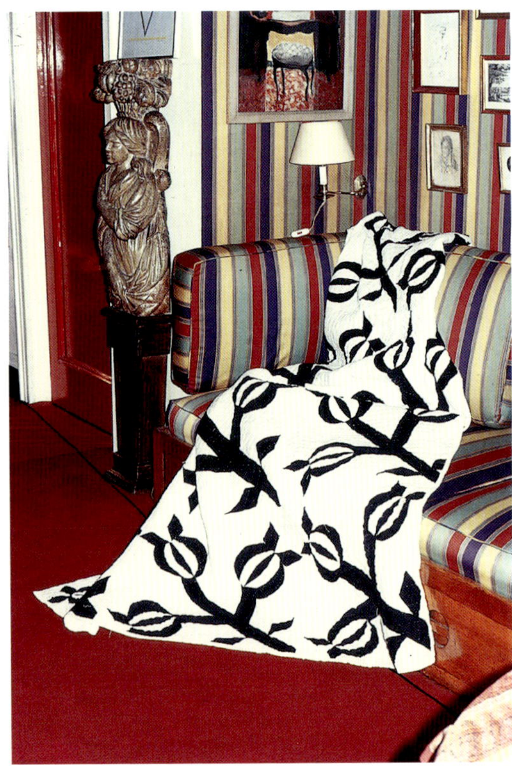

Fig. 23. Diana Vreeland's Freedom Quilting Bee quilt (1966) by Lucy Mingo in Vreeland's living room, New York

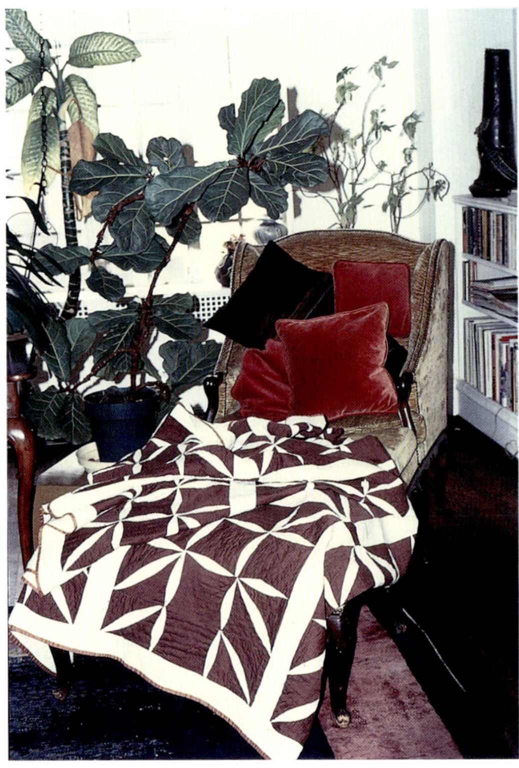

Fig. 24. Lee Krasner's Freedom Quilting Bee quilt (late 1960s) by an unknown artist in Krasner's living room, New York

totally inappropriate. However, sometimes the fabrics proved inspirational; for instance, the by-product of what was surely one of the most tedious commissions, the 1972 contract to make corduroy pillow covers for Sears, Roebuck and Company, introduced cotton corduroy in the typically fashionable colors of the early 1970s (reds, oranges, golds, avocado green, and peacock blue) into the quilters' lives. The leftover scraps brought a renewed energy to many of their quilts (pl. 29).

The reception in the mid-1960s of the Freedom Quilting Bee quilts remained split; while some artistic types began equating the patterns on the quilts with modern art movements, for the most part the quilts were still considered in terms of design, craft, and folk art. A major attempt to transform quilts in general into works of abstract art came in 1971, when Jonathan Holstein and Gail van der Hoof created the exhibition "Abstract Design in American Quilts" (July–October 1971) at the Whitney Museum.[19] New Yorkers Holstein and van der Hoof started studying and collecting quilts in 1968, when Holstein was working as a photographer of paintings and sculpture and also writing about art.[20] It is not known if they were influenced by the Freedom Quilting Bee auctions of two years earlier. Before Holstein had ever seriously looked at a quilt, he counted artists Barnett Newman, Robert Murray (born 1936), and Roy Lichtenstein (1923–1997) among his friends.[21] Holstein describes his and van der Hoof's growing interest in quilts as follows: "By late 1968 we were intrigued enough with quilts to spend a good deal of time looking at them in shops and markets, and there

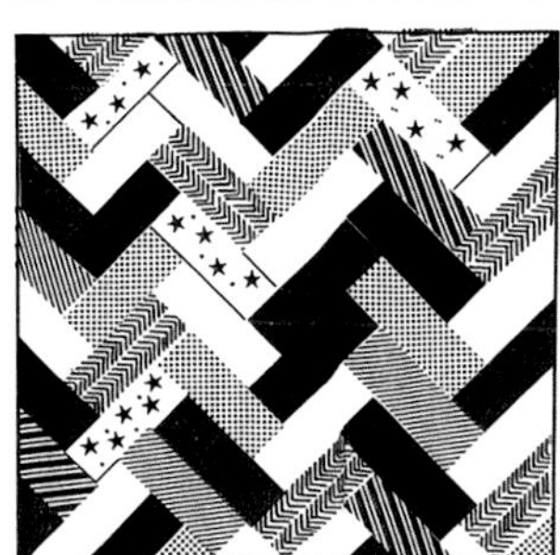

Q2 Coat of Many Colors

Traditional design giving the effecof a stained glass window. Combination of solids ad prints with coordinated solid border and backing, or for :more contemporary feeling all solids may be had at no adde charge. Made of finest cotton and/or cotton blend, mush-backed and dacron-filled.

Color Selection: Vivid multi-cors with yellow border and backing. Earth colors of browns, ısts, golds, beiges, sea colors of blues and greens in varyıg shades, combined with white.

May be ordered in twin, double, ueen, king and baby sizes.* See order blank for prices.

**Baby-size quilt used by many cutomers as wall-hanging, framed or unframed, bringing wenth and color to a room—enduring as a work of art.*

Q5 Rainbow

Set up in Grandmother's Choiceattern this pattern is made of the same fine materials and ailable in the same sizes. Done in vivid colors of the rainbv, all solid with blue

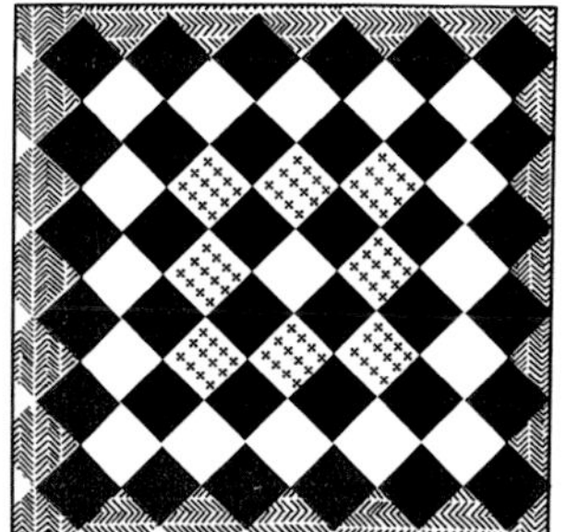

Q3 Grandmother's Dream

Both of these popular and traditional patterns made of the same fine materials and available in the same sizes and color selections as Q2 Coat of Many Colors.

May also be ordered in red, blue or yellow combinations of prints and solids at no additional charge. See order blank for prices.

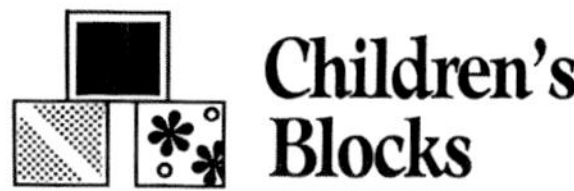

Children's Blocks

Small children delight in playing with these colorful blocks, in stacking and in throwing them—a safe and educational toy. Available in rainbow solid colors or primary calico prints. Made of fine cotton, dacron-filled, approximately 3" square. Be sure to state color preference on order form.

Fig. 25. Freedom Quilting Bee brochure, 1980s

certainly came a day when a particular quilt fit all of our evolving perceptions. There it was. I'm sure it looked just like one or another of the snapshots of paintings we carried around in our minds, and we bought it."[22]

In deciding to create a collection, they were only interested in quilts that "were in [their] opinion of great aesthetic merit, which worked for [them] as 'paintings,' creations in which the maker had posed and successfully solved interesting aesthetic propositions." Holstein explained further, "We felt that if we followed that ruthlessly, we would build a collection of the greatest visual interest and impact, one from which, eventually, a significant exhibition could be drawn."[23] From the beginning van der Hoof and Holstein had little interest in quilts as textiles, whether decorative or useful; to them, quilts had meaning and value only when they were equated with formal works of painting. While they could not state that quilts made in the nineteenth and early twentieth centuries, decades before the widespread popularity of abstract art, were exactly one and the same as paintings, they posited that the abstract patterns created in American pieced quilts represented "indigenous American aesthetic attitudes" that were later taken up by abstract painters.[24] They approached the Whitney Museum about doing a show, and the staff was receptive to their idea of creating an exhibition of about sixty quilts, hung according to "aesthetics" (i.e., which quilts looked good next to each other). They created the basic layout by taking the quilts they had selected out to Roy and Dorothy Lichtenstein's house on Long Island and ranging them around the lawn surrounding the house. Together with the Lichtensteins, they climbed onto the roof to view them, deciding on which looked good together by shouting down to the Lichtensteins' sons, who then moved the quilts around.[25]

"Abstract Design in American Quilts," which was meant to be a quick and inexpensive summer filler show, ended up being a popular and critical success. Perhaps the most surprising accolades came from Hilton Kramer, the highly conservative *New York Times* art critic:

> What is so impressive, then, is not the originality of the designs—these designs were, in the most literal sense of the word, conventional—but the dazzling sensibility for color and visual construction that the execution of these designs, with their personal and regional variations, display with such appealing vigor. For a century or more preceding the self-conscious invention of pictorial abstraction in European painting, the anonymous quilt-makers of the American provinces created a remarkable succession of visual masterpieces that anticipated many of the forms that were later prized for their originality and courage.[26]

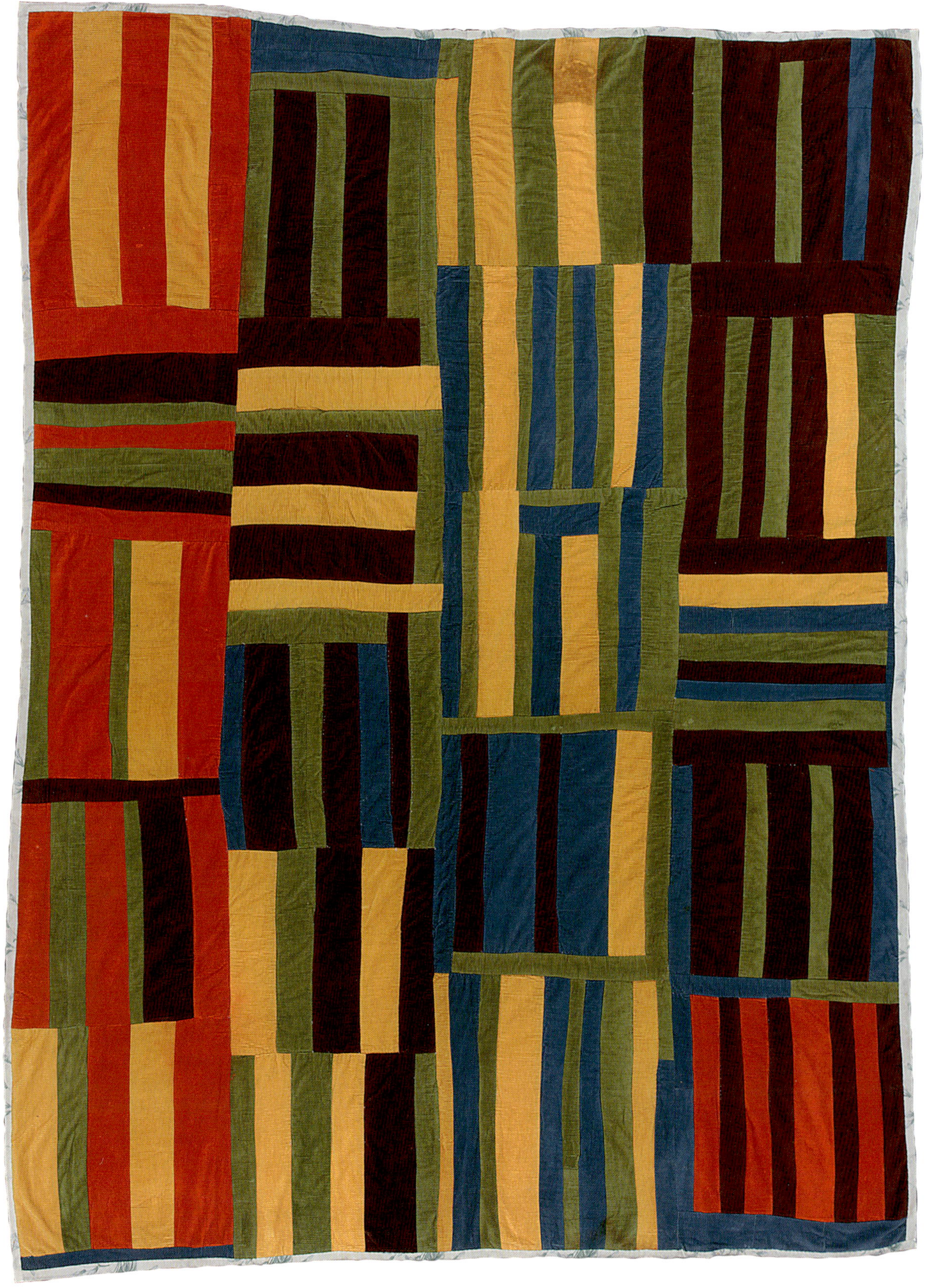

As a quilt scholar who came to the field about fifteen years after the Whitney show, I find several things troubling about the concept of this influential exhibition. First, within the title the tiny word "in" made a totally unfounded connection between an abstract art and American quilts. While American pieced quilts do display abstract, geometric patterns, the intention of the almost-always female quilter was to create a beautiful and satisfying pattern that would prove her artistry in the medium. These women were indeed quilt artists, but for the most part their intention was to put a quilt on a bed where it would be admired and also serve a practical use as a bedcover.[27] By hanging quilts on a wall in a white gallery space and equating a nineteenth- or even a twentieth-century quilt with canvases painted predominantly by men working on the intellectual ideas underpinning Abstract Expressionism, the work of mostly anonymous women quilters is diminished and becomes something like a party trick—that is, "Isn't it amazing that these untutored rural women were able to make something almost as good as our favorite paintings of the late twentieth century?" Under this mind-set, quilts are valid as authentic works of art only when they are defeminized by connecting them with a formal, predominantly masculine style of "fine" art. Then, they can be removed from the uncomfortably domestic "decorative" arena.

For many museums and collectors, "Abstract Design in American Quilts" and reviews like Kramer's gave them the imprimatur they needed to start collecting quilts as legitimate works of art. After the exhibition, the boldly patterned quilts of the Amish of Lancaster County, Pennsylvania, with their broad areas of densely saturated colored wool, became a hot area of collecting (fig. 26). At the Metropolitan, gifts of donated quilts were accepted starting in the 1920s and 1930s (fig. 27), but the museum purchased only one, a specially commissioned appliqué quilt in 1945.[28] After the Whitney show, numerous quilts were purchased for display in the American Wing. In 1973–74 alone, fifteen were bought, the majority of which were by Amish or Mennonite makers from Pennsylvania, except for one of the other newly appreciated stars of the quilt world, a Baltimore Album quilt. Following these purchases, in 1974 the museum held its first quilt exhibition, "12 Great Quilts from the American Wing."[29]

By the mid-1970s, it was generally accepted that quilts were objects worthy of displaying on the walls as "masterpieces." For many new collectors, their interest in quilts was in their formal visual properties, much in line with the Whitney show, but at the same time, a new field of serious study emerged, in which mostly female quilt scholars focused on materials, techniques, regional styles, history, and genealogy. The quilt market expanded during the 1970s and 1980s. Although it contracted again from the 1990s on, the field of quilt scholarship continues to grow in size and scholarly depth.

Many collections and thematic exhibitions have been mounted since the 1971 show, but perhaps none had the impact of "The Quilts of Gee's Bend" (2002–8).[30] What was the genesis of this enormously influential and long-lived show? In 1997, Georgia native Bill Arnett, collector, writer, curator, and entrepreneur, was reading Roland L. Freeman's book *A Communion of the Spirits: African-American Quilters, Preservers, and Their Stories* (1996) when he came across the image of Wilcox County quilter Annie Mae Young and her great-granddaughter Shaquetta Young (fig. 28). Arnett was so taken with the denim-and-corduroy quilt in the image that soon afterward, he and his son Matt visited Young. This initial trip led to Arnett's coming into contact with more than 150 other quilt makers from the area and ultimately, in the course of many visits over a four-year period, purchasing hundreds of their works. Arnett's interest in the quilts may have had its start in several earlier collecting forays, the most pertinent being West and Central African art, and starting in the mid-1980s, his fascination with the work of self-trained artists of the Deep South such as Thornton Dial and Lonnie Holley.[31] Arnett collected works that he described as

(opposite) Pl. 29. **Willie "Ma Willie" Abrams**, *Roman Stripes quilt*, ca. 1975

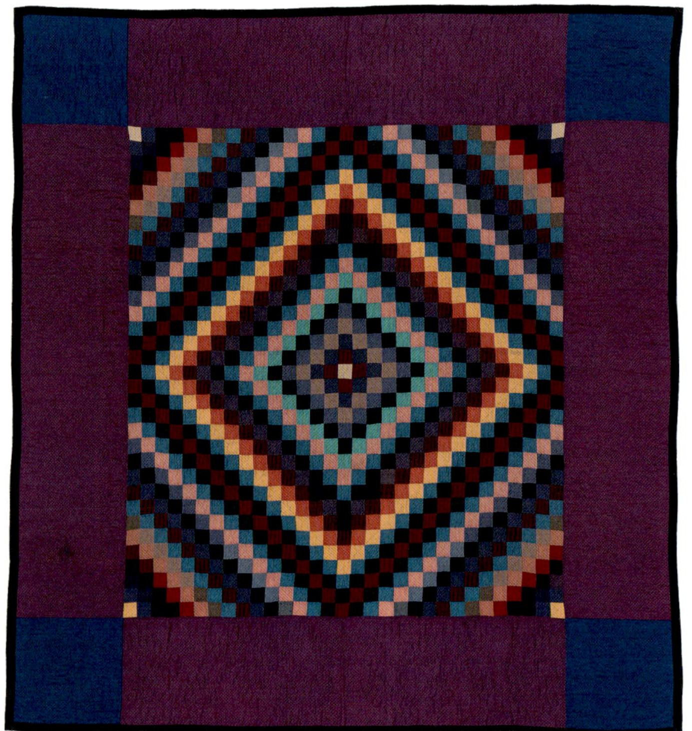

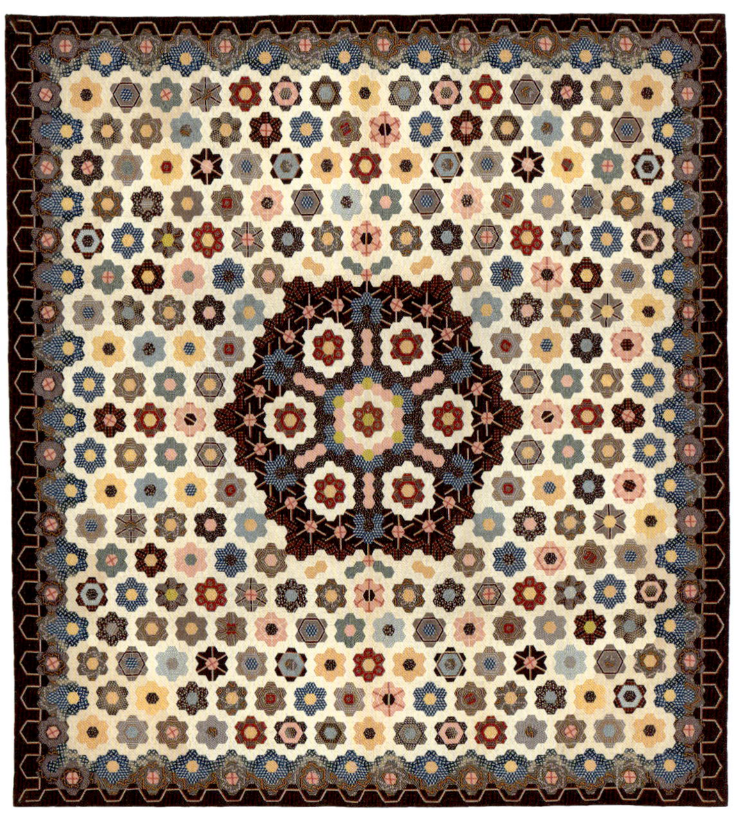

Fig. 26. **Amish maker**, *Sunshine and Shadow quilt*, Lancaster County, Pennsylvania, ca. 1930

Fig. 27. **Elizabeth Van Horne Clarkson**, *Honeycomb quilt*, New York, ca. 1830

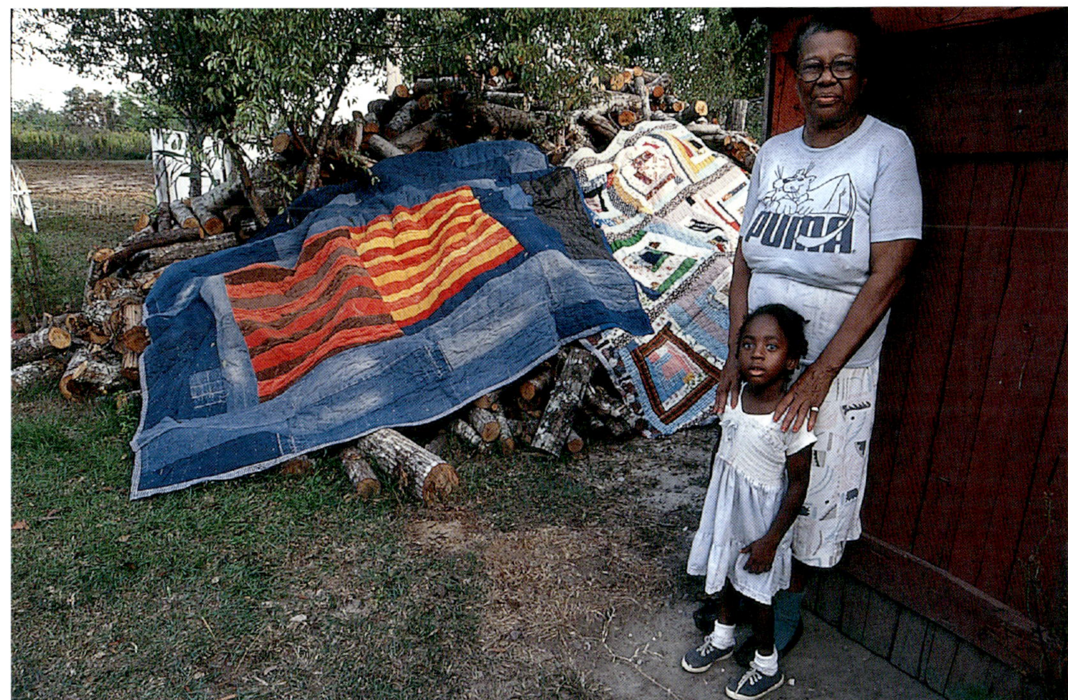

Fig. 28. Wilcox County quilter Annie Mae Young and her great-granddaughter Shaquetta Young, 1993

"found-object assemblages," which he believed were "the basis of southern African American art and aesthetics, evolving into a highly sophisticated visual language."[32] He believed that these assemblages and the Gee's Bend quilts that he collected in the 1990s were actually a means of subversive communication among blacks in the South. "As means of encoding information, both media [assemblages and quilts] can hide absolutely private meanings within often public manifestations. As a result, these 'vernacular' arts that developed among blacks in the South were highly personal expressions, indecipherable by the general population of whites and many blacks, and easily overlooked or dismissed as meaningless by potential adversaries. Because found-object assemblages and quilts are both created with materials that often possess symbolic, commemorative, or metaphysical significance to their makers, they may bear any number of messages."[33] Arnett put the assemblages and quilts in the same category, saying they were "two sides of the same coin; a quilt is simply a two-dimensional assemblage pieced together with the same philosophies and techniques as the three-dimensional one."[34]

Neither Arnett nor any of the people who worked on the 2002 Gee's Bend show were textile experts. Like Holstein and van der Hoof in 1971, they were looking at the quilts to prove something other than what could be found in the materiality of the actual object. In fact, Arnett's take on quilts came directly out of several popular sources written in the 1980s and 1990s. Art historian Robert Farris Thompson's *Flash of the Spirit: African and Afro-American Art and Philosophy* (1983) may have been the first such book that made the visual connection between West African strip-woven textiles and African American strip quilts. He believed that the knowledge of these "rhythmized textiles" were carried with enslaved Africans to the New World, where their traditional patterns continued to be passed down in the quilts created by their descendants.[35]

Thompson's student Maude Southwell Wahlman expanded on her mentor's work in *Signs & Symbols: African Images in African American Quilts* (1993) and posited that the patterns Thompson believed were carried down from Africa through generations were also means of communication: "Contemporary African American quilters . . . use bold colors and large designs as part of their textile aesthetic, perhaps due to memories their ancestors would have had of the communicative function of African fabrics."[36] She also wrote that some patterns had protective or religious significance, often without the quilters' knowledge: "However, because knowledge of some folk-art techniques is usually passed from one generation to the next by example, often without verbal explanations for the religious significance of forms, many African Americans are unaware of the meanings behind the forms they use in their art."[37] Additionally, Wahlman believed that the reason that these quilts "retain an African aesthetic preference for improvisation, for variations on a theme, for multiple patterns, and for unpredictable rhythms and tensions [was because] improvisation and multiple patterning are also protective, for copying is impossible."[38] Arnett was clearly influenced by Wahlman's book, and in fact his Tinwood Books imprint published the revised edition in 2001.

The thesis that these quilts were something other than what they appeared and had hidden messages that only white academics could tease out of them was another strategy to raise the quilts above the status of folk art or craft. However, the opinion that Wahlman and Arnett both reiterate about most African Americans being unaware of the symbols and signs in their quilts makes the concept both paternalistic and suspect.[39]

In 2000 Arnett assembled a team of curators and art historians to create "The Quilts of Gee's Bend" and the accompanying catalogue *Gee's Bend: The Women and Their Quilts*. To the team's credit, the quilts were not presented in the catalogue in the now-familiar trope of quilt = abstract painting. In fact, curator Jane Livingston wrote about the quilts in opposition to Op art and Abstract Expressionism as an equally valid "other art," saying "the 'other' art is, of course, the rich and various tradition of 'vernacular,' or 'self-taught,' or 'folk,' or 'visionary,' or 'outsider' art that has finally reached a point of general acceptance in most of the cultural establishment."[40] However, Livingston feared that the quilts would be looked at as merely "craft" since "quilts, especially those after the 1950s, have been generally categorized not as visionary or folk art but as *craft*, and have consequently been relegated to a traditionally subordinate and less serious, though much beloved, genre."[41] In order to combat this dreaded correlation with "craft," the catalogue is filled with reiterations of the quilts' artistry and the quilters' "genius." The first sentence of the introduction by curator Alvia Wardlaw reads "*Gee's Bend: The Women and Their Quilts* presents the genius of a group of *exceptional* women who, for well over a century, have created *distinctive works of art* for their homes and families." The women are called "textile artists" who "are in a league by themselves," and the paragraph ends with "*Gee's Bend: The Women and Their Quilts* presents a particular place and its people, who have created a body of art so rich in its content and so remarkable in its execution that it now enhances dramatically the American cultural landscape."[42]

The exhibition of seventy quilts by fifty-four makers opened at the MFA, Houston, on September 8, 2002. As Wardlaw continued, "From the beginning, all involved agreed that this exhibition was much more than a collection of quilts, albeit extraordinary ones. It was a study of an entire area in need of documentation."[43] At most venues, the quilts were augmented with a strong sociological component meant to illuminate the area of Gee's Bend, the quilters' lives, and the struggles for both economic and artistic survival: wall texts describing the area, biographical materials on the quilters, archival photographs from the 1930s of the town and its residents, and a twenty-minute film. Though at first considered an unlikely choice for traditional fine-art museums, the show next traveled to the Whitney.[44] While at the Whitney, the show received a rave review in the *New York Times*, but unfortunately, the critic once again equated the strongly graphic quilts with contemporary painting. Michael Kimmelman wrote that the quilts "turn out to be some of the most miraculous works of modern art America has produced. Imagine [Henri] Matisse and [Paul] Klee . . . arising not from rarefied Europe, but from the caramel soil of the rural South in the form of women, descendants of slaves when Gee's Bend was a plantation." He went on to comment: "Eyes of New Yorkers attuned to modern art will find echoes of painterly equivalents: here a Barnett Newman, there a Frank Stella, here a Josef Albers, there an Agnes Martin. The chances that poor black women in a remote corner of Alabama ever saw, much less were influenced by, any of them is slim to nil. . . . What we can say for certain is only that an ethos that permits us to appreciate the work of modernist painters also lets us recognize the virtues of Gee's Bend quilts."[45]

By the end of the three-month run, more than 200,000 people had seen the Whitney presentation. As one of those visitors, I remember being entranced by the quilts and the exhibition, which was beautifully installed in a spare, elegant way that responded to its setting in the Marcel Breuer–designed modernist building. Cultural historian and curator Michael J. Prokopow described the show in his review for the scholarly journal *Winterthur Portfolio*: "Occupying the entire third floor of the Whitney Museum and organized on stylistic and chronological grounds, the exhibition displayed the quilts as if they were canvases. And to be sure, the compact white galleries of Marcel Breuer's fortresslike building . . . were decidedly changed by the presence of the quilts. For although the critical and popular commentary that both preceded and followed the exhibition's opening emphasized that it was one of a kind and should not be missed, the extraordinary mood that pervaded the galleries was not discussed. If anything, the exhibition fostered a type of solemnity and awe."[46]

That awe, which I experienced, came through the materiality and expressive nature of the quilts themselves. I remember being particularly touched by those made from recycled worn blue denim work clothes, such as plate 30, which spoke to the extreme poverty of the area, where every last bit of cloth needed to be used and reused until it was nothing but scraps, and then might be reused as the filling of yet another quilt.[47] The worn clothes were a testament to the hard labor of working in the fields, and the fact that after they were done being useful as clothes they made their way into quilts made me think of the dire necessity of keeping a family warm year-round in a wood cabin. To this middle-class New Yorker, used to a desk job, central heating, and being able to go to a store to purchase a down comforter to put on my bed in winter, these quilts bluntly revealed the harsh reality of day-to-day life in the Deep South in the middle decades of the twentieth century. As Prokopow noted:

> In moving from room to room, with quilt after quilt rarely failing to astonish, it was striking how at a certain point the quilts ceased being art objects, despite the curators' efforts to secure their status as art. Their compositions, their capacity to startle and surprise, the poignant obviousness of their purpose, and their very materiality—including pieces of dungarees and work clothes, faded where knees and elbows had bent in toil—combined to make the viewing of the quilts much more than the type of aesthetic and emotional engagement of, say, seeing [Willem] de Kooning's early abstract work for the first time. For in the ways that certain works of art and certain exhibitions generate particular and palpable moods . . . *The Quilts of Gee's Bend* created a profoundly striking mood in the Whitney Museum's galleries.[48]

Why did these quilts, presented as works of modern art, have a very different effect on their viewers than a painted canvas might? I will not say because they are not "art," because I believe they are. Sometimes called "folk," "self-taught," or "outsider" art, they are just a type of art different from painting or sculpture. I choose not to distinguish between folk art and art; as a long-time American decorative-arts curator, specializing in textiles and interiors, I study a lot of handmade material that could be considered "folk art." However, in my eyes, anything created with the intent to give visual pleasure to those who view it can be called "art."

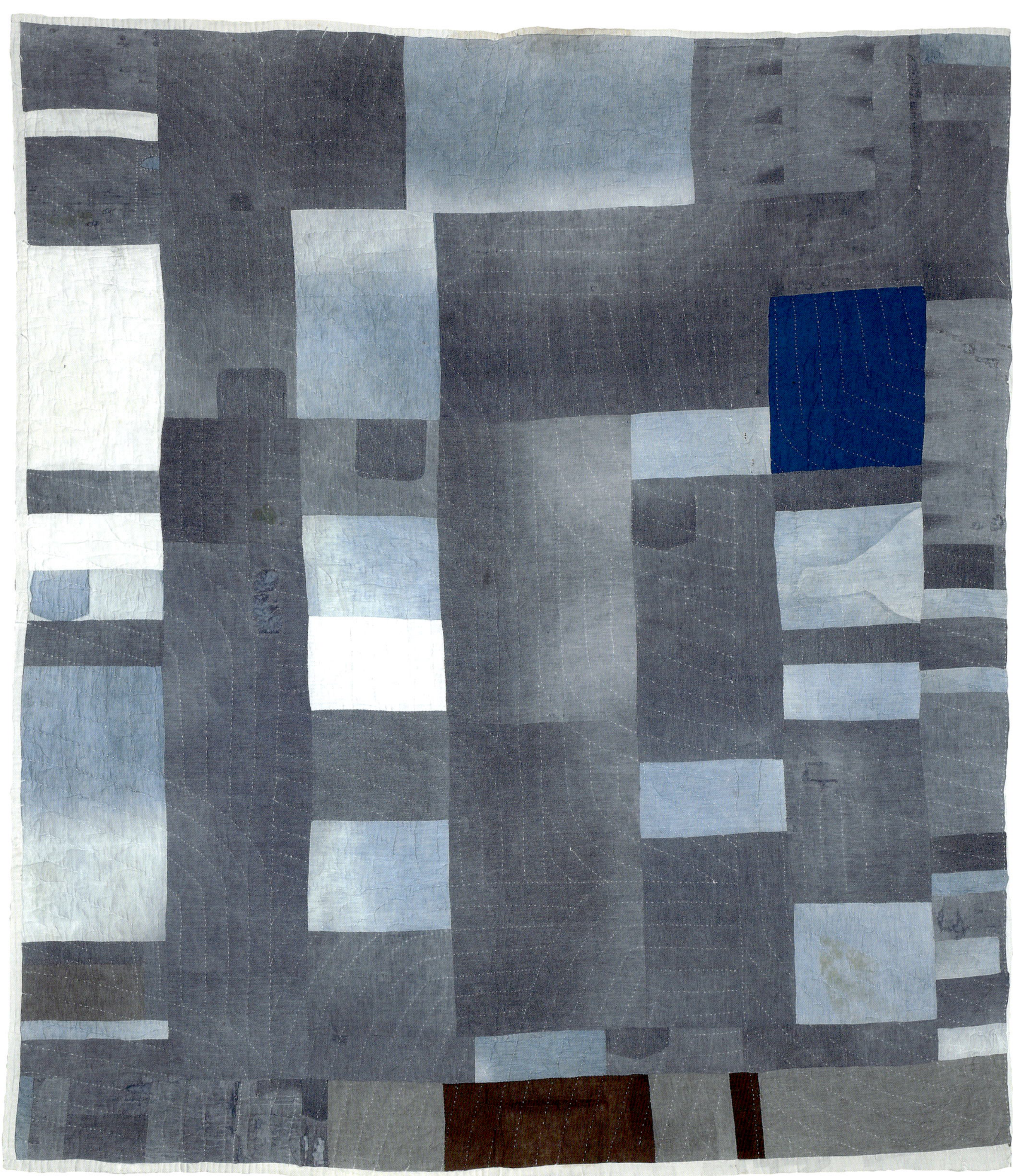

Pl. 30. **Lucy Mingo**, *Blocks and Strips work-clothes quilt*, 1959

Yet quilts, besides being pieces of art, are more. Most are about design, pattern, and color, but they are also about warmth, handwork, and family. The Gee's Bend quilts speak about poverty and deprivation, isolation and the handing down of design traditions from generation to generation. Each tells a rich story, as most quilts do, no matter their maker. As curator Ulysses Grant Dietz of the Newark Museum has written: "I am inclined to see these connections between modern art and African American quilts as false cognates—accidental intersections with no cultural weight beyond delightful coincidence. For me, the most valid way to discuss quilts is through their own virtues. . . . These quilts would exist, and would mesmerize and inspire, even if modern art had never existed."[49]

Historically, in the eighteenth and nineteenth centuries, it was rare for an American woman to become a painter or sculptor. The rise of the female professional artist did not really begin in any meaningful way until the end of the nineteenth century, and the path toward being considered on equal terms with male artists is still somewhat rocky today. That path was even more difficult for women artists of color. However, there have always been artistic women. Even when unable to obtain training, materials, or time, they still had the impulse to make art. Textiles, a material traditionally assigned to the female domain, were an accessible, uncontroversial place to create. Like other artists, people make decisions about color, texture, and composition when they create a quilt. Sometimes they use traditional, well-known patterns, while at other times they create more free-form quilts. The Gee's Bend quilters, and many other African American quilters, mostly employed traditional nineteenth-century pieced patterns, although some quilts appear freer and more spontaneous than those made by white quilters from the same patterns.

The Gee's Bend quilts in the Museum's collection are primarily based on five traditional patterns: Log Cabin (sometimes called Bricklayer by the Gee's Bend quilters), small and large strip quilts, center medallion quilts that have been translated into the Gee's Bend Housetop pattern, Flying Geese variations, and Crazy variations. Some Gee's Bend quilts do not exactly fit into one category only; several blend patterns such as Housetop and Log Cabin. By breaking and blending patterns, the designs are filled with action and vibrancy. Although it may be tempting to assign specific meaning to the patterns used, without the quilters specifically explaining their intentions, it is hard to subscribe to this speculation. The patterns seem more practical than symbolic.

The Log Cabin pattern, which became extremely popular across the United States between about 1860 and 1880, seems a natural style for the Gee's Bend quilters to embrace. Many homes in Gee's Bend were log cabins in the years when the many of the quilters grew up (fig. 29). Some quilters got the ideas for their designs from their immediate environment, such as Mary Lee Bendolph, who said: "Most of my ideas come from looking at things. Quilts is in everything. . . . I see the barn, and I get an idea to make a quilt. I can walk outside and look around in the yard and see ideas all around the front and the back of my house."[50] But more practically,

Fig. 29. **Arthur Rothstein**, *Girl at Gee's Bend (Artelia Bendolph)*, April 1937

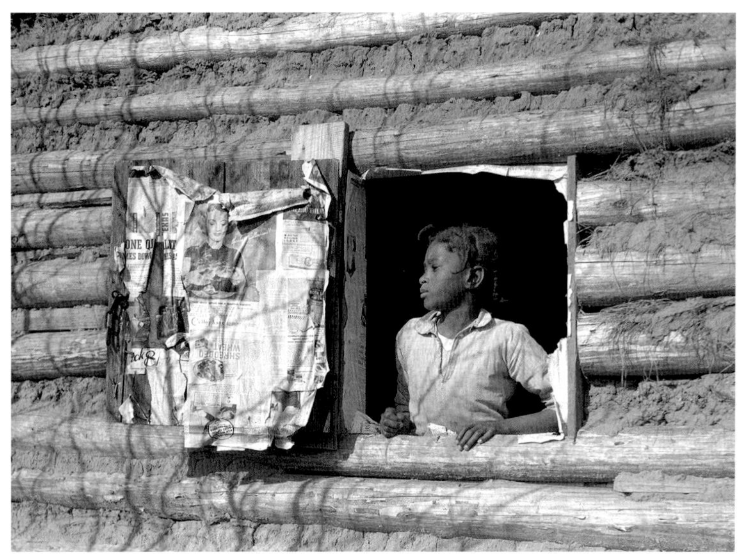

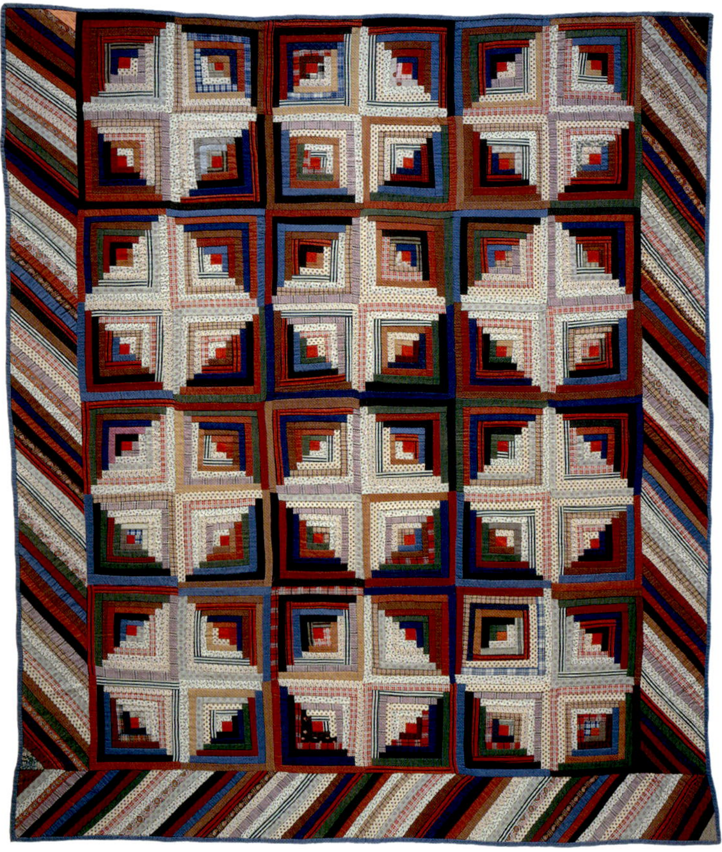

Fig. 30. **Unknown maker**, *Log Cabin quilt*, possibly Pennsylvania, ca. 1865

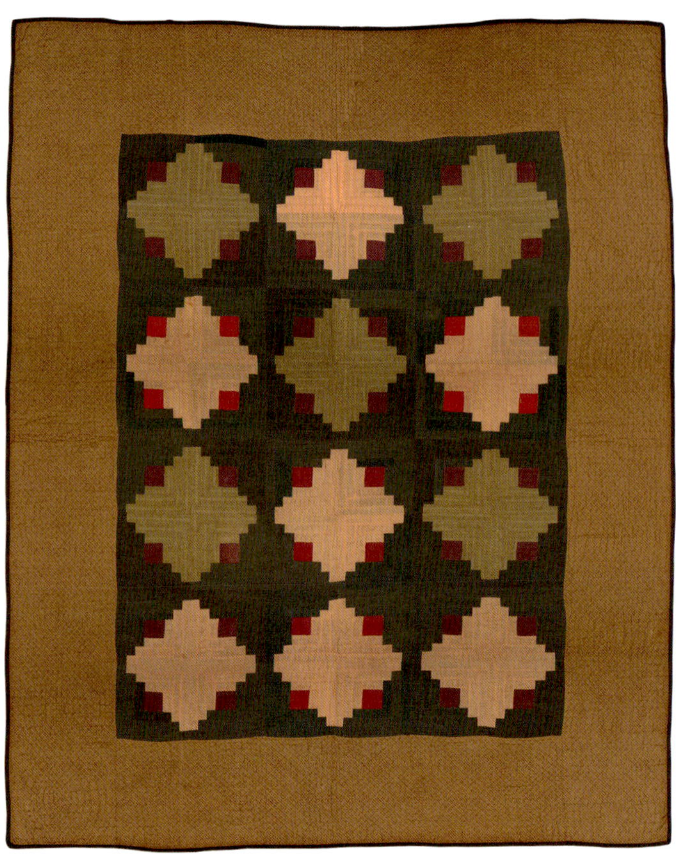

Fig. 31. **Unknown maker, possibly Mennonite**, *Log Cabin quilt*, Pennsylvania, ca. 1900

the Log Cabin pattern only calls for very small bits of assorted fabric to be pieced together; it is useful for those without the means to buy new yardage, but with plenty of various scraps at their disposal. Figures 30–31 and plates 31–33 show some Gee's Bend variations on this pattern and related examples from the Metropolitan's collection that demonstrate other ways the pattern can be laid out. A quilt (pl. 34) by Lucy T. Pettway, made with large and small strips of fabric in the common patterns of both Housetop and Bricklayer, may be one of the only representational quilts. It has been interpreted as an aerial view or map of the old Pettway property, with the large plantation house at the top, the smaller slave cabins in two lines below it, the blue Alabama River to the right, and the fields to the left.[51]

Another extremely popular way of building up a design, similar to the Log Cabin style, was based on small or large rectangular strips of fabric that were joined together vertically or sometimes both vertically and horizontally. The smaller strip quilts seen in plates 29 and 35 are based on the Roman Stripes pattern that was widely seen in the greater United States in the last three decades of the nineteenth century. In that period, the pattern was somewhat akin to the Crazy quilts of the 1880s and often used small bits of leftover silks and velvets from dressmaking (fig. 32).

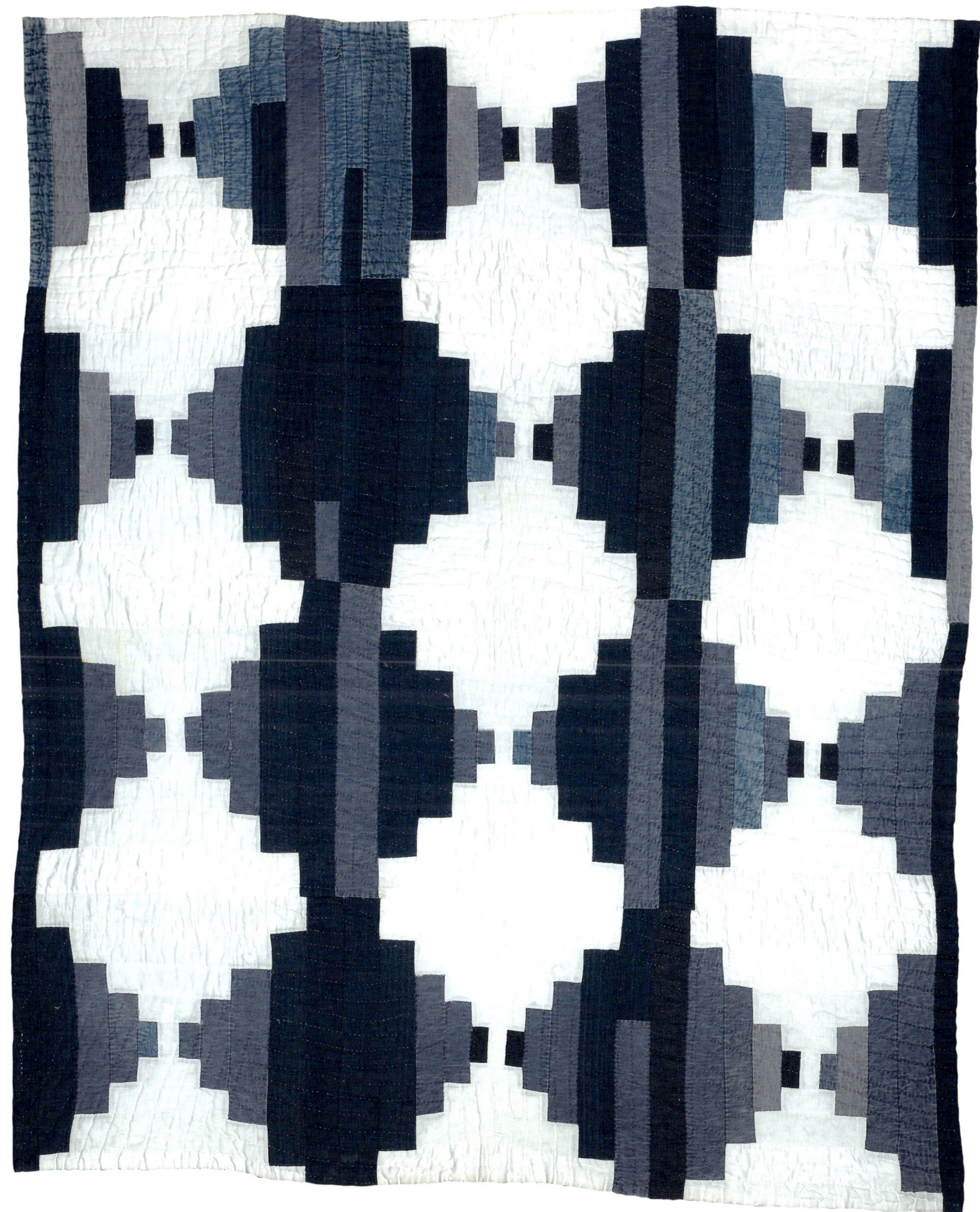

Pl. 31. **Linda Diane Bennett**, *Bricklayer quilt*, ca. 1970

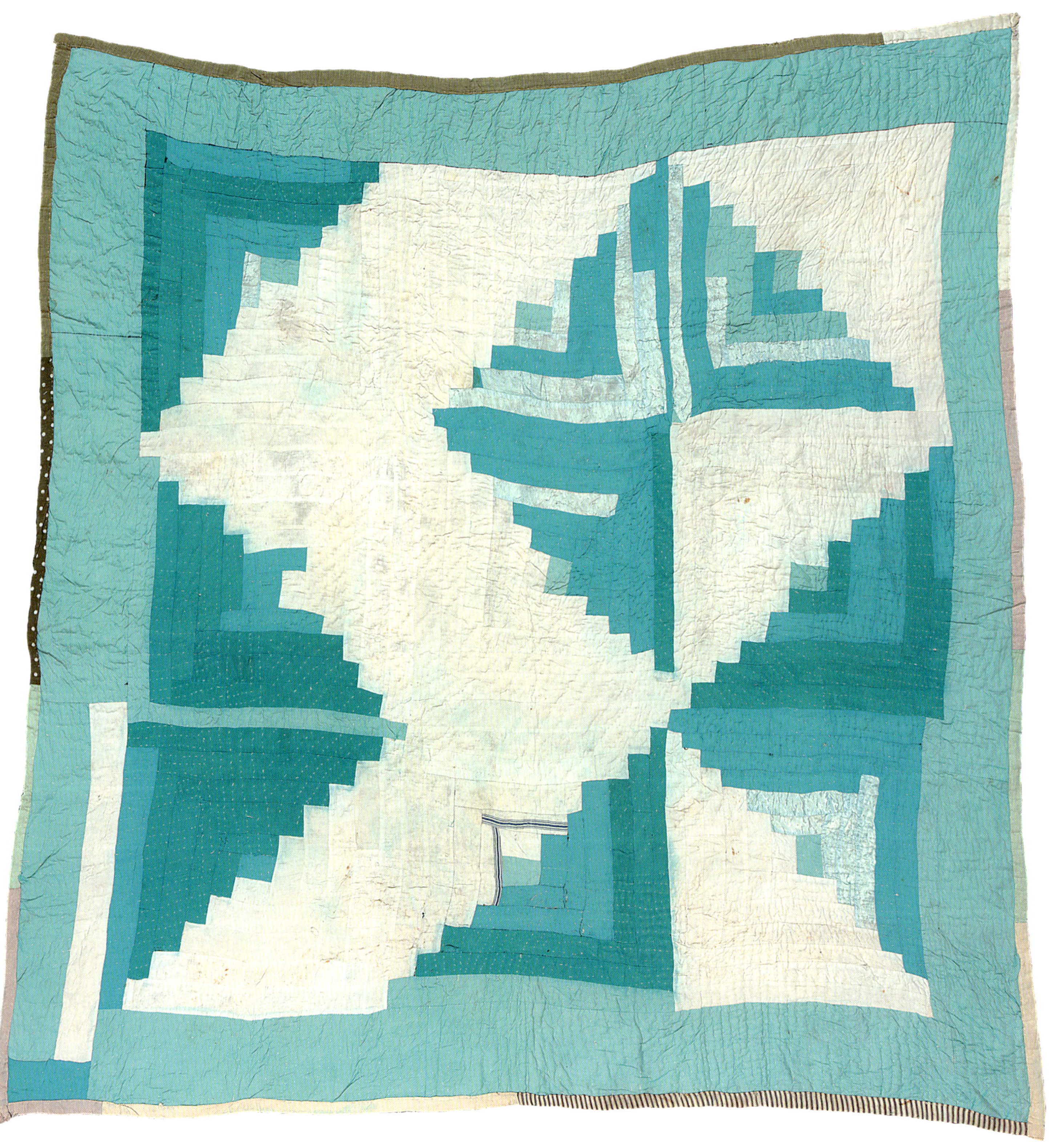

Pl. 32. **Mary Elizabeth Kennedy**, *Log Cabin quilt*, ca. 1935

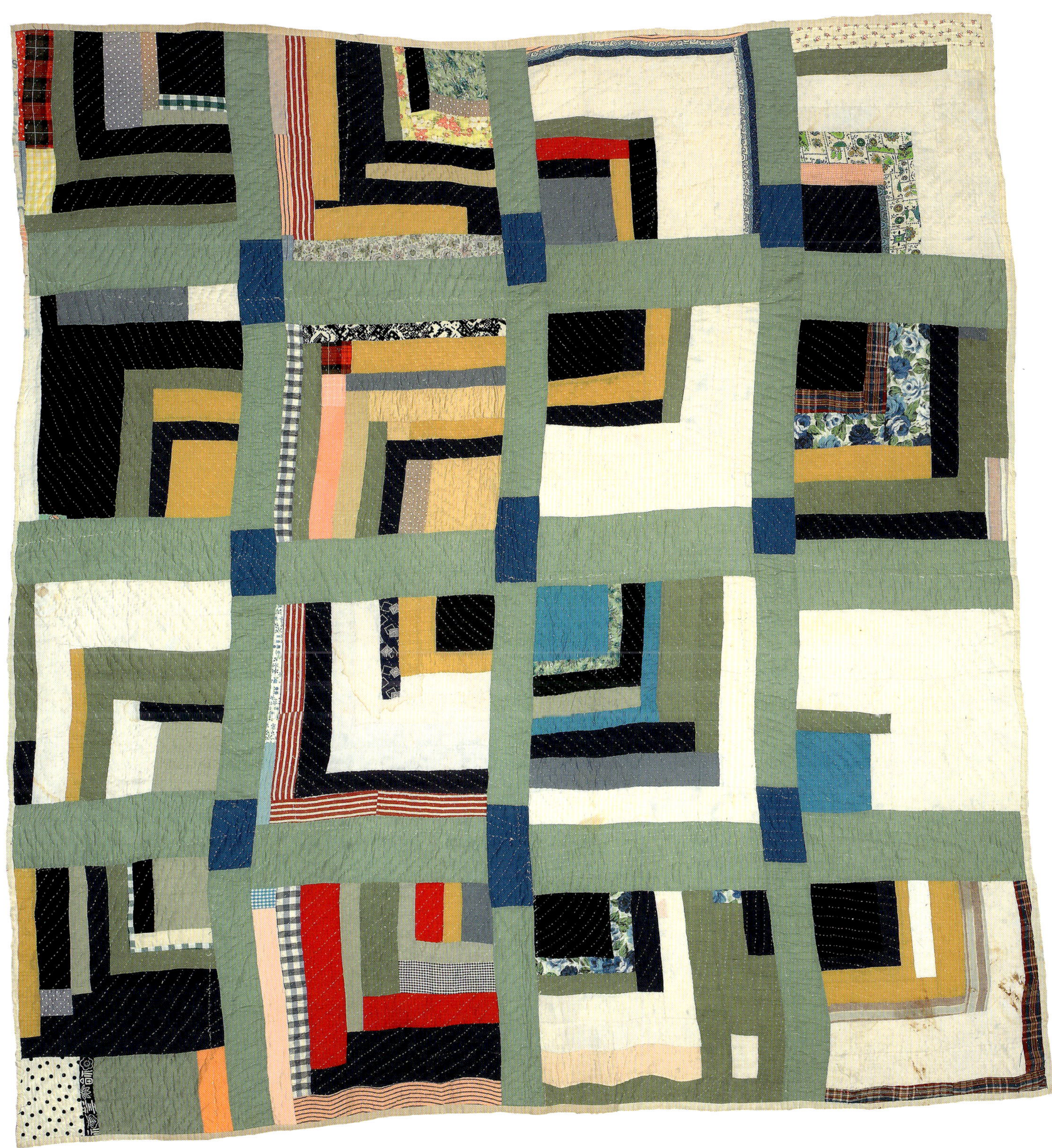

Pl. 33. **Martha Pettway**, *Log Cabin quilt*, 1930s

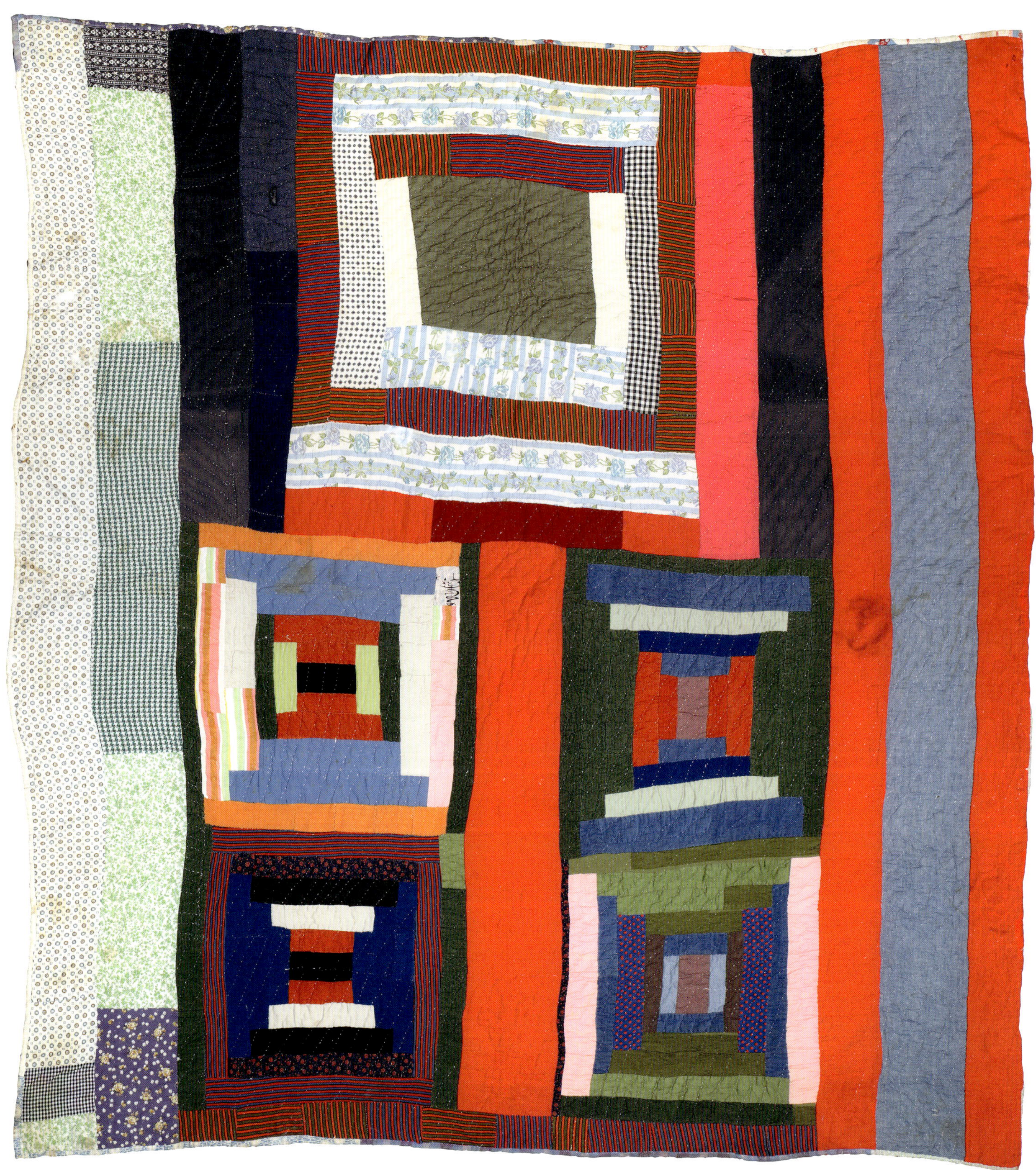

Pl. 34. **Lucy T. Pettway**, *Housetop and Bricklayer with Bars quilt*, ca. 1955

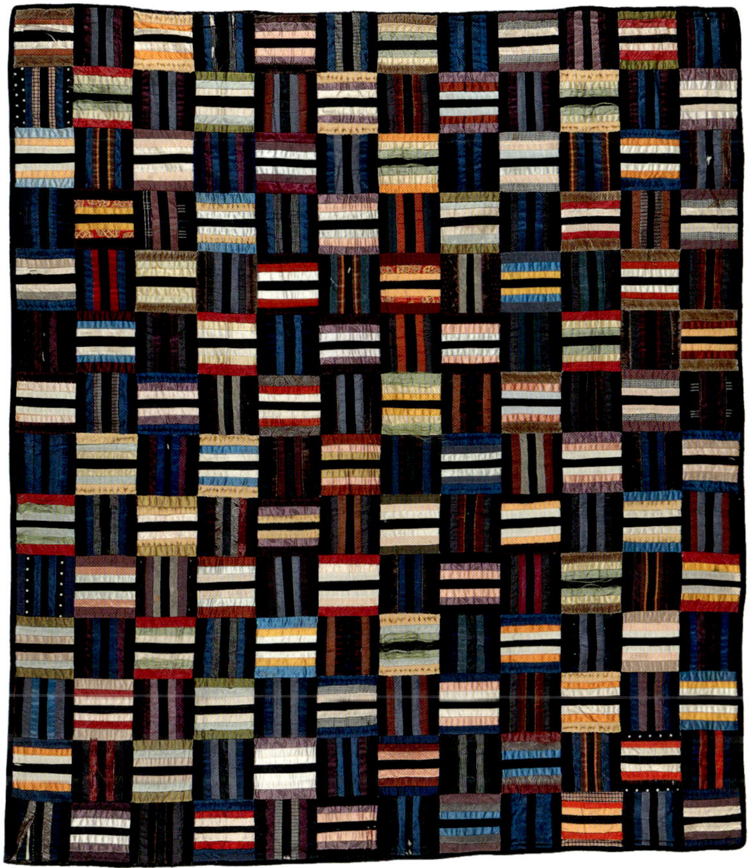

Fig. 32. **Julia Perry Brigham**, *Roman Stripes quilt (or decorative throw)*, Wyoming County, New York, ca. 1865

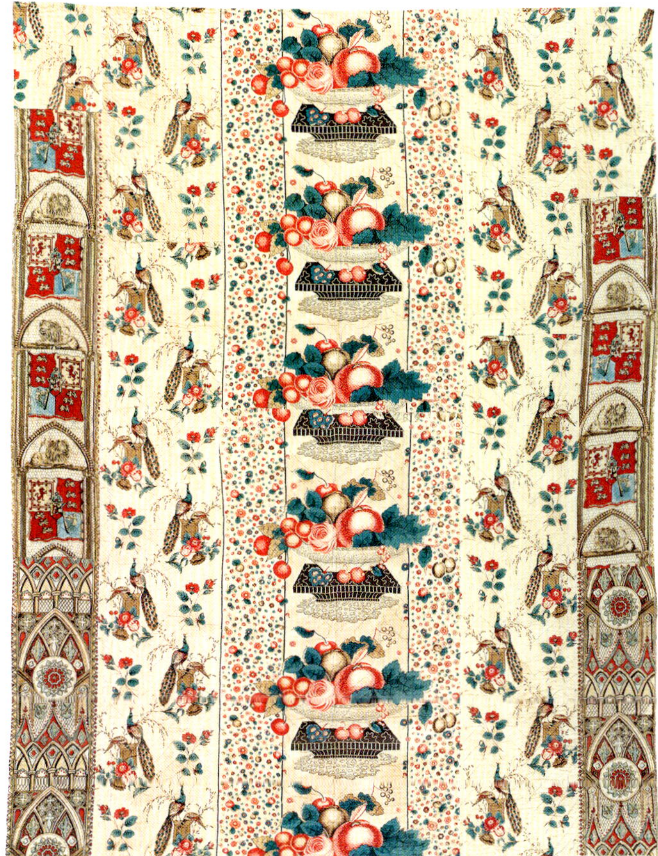

Fig. 33. **Unknown maker**, *Strip quilt*, New Hampshire, ca. 1840

Larger strip quilts from Gee's Bend arise from a similar tradition of preserving scraps of cloth like those found in quilts from the first half of the nineteenth century, when yardage of brightly colored printed cloth was expensive, hard to acquire in America, and therefore treasured. The American Wing owns two quilts pieced of long strips of printed English chintz in festive colors. One of them, figure 33, is composed of four different fabrics, which are somewhat awkwardly pieced at the sides, since the quilter was working with leftover fragments. For Gee's Bend quilters, sometimes leaving intact long strips of whatever fabric they had would produce a strong visual statement (pls. 28, 36). As Young said: "I like big pieces and long strips. However I get them, that's how I used them. I liked to sew them however they be. I work it out, study the way to make it, get it to be right, kind of like working a puzzle. You find the colors and the shapes and certain fabrics that work out right."[52] Her quilt, the one that started Arnett on his mission to collect the quilts of Gee's Bend, is composed

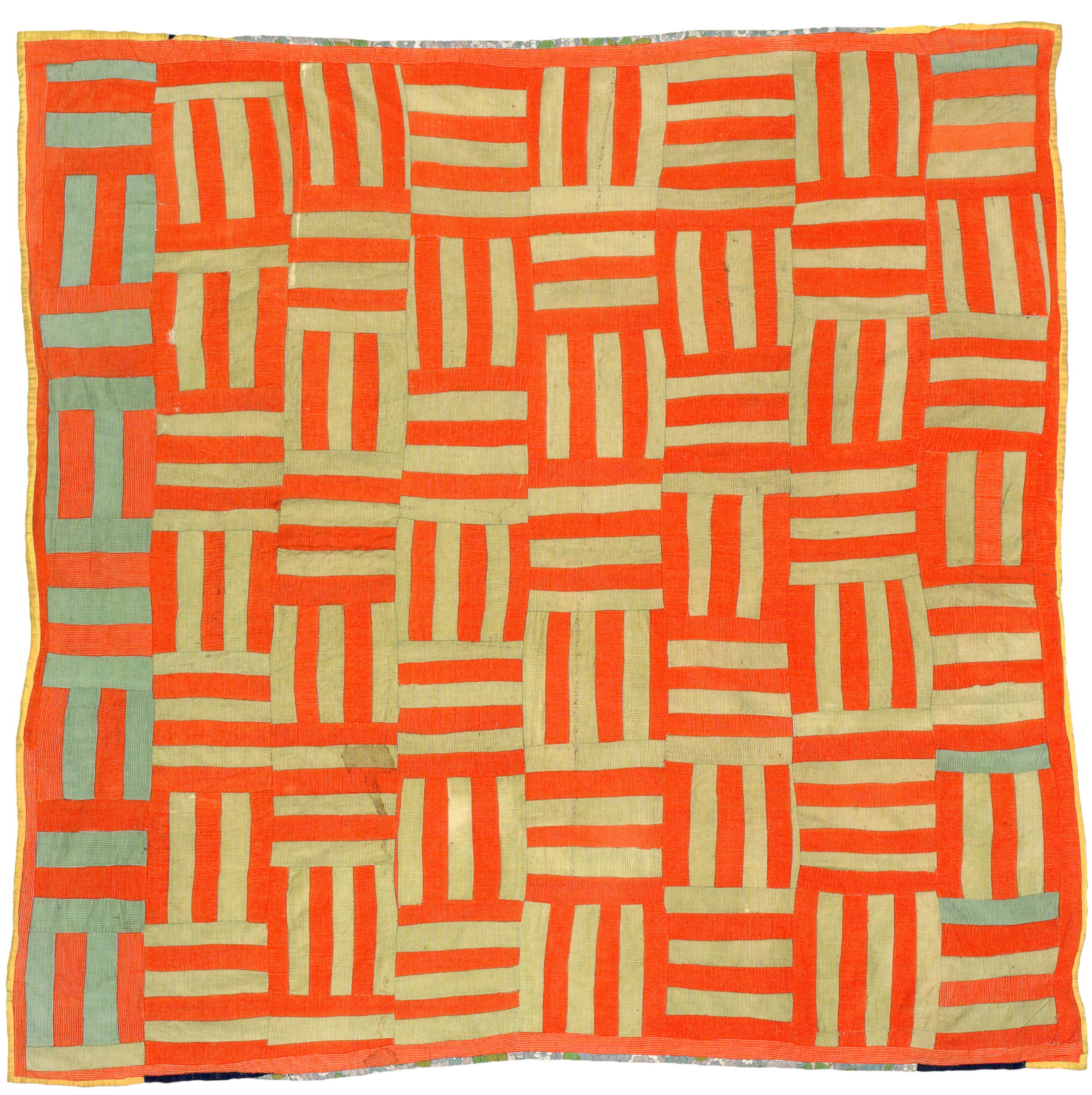

Pl. 35. **Nettie Jane Kennedy**, *Basket-Weave quilt*, 1973

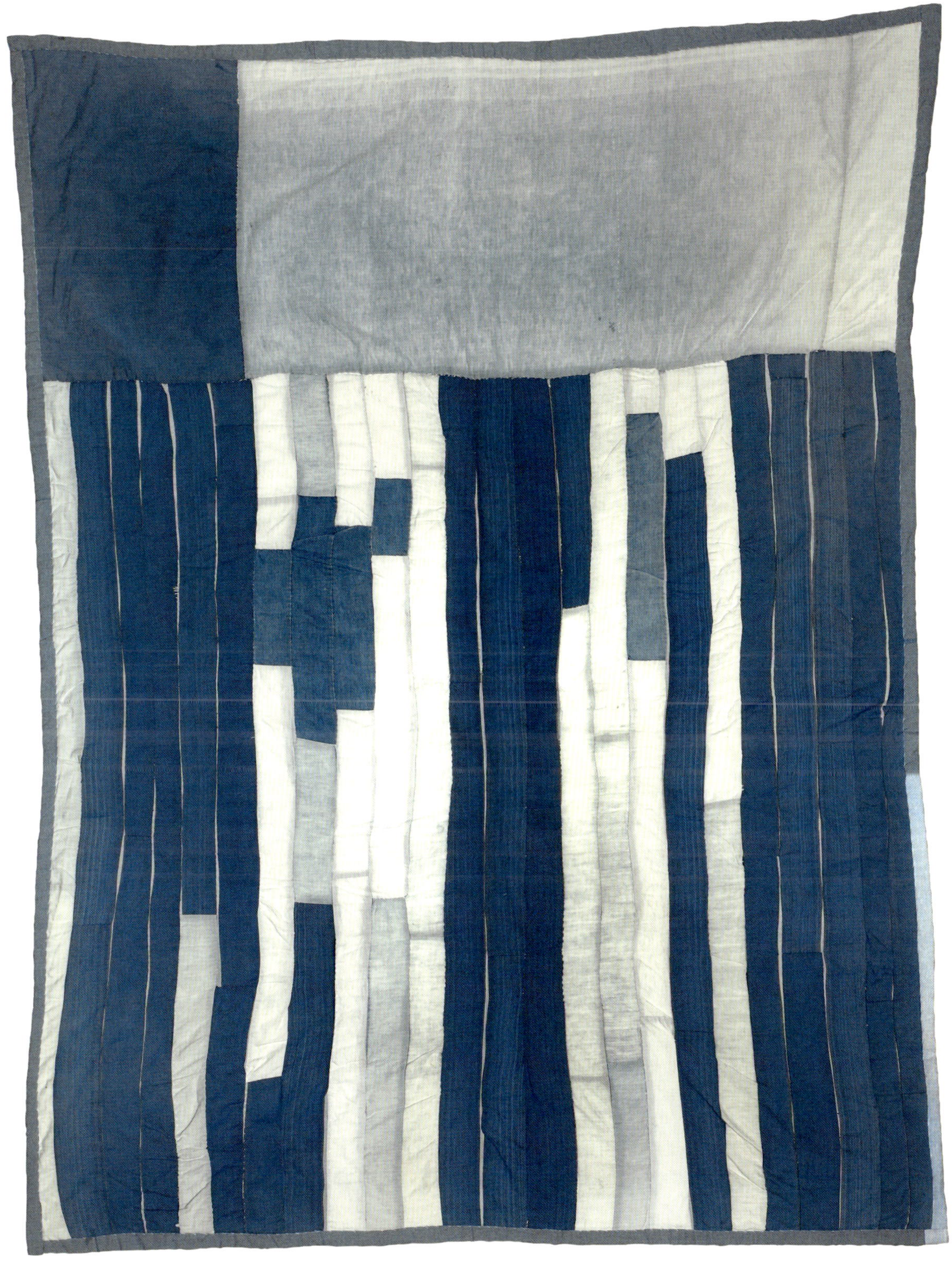

Pl. 36. **Emma Lee Pettway Campbell**, *Blocks and Strips work-clothes quilt*, ca. 1950

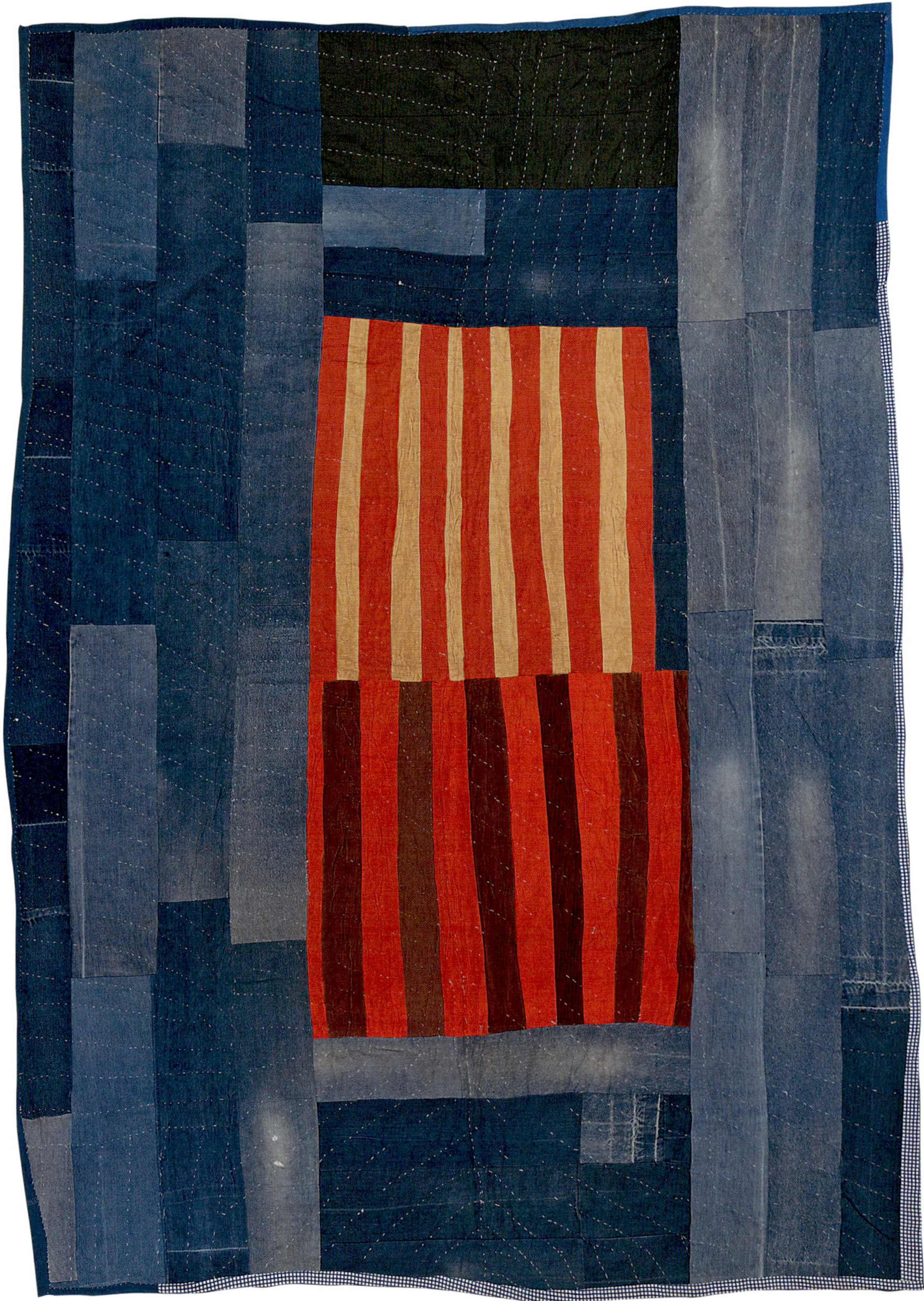

Pl. 37. **Annie Mae Young**, *Strip Medallion quilt*, 1976

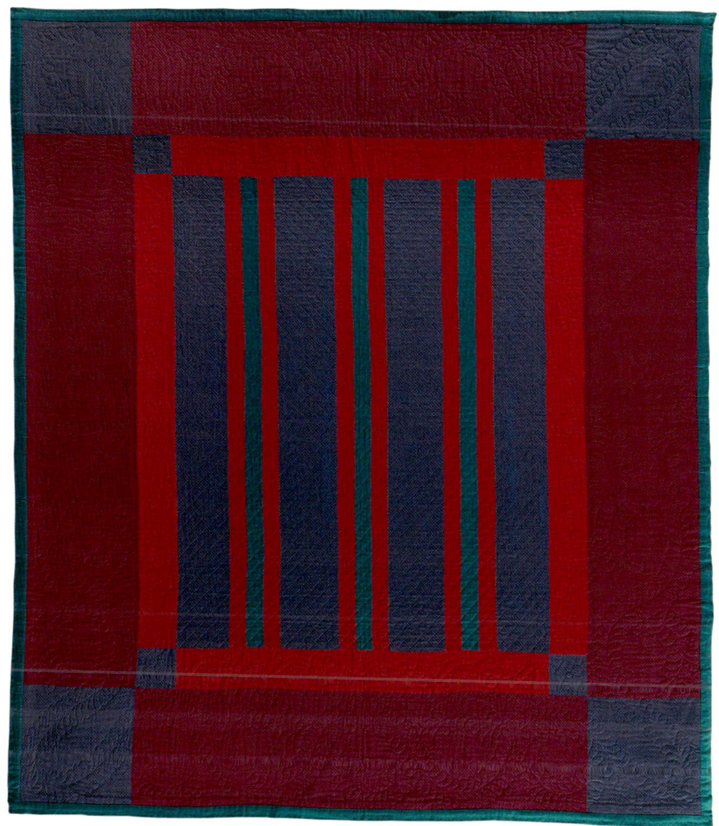

Fig. 34. **Amish maker**, *Split Bars quilt*, Lancaster County, Pennsylvania, ca. 1930

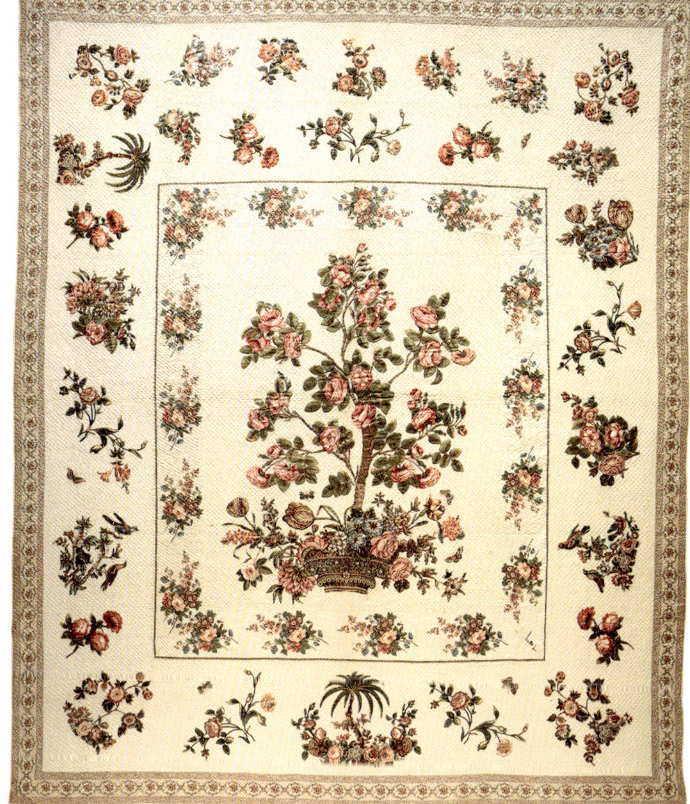

Fig. 35. **Mary Malvina Cook Taft**, *Chintz appliquéd quilt*, Sag Harbor, New York, ca. 1835–40

of a border of long strips made from used denim work clothes, with a glowing center of red, gold, and brown corduroy (pl. 37). It bears a remarkable overall resemblance to the Split Bars quilts made by the Lancaster County Amish (fig. 34). The centrally focused design of each proves that certain compositions readily please the human eye.

Several other Gee's Bend quilts in the Metropolitan's collection are designed with a central focus. The Housetop pattern of concentric bands of squares is reminiscent of medallion quilts from the early part of the nineteenth century, which started with a central square or rectangle, most often appliquéd with a fancy chintz, and then bands of decorative fabric built around the large center block were attached (fig. 35). The Gee's Bend quilters particularly favored the Housetop pattern, one that is not often found in other areas of the country (pls. 38–40).

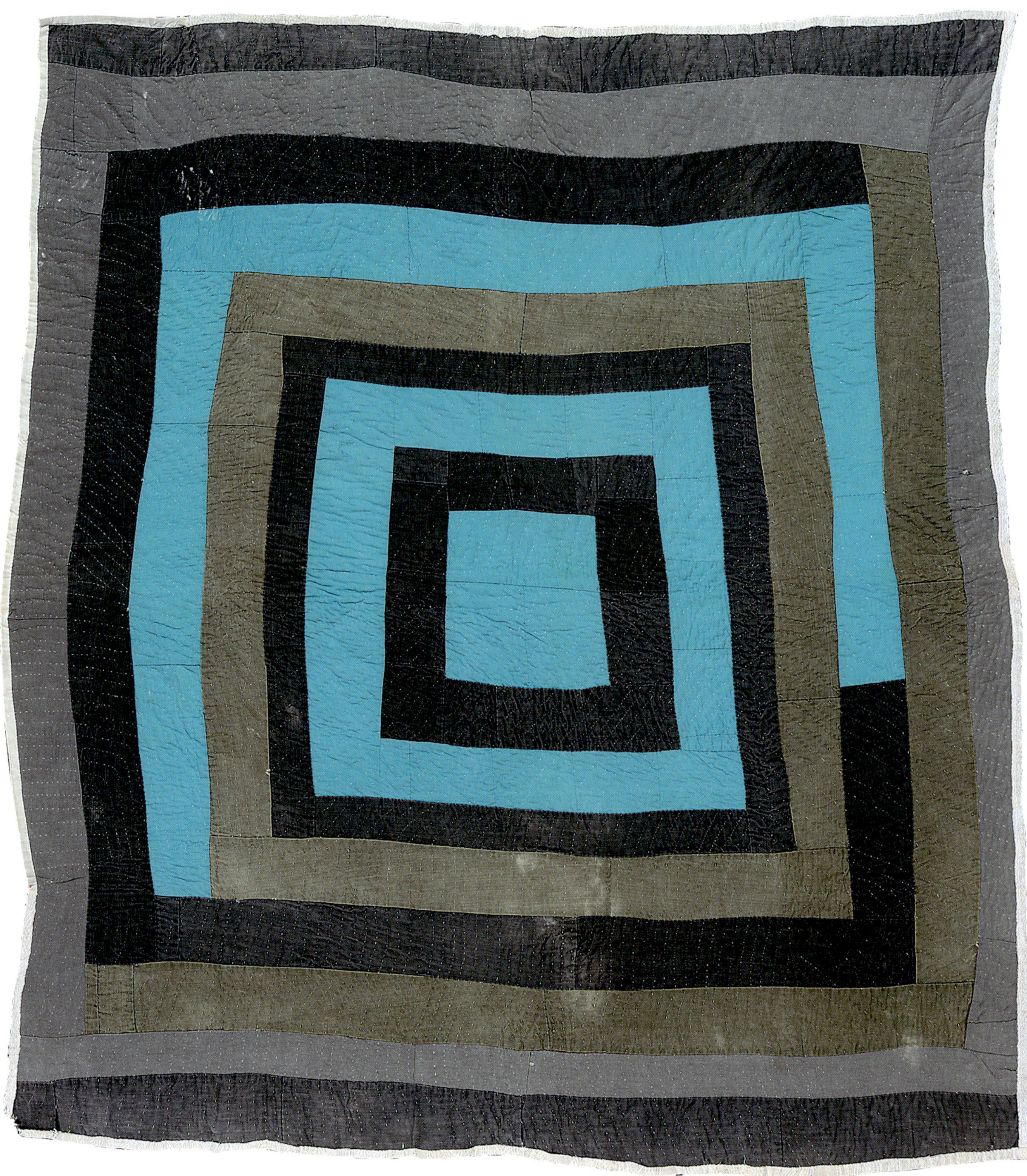

Pl. 38. **Loretta Pettway**, *Housetop quilt*, 1963

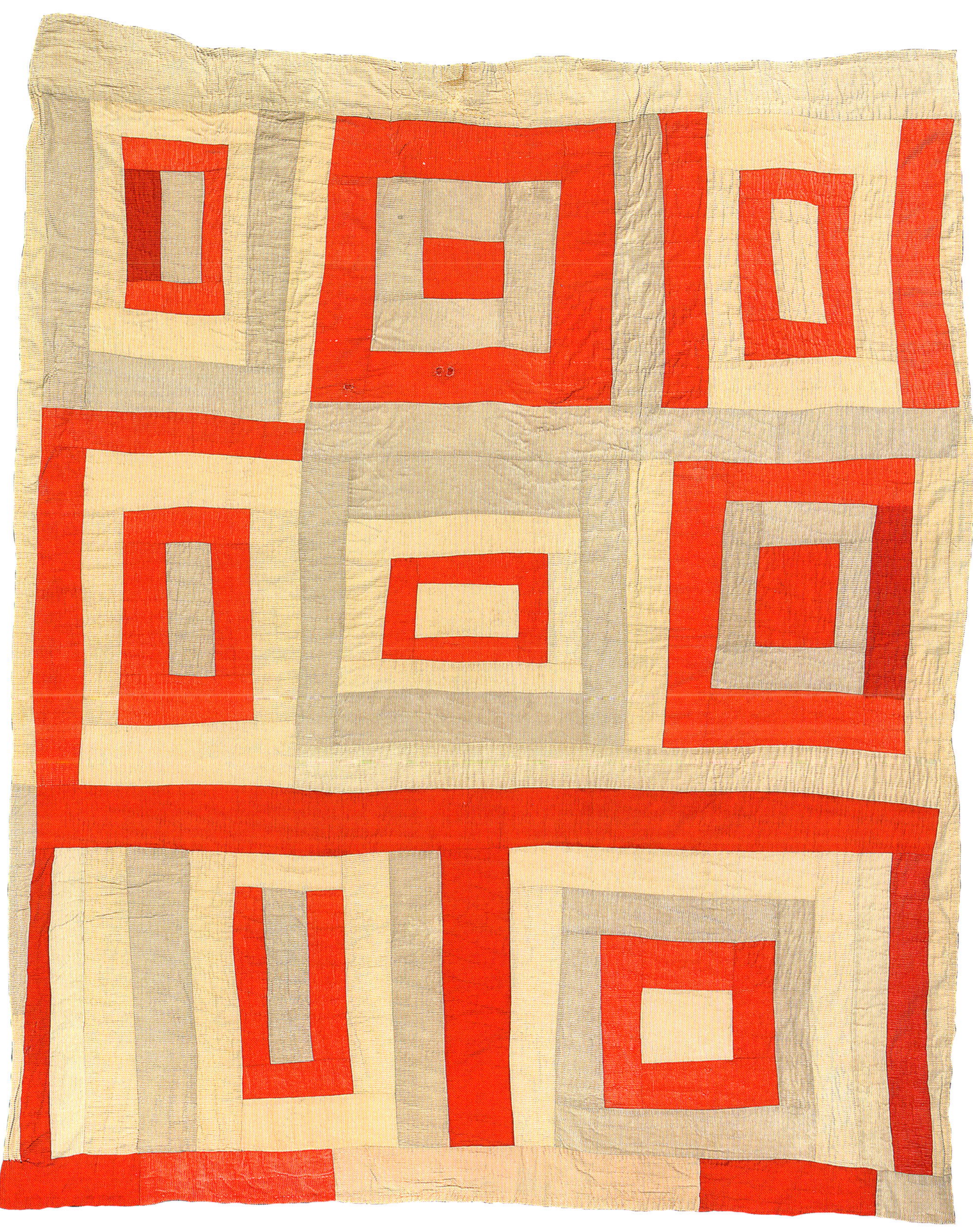

Pl. 39. **Lola Pettway**, *Eight-Block Housetop quilt*, ca. 1975

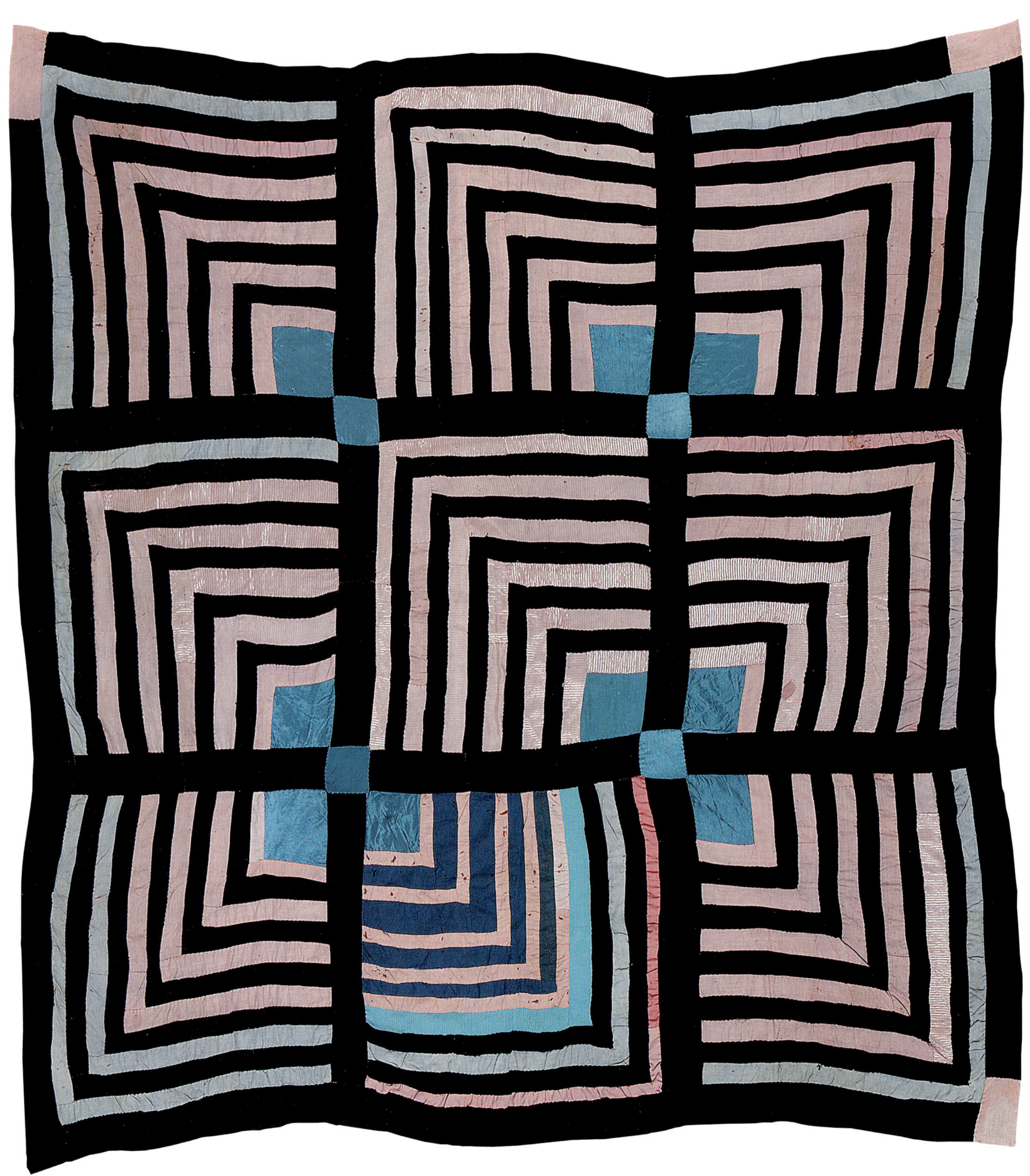

Pl. 40. **Sue Willie Seltzer**, *Nine-Block Housetop quilt*, ca. 1955

The Flying Geese pattern, which is based on repeating small triangles, was also popular in Gee's Bend. It, too, has earlier American origins; there are two examples in the Museum's collection that date to as early as the 1840s. The triangles can be pieced in many variations, as illustrated here (figs. 36–38, pls. 41–44). In the Gee's Bend quilts, small scraps of a number of different fabrics were not an option, since the way the artists put the pattern together needed an overall consistency. It is likely a quilt of this pattern would not have been attempted without large amounts of the same fabrics available.

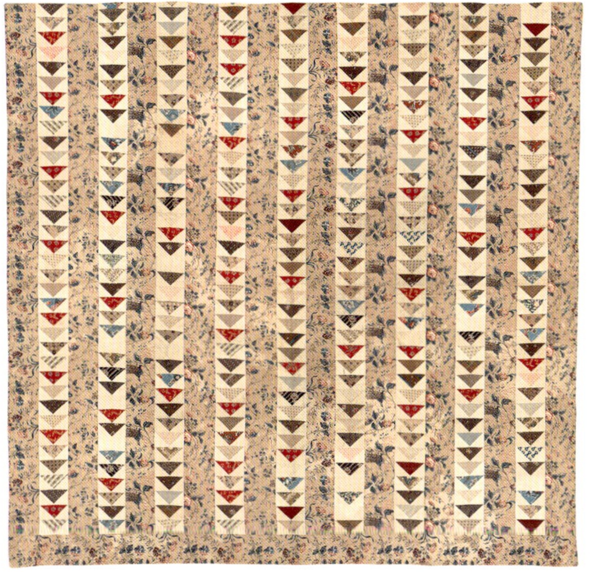

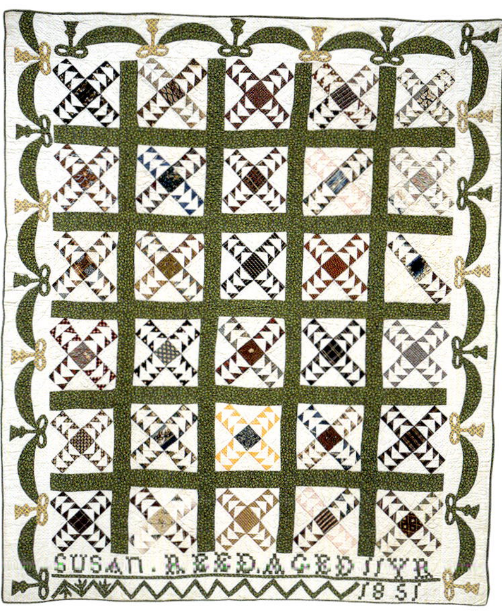

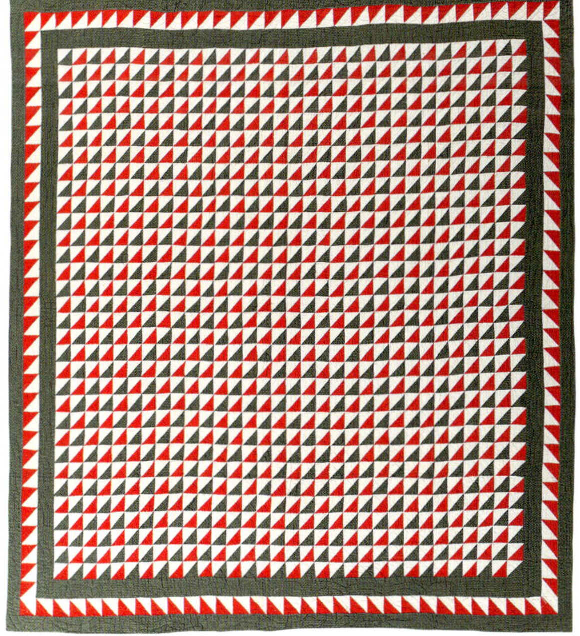

(clockwise from top left)
Fig. 36. **Unknown maker**, *Flying Geese quilt*, ca. 1840–50

Fig. 37. **Susan Reed Ruddick**, *Wild Goose Chase quilt*, Forestburgh, New York, 1851

Fig. 38. **Annie E. Freshour Schaeffer**, *Birds in Air quilt*, Lewistown, Maryland, before 1891

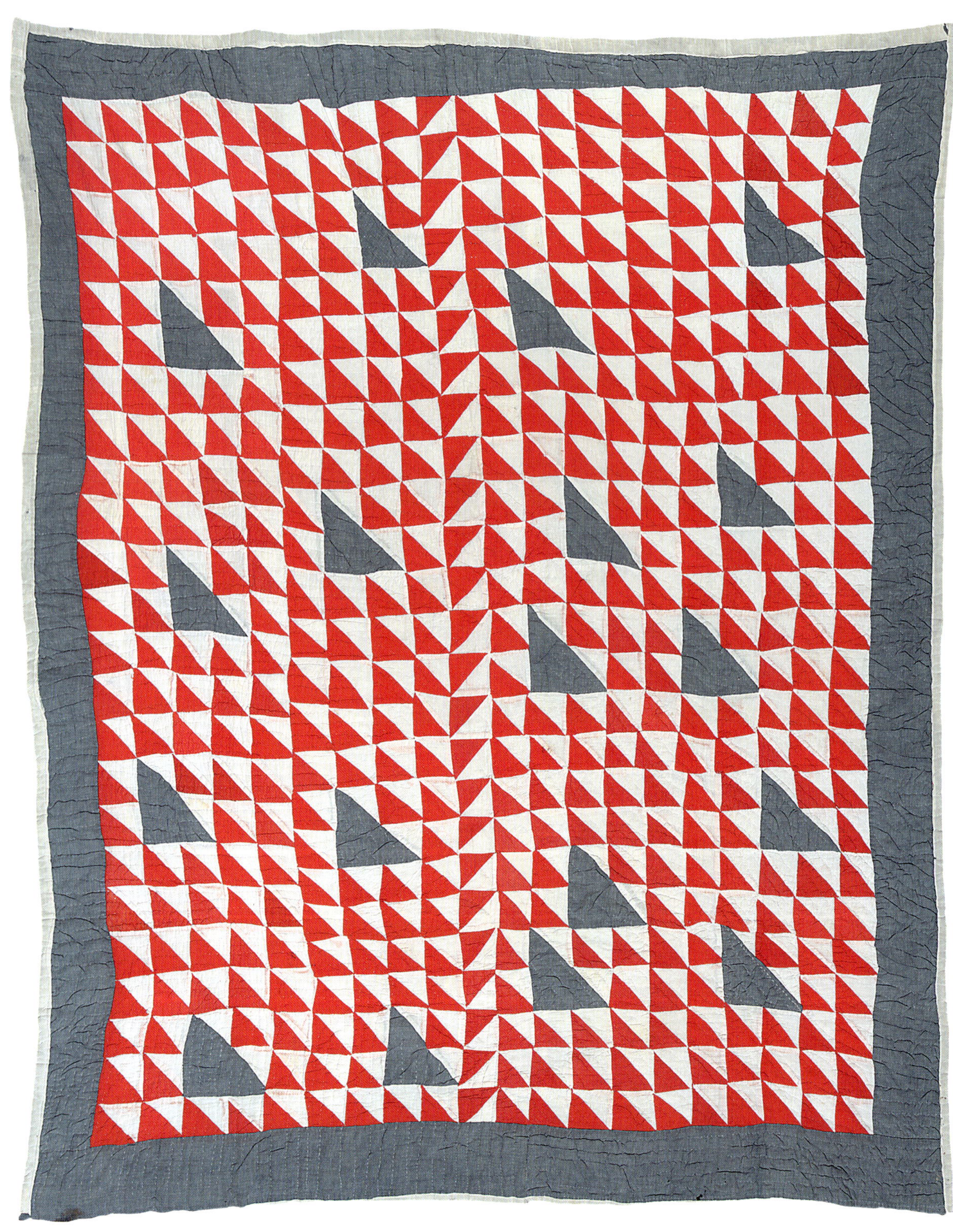

Pl. 41. **Annie Bendolph**, *Thousand Pyramids quilt*, ca. 1930

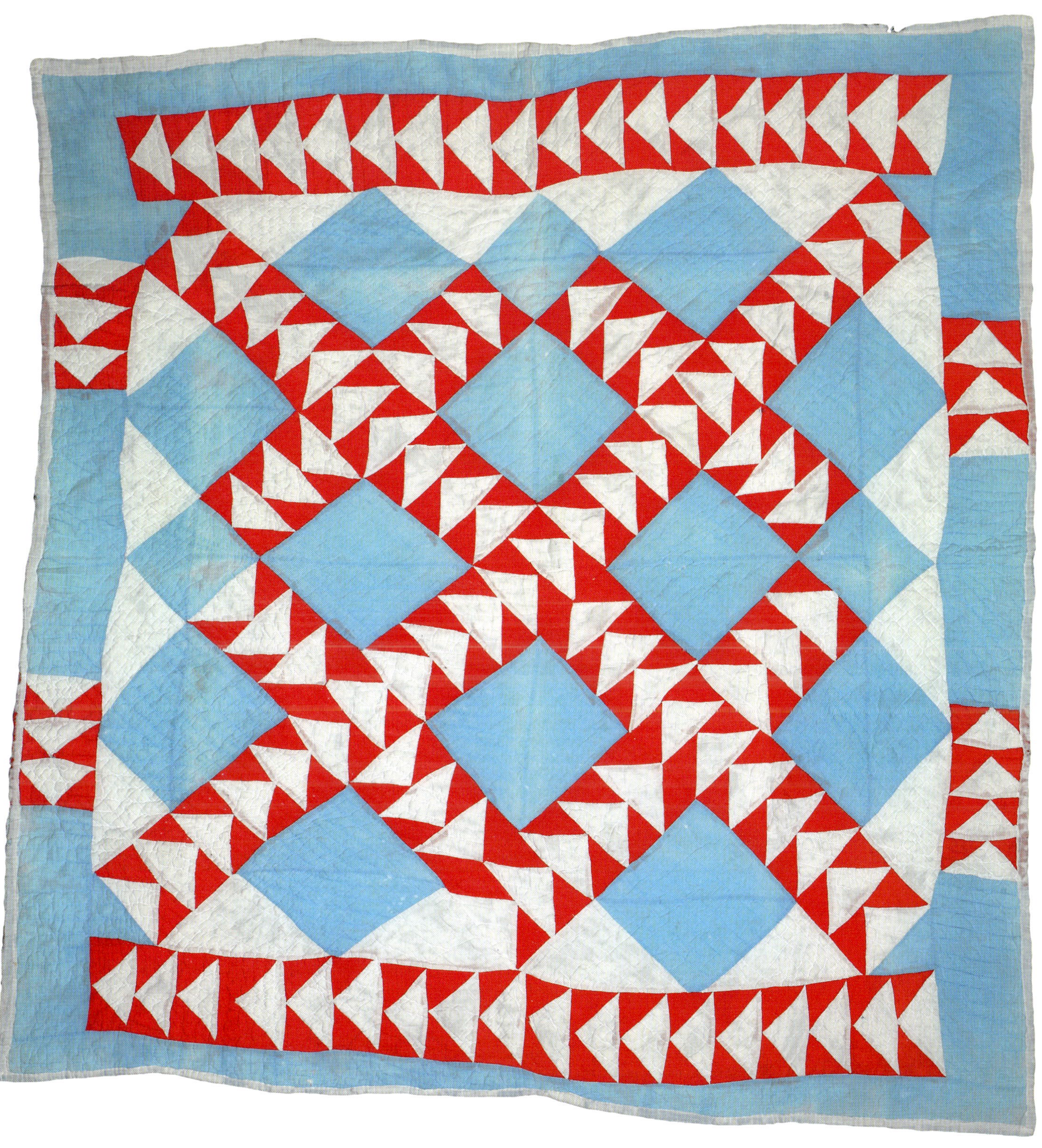

Pl. 42. **Annie Bendolph**, *Wild Goose Chase with Flying Geese border quilt*, ca. 1930

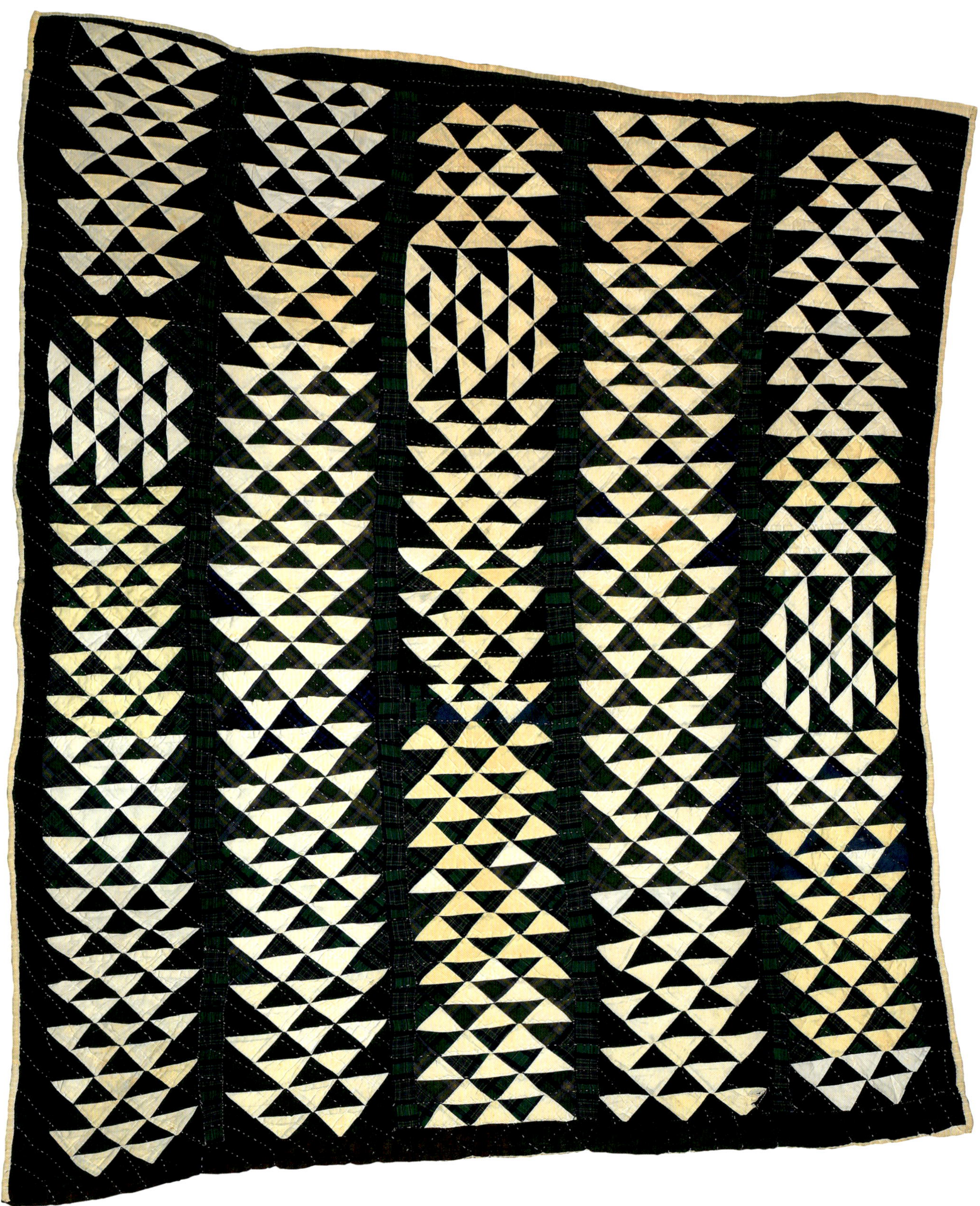

Pl. 43. **Mertlene Perkins**, *Birds in Flight quilt*, 1940s

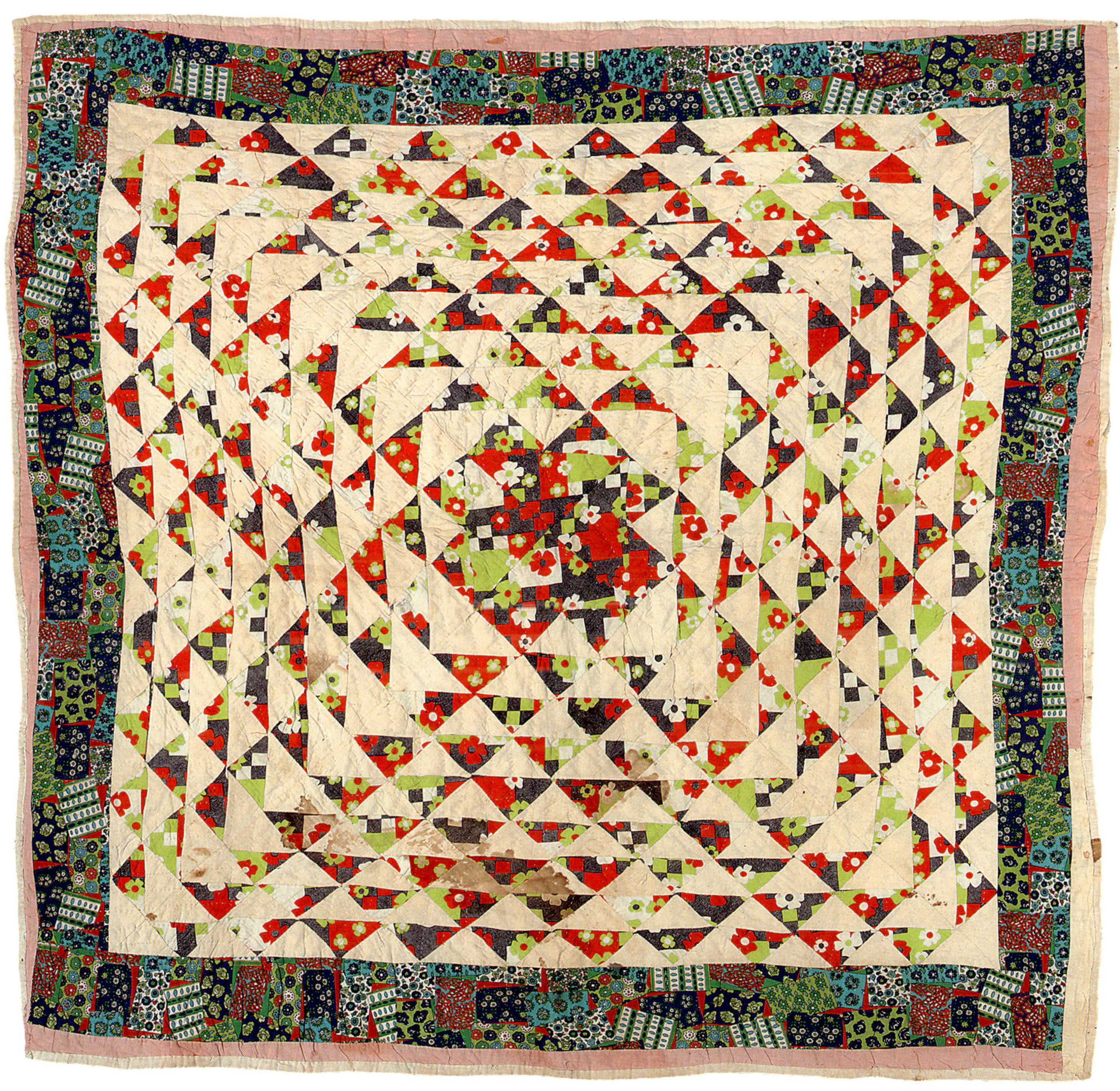

Pl. 44. **Pearlie Kennedy Pettway**, *Triangles quilt*, ca. 1960

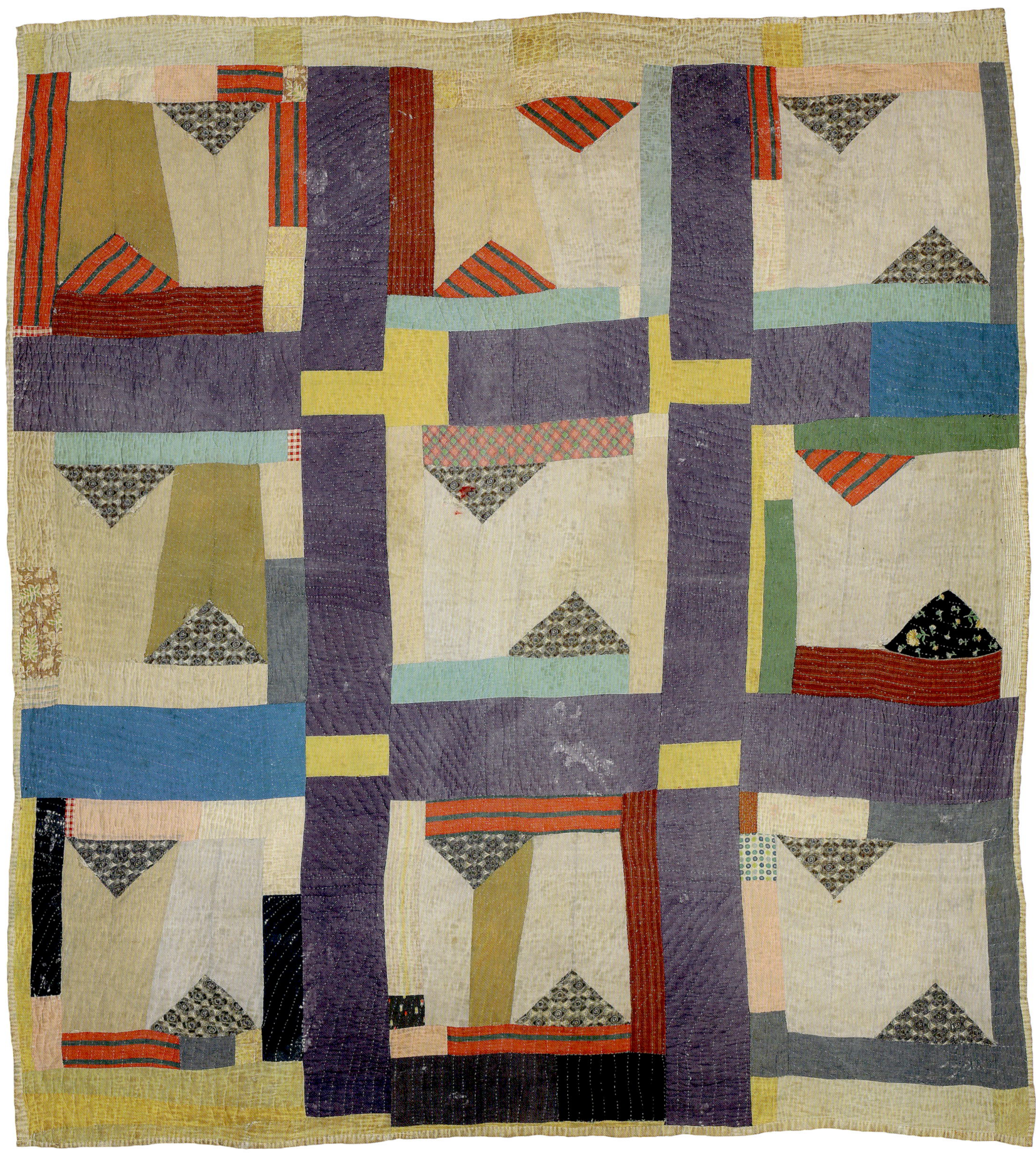

Pl. 45. **Martha Pettway**, *Nine-Block quilt*, 1930s

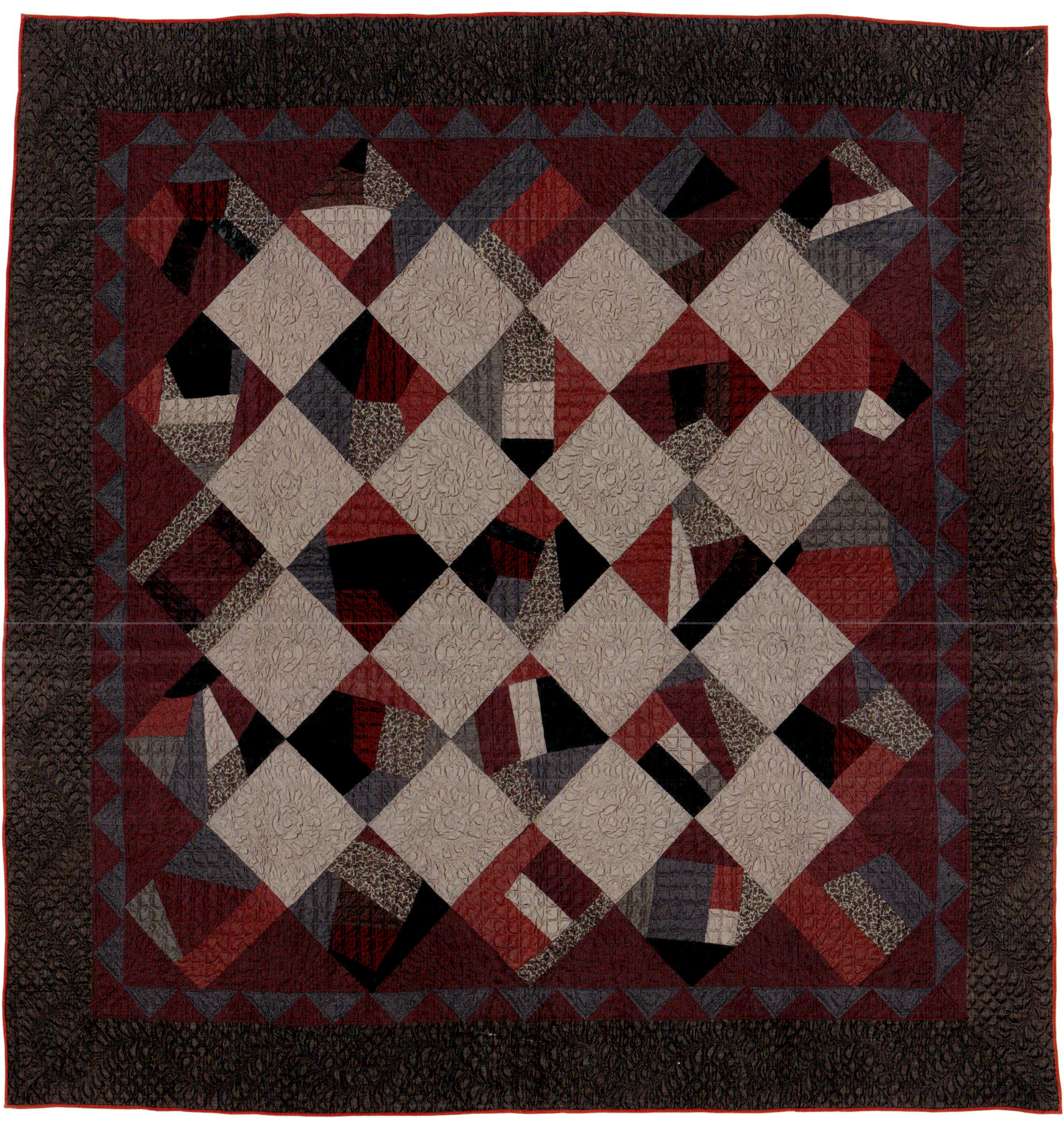

Fig. 39. **Unknown maker, probably Quaker**, *Crazy quilt*, Pennsylvania, ca. 1885–1900

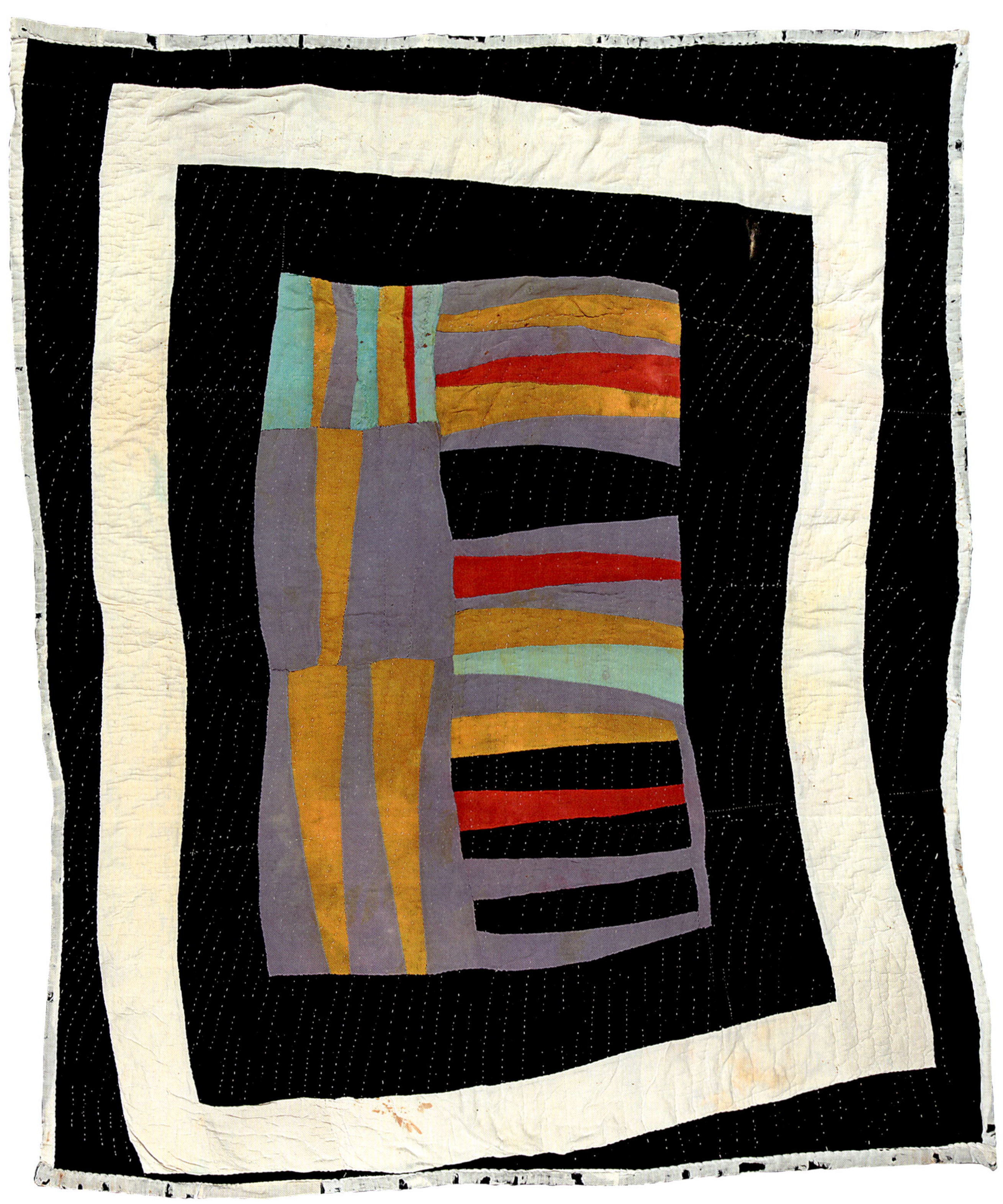

Pl. 46. **Loretta Pettway**, *Medallion quilt*, ca. 1960

A final group of Gee's Bend quilts that does not quite fit any other mold is reminiscent of the late nineteenth-century Crazy quilts, in which eccentrically pieced together bits of fabric were formed into blocks, and then the blocks were placed in a grid to form an orderly composition (pls. 45–46). Surprisingly, Crazy quilts were popular in all regions and communities, though they were more and less Crazy depending on who was making them, as evidenced by the atypical Pennsylvania Crazy quilt thought to have been made by a Quaker quilter (fig. 39). The Crazy pattern allowed more freedom and room for improvisation, traits clearly valued by the Gee's Bend quilters.

While the quilts of Gee's Bend, in particular, speak loudly of extraordinary creativity in the face of hard circumstances, the most important takeaway should be that these quilts, like most, are original works of art, with no more than a superficial visual relationship to abstract paintings. They most likely were not meant to reference African textiles or secret codes. More convincing even than the beautiful final product, the mindful individual creative process that brought the quilts into being attests to their status as works of art. The quilters themselves should have the final word. Gearldine Westbrook (1919–2016) stated that when faced with her pieces of fabric: "You just had to find a way to do it yourself. . . . When you sit down, you got to get yourself a mind of your own, figure out a way to put them together." Mary L. Bennett (born 1942) believed that a quilt is something beautiful made first and foremost for her own visual pleasure: "I just taken me some pieces and put it together, piece them up till they look like I want them to look. That's all."[53]

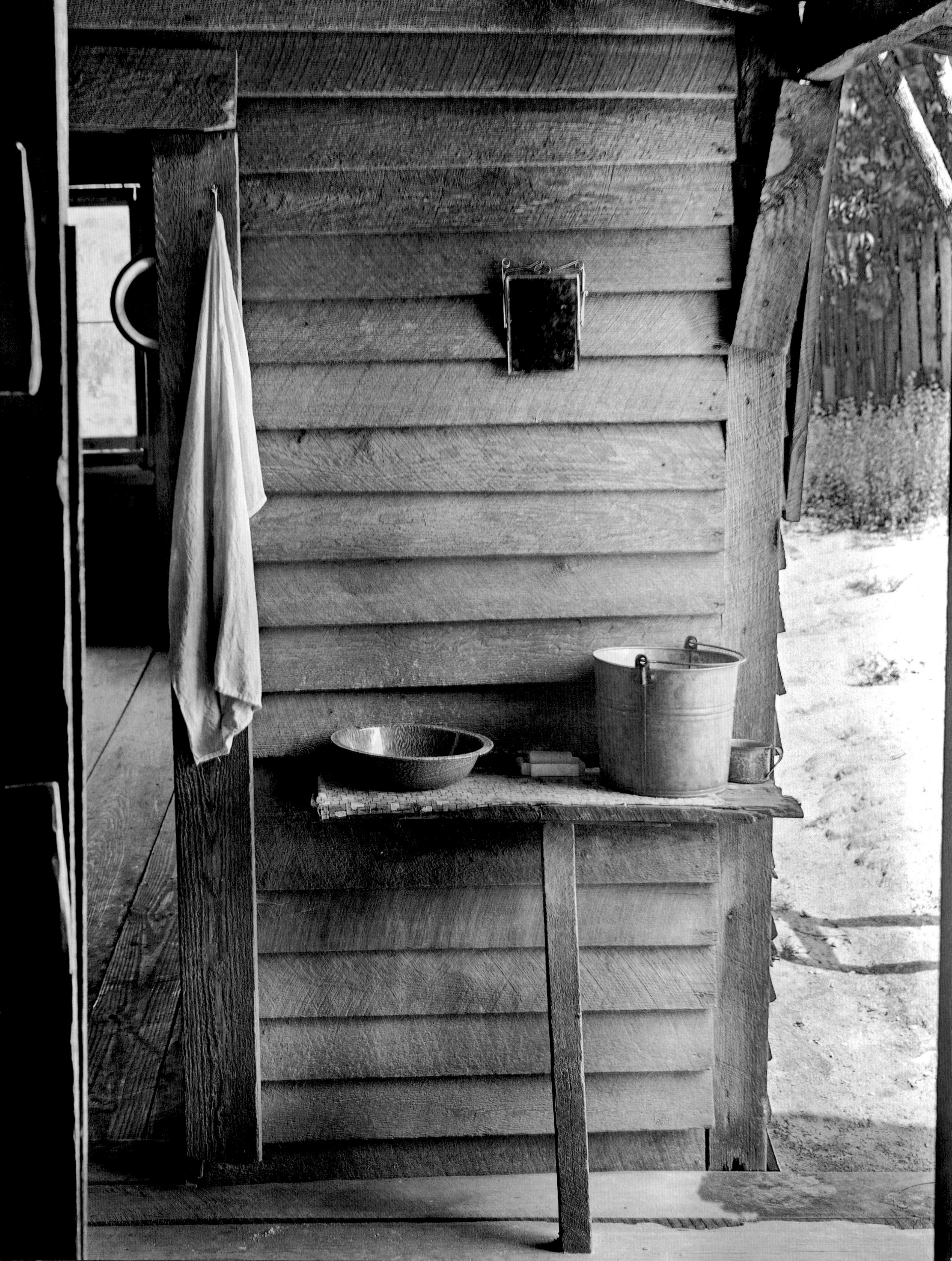

THE OLD COUNTRY

DARRYL PINCKNEY

In 1877, federal troops were withdrawn from the former Confederacy, and by the end of the nineteenth century the repeal of Reconstruction was complete. The Supreme Court had upheld segregation and steadily undermined the Fifteenth Amendment to the Constitution, deciding that the welfare of citizens was a matter for individual states. It would be a century after the Civil War before black people again voted in significant numbers or held meaningful political offices in the South. Woodrow Wilson segregated federal facilities in Washington, D.C., and even before World War I, because lynching was such a threat for black men, black families that had the means were sending their sons out of the South in order to save their lives. The Old Country. That's what blacks, who went north to a new world, called the South, where they were from, the Old Country (fig. 40).

After the defeat of Reconstruction, the Black Codes, the restrictions imposed on the free movement of black men, assured the South a steady supply of cheap labor. The agricultural economy of the region would prove yet another form of imprisonment. Though many blacks stayed near where they had been enslaved, those who moved on within the Black Belt of the South found themselves similarly oppressed under the sharecropping system. Reconstruction's promises of reparations would never be fulfilled. Plantation owners got their holdings back, and the once enslaved were turned into a peasantry. Black farmers paid rent in cash or gave the landowner a percentage of their yield. Cotton cultivation depended on human strain, making black people tenants with little chance of breaking the cycle of indebtedness. "Dat's all dey is to expect—work hard and go hongry part time—long as we lives on de other man's land. Dey ain't nothin' in sharecrappin', not de way it's run," a sharecropper's wife is quoted as saying in *These Are Our Lives* (1939), an oral history of black and white experiences in the rural South.[1]

All along, popular literature, drama, and film were creating a culture of nostalgia for what had never been, a land of cavaliers, chivalry, and social grace. The romance of the Confederacy was in part a pastoral that appealed to an audience frightened by industrialization. This distorted history of the South also provided a social education for European immigrants, told them how to become American, and reinforced the racial hierarchy. When William Faulkner burned down the big house in *Absalom, Absalom* (1936), he was trying to destroy the plantation tradition he had once thought it his life's work both to represent and question, but Margaret Mitchell's *Gone with the Wind* (1936) showed the accumulated power of that tradition as entertainment.

The South of the Great Depression was aristocratic, fallen, a retelling of the same romantic myth. One price of reunification was that politicians in the North left the South to rule itself. The image of the South as decayed, full of the bypassed, passed-over, and perverse was a continuation of this accommodation. It was a wounded region, not only because of defeat in the war, but also

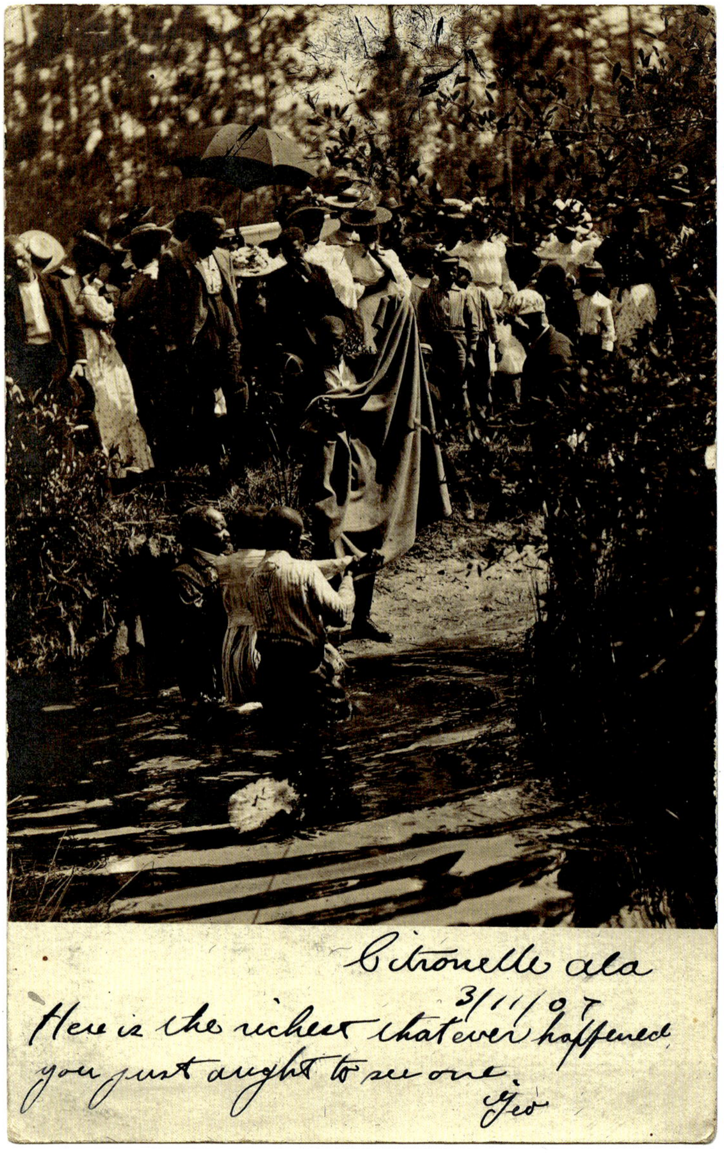

Fig. 40. **Unidentified photographer**, *River Baptism, Citronella, Alabama*, 1907

because black people were anxious to get out of the South. World War I halted the flow of European labor to Northern factories, and black agricultural workers were easily enticed to take their places. The Great Migration meant the abandonment of the Old Country. As a way of life that might be dying, the black South became interesting for its peculiar folkways, as a cultural repository.

In the 1920s, anthropologists began to judge cultures not by standards imposed from the outside but by how well people had adapted to their environments. In *Mules and Men* (1935), Zora Neale Hurston presented the folklore of the black South as the collective wisdom and philosophy of a people, as well as part of the arsenal of group survival.[2] Her work was completely unlike anything that had come before, even that of the most sympathetic white recorder of tall tales, because she shared the culture of the people she was interviewing and could insert herself directly into the scenes she describes. Moreover, the intelligence she uncovered in vernacular language was central to her argument for the complexity of black culture in the South.

However, in his review of *Mules and Men*, Sterling Brown, poet and cultural critic, observed that her book was not bitter enough to be a really true picture of the black South.[3] W. T. Couch, the editor of *These Are Our Lives*, omitted stories he found sordid.[4] In this period, anthropologists and folklorists avoided in their studies the underlying threat of violence against black people, the vulnerability of black women, and the social consequences of poor conditions under which the majority of blacks in the South lived. Yet although black communities were studied in isolation, it was not as though the larger social context did not impinge on them. The trickster figure in black folklore derives its importance not only as a cultural survival from West Africa, but also because the trickster always wins, beats his oppressors, outwits them.

In the case of the Scottsboro Boys, nine black youths convicted of the rape of two young white women in Alabama in 1931, the black South had its first

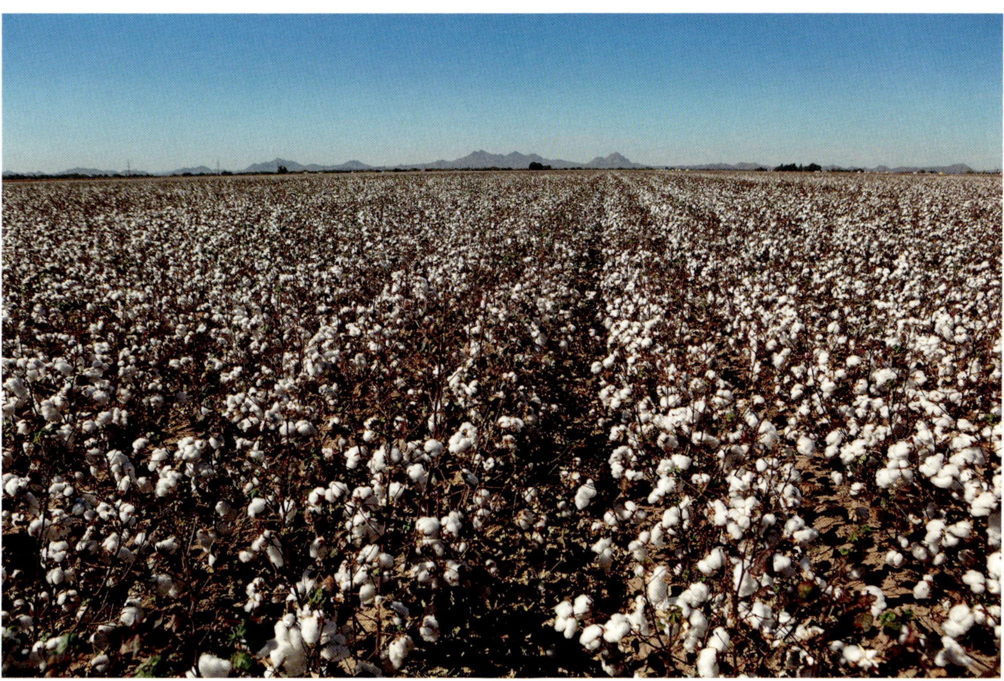

Fig. 41. Cotton fields ready for harvest

protest movement since the enslaved had abandoned the plantations and amassed behind the advancing Union Army. The fight for justice for the Scottsboro Boys created a sense of racial solidarity that cut across class lines among blacks and opened connections to black people up North as well as in Europe and Africa. Meanwhile, the Great Depression exposed the interracial reality of rural poverty and that a large percentage of sharecroppers were white, even if tenant farmers represented only a third of white farmers as opposed to 85 percent of black farmers. The thin white faces in the photographs of Walker Evans became symbols of interracial possibility. The union movement took hold among black and white sharecroppers, and legislators began to reform land ownership. But mill owners and state officials resorted to violence in order to put a stop to union organizing among textile workers. Moreover, to secure passage of his New Deal legislation, Franklin Delano Roosevelt had had to appease Southern lawmakers by excluding black workers, domestics, and agricultural workers from its compensations. However, mechanization was already changing the economic practices (fig. 41), adding to the next wave of migrants exiting the Old Country for a better life.

If the real South had been hidden from the white people who did not want to see their region for what it was, what were the black people of the South looking at when they woke up down home and were not in a position to be fortified? Richard Wright in his autobiography, *Black Boy* (1945), evokes a loveless Mississippi childhood of hunger and fear.[5] Ralph Ellison suggests in a memoir in the essay collection *Going to the Territory* (1986) that Wright concentrated on the injustices against blacks almost at the cost of not seeing any value in the lives black people made wherever they were, Ellison's "artistically induced catharsis," in spite of daily oppression.[6] Ellison was from Oklahoma, and although he went to Alabama to become a student at Tuskegee College, he also knew something about the hobo's life during the Depression. Radical politics led him to

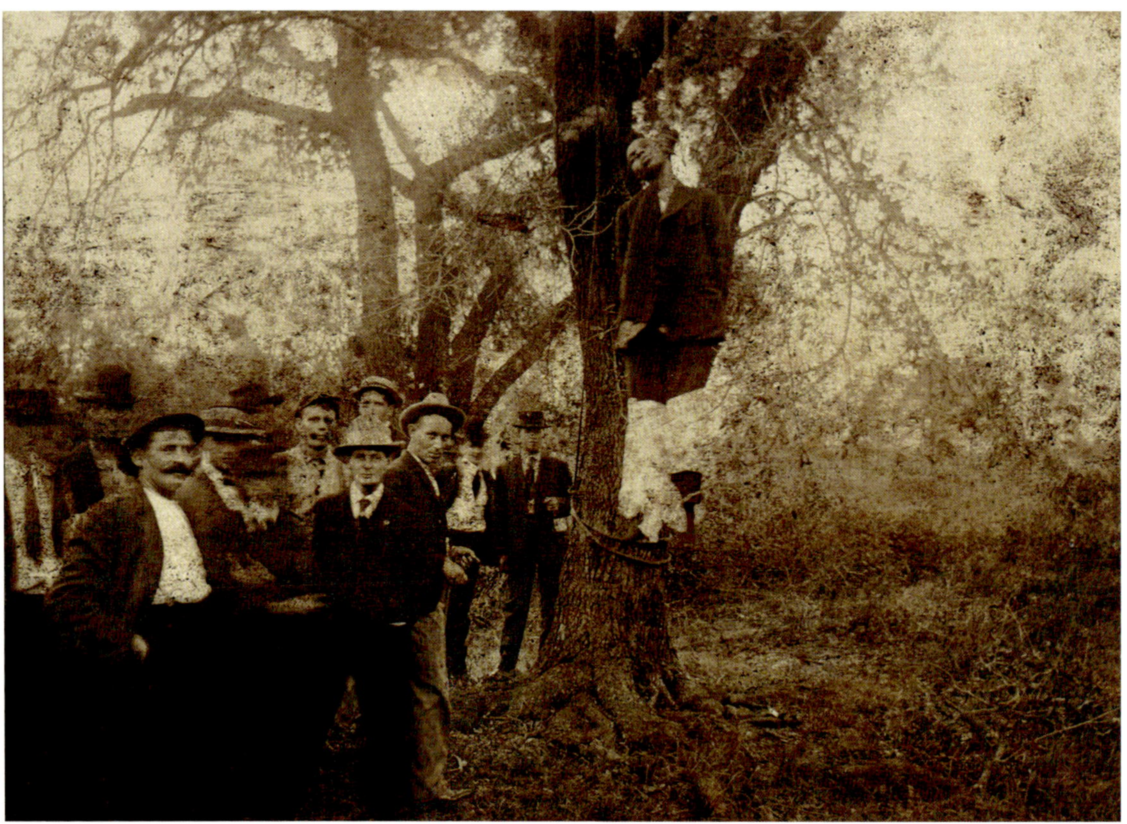

Fig. 42. **Unidentified photographer**, *The Lynching of Dick Robinson and a Man Named Thompson, Pritchard Station, Alabama*, October 6, 1906

question the historical function of arts and culture in black America. Art and literature were a form of witness, and culture was valued as evidence of and propaganda for black advancement. The folk utterance was not political, but it was resistance because creativity affirmed the humanity of black people that American history had tried to deny. But Ellison wanted to imagine that black musicians and black artists in general took for themselves the freedom to choose among influences. Moreover, for Ellison, the influence of black life on the nation had been so profound that American culture was black culture.

After World War II, women who had entered new occupations in order to fill the places of absent men found themselves sent home. However, black veterans of World War II, the GI Bill generation, were determined that what had happened to their fathers when they returned from World War I would not happen to them. They would not be put back in their places. The South was still viewed in popular culture as a left-behind section of the country, its torpor a contrast to the dynamism of the urban North and the seductiveness of the West. Racial strife had been acute in cities up North and out West, but it was always the South where the drama of desegregation would first take place, in the land of "For Whites Only" and "For Colored" signs.

Congressman John Lewis once remembered that in 1960 the safest method of transportation for him in Mississippi had been to travel the back roads at night in an automobile at eighty to ninety miles an hour with the headlights off.[7] Anne Moody's autobiography

Coming of Age in Mississippi (1968) reminds us how uncertain the outcome of the Civil Rights movement had been at the time.[8] No one knew what would happen. The road between church and home had always been dangerous. One could get lynched for crossing the wrong party's path (fig. 42). Maybe customs shaped by a degree of violence and surveillance put into black lives not only the desire for shared spaces, public spaces that were relatively safe, community spaces, but also an even deeper need for private spaces, secret spaces, zones in the head.

What would a black art of the South, then or now, or an art of any people there, reflect under those circumstances? It could be a reordering of the landscape, a conversation between an artist and the physical world, an act that takes place in the realm of doing, making, creating something beautiful, against the odds, for whatever it said to others and to the self. Art is control, and also self-control. But these artists are also making objects in what is understood as primarily an oral culture. The majority of poor blacks could not for a long time have many possessions. Black artists in the South who became known in the 1960s were thought of as the naive exponents of religious fervor, as in the case of Sister Gertrude Morgan (1900–1980), the missionary, or that of James Hampton (1909–1964), the short-order cook. They were prisoners who had run out of chances like Frank Jones (1900–1969), or they were visited by an abundance of dreams like Minnie Evans (1892–1987). Several of them began to make art late in their lives, when perhaps they had little to lose and still everything to say.

Amiri Baraka's *Blues People* (1963) relates his anxiety that for black culture to become mainstream is for it to lose something—its edge, its integrity, its inspiration from the margins.[9] The mainstream represented theft, or dilution of some essential quality of blackness. But maybe the theory that black culture was always ahead of the curve and therefore stolen from was in itself a kind of compensation for that very marginality. In his review of *Blues People* in the *New York Review of Books*, Ellison took issue with Baraka, as he had with Wright, arguing that he had too narrow a view of what influenced an artist, what disparate influences make up a given culture.[10] Black vernacular culture has largely been known through music—spirituals, blues, gospel, jazz, soul, R & B, hip-hop—than through literature. We know what it sounds like and what it says. By comparison, we have only glimpses or suggestions of what it looks like. Another form of visual expression, photography immediately assumed a documentary function in black life, as would film, which left the visual arts under a similar pressure to speak out, instead of remaining hidden, private, and by the very nature of race in America, inherently on the outside.

An early essay of Zora Neale Hurston's, "Characteristics of Negro Expression," first printed in Nancy Cunard's anthology, *Negro* (1934), explains that visual expression or visual culture in Southern black life was primarily a matter of decorating cabin walls or the self.[11] There is no folk art peculiar to the black church. Hurston did not discuss the artisanal, or black furniture makers. She is honored in quilts today, but her social anthropology searched black culture for metaphor, not domestic history. Years ago, blacks in Southern cities would have had to travel to see art collections other than those on display in rare black institutions, such as the collection formed by Hale Woodruff (1900–1980) at Atlanta University or the bequest by Georgia O'Keeffe (1887–1986) to Fisk University, Nashville. Elsewhere in the South, art museums and galleries were not easy thresholds to cross. *Zinnias: The Life of Clementine Hunter* (2013), Robert Wilson's opera about the self-taught painter of happy subjects in Louisiana who was probably one hundred and one years old when she died in 1988, makes the point that Hunter could not attend the opening of her first exhibition because the gallery was segregated. What art had Bill Traylor seen when in 1939 at age eighty-five he began to draw with pencil on shirt cardboard? W. E. B. Du Bois stressed the importance of beauty and the fact that many millions of black people were, as he said, "choked away from it."[12]

Not all of the arts move at the same pace, but the striking presence of black visual artists in contemporary art would astonish their forebears. This art is asking the art formerly known as outsider art why it keeps calling itself a folk art. It is art from the black South. We leap to interpret pieces situated in the landscape, pieces maybe made from scrap material found in the artists' environments. But maybe black art from the South has become a historical category, like Color Field painting. The art from the black South reflects the influence of the cult of primitivism and how those assumptions have defined what some people expect from black culture: authenticity.

White and black critics alike disapproved of the adaptations of Negro spirituals that the black composer R. Nathaniel Dett made in the 1930s because his arrangements were somehow too European. Alfred H. Barr Jr., Director of the Museum of Modern Art, New York, was suitably impressed by photographs of the limestone carvings of William Edmondson (1874–1951), a hospital orderly in Nashville, to make Edmondson in 1937 the first black artist to have a solo exhibition at MoMA. Meanwhile, formally trained Augusta Savage (1892–1962), who worked in New York around the same time as Edmondson, lost most of her sculpture because she could not afford the storage costs. It has been a constant problem in both black and white America that extensive education in the liberal or fine arts for a black person was seen as taking one away from one's black roots. Black artists must be natural, uninterfered with, the prejudice said, which had a distant connection to the unsavory view that cultures described as primitive could reveal more about human behavior than could advanced societies because they were more elemental, down to earth.

Black people have been moving back South since the 1980s, a time when manufacturing in the North was in decline. According to the U.S. census, in 1900 89.7 percent of black Americans lived in the South; in 2000, 54.8 percent of black Americans lived there, but the majority in its cities, not in small towns or rural areas.[13] People have returned, but not to the land. The United States ranks third in the world in the export of cotton, but the South is a changed economy, as trapped in whatever is going on as anywhere else. As the Old Country begins to disappear, as the South becomes culturally similar to every other region of the United States, the question is what is the relationship between the context of black life in the South and the work it once framed so strongly and automatically.

Perhaps the present collection arrives with a new kind of independence, unburdened by any historical imperative—a fiery ocean view painted on wood and Masonite; a self-portrait on wood; the lode from Gee's Bend; and a good number of works on paper, including a forest done in tempera, ink marker, and yellow ink (pl. 25) and a boat on the Mississippi in marker, crayon, and graphite. Here place mats have met spray paint (pl. 18) and over here are graphite, charcoal, watercolor, and coffee (pl. 13). The symbolism remains private in a work done in 1981 about the child murders in Atlanta (pl. 10), while other works yield their meanings more freely. But who is the white guy, the pink guy, identified only as "Head of the Penitentiary," and under what circumstances was the portrait made? Can the artist's biography answer the question? For some works, especially those valued culturally and financially, their stories are added to or lost as they move around the world, hand to human hand. But the history still tells us that the sheer existence of this art was not predicted, and maybe that is the most important thing history can tell us about it.

NOTES

Introduction: Troubling the Waters

1. The Souls Grown Deep Foundation holds approximately twelve hundred works by one hundred sixty-five artists donated by William S. Arnett in 2010 from his collections dating back to the 1970s.

2. In addition to the Souls Grown Deep Foundation's gift to The Metropolitan Museum of Art, the Ackland Art Museum, University of North Carolina, Chapel Hill (twelve works); Fine Arts Museums of San Francisco (sixty-two works); High Museum of Art, Atlanta (fifty-four works); New Orleans Museum of Art (ten works); and Philadelphia Museum of Art (twenty-four works) received related collections of art in 2017 through the Souls Grown Deep Foundation's strategic gift and purchase agreements. In addition, the Southern Folklife Collection at the University of North Carolina, Chapel Hill, received an important donation of more than nine thousand photographs and archival video and audio recordings documenting the artists of the Souls Grown Deep Foundation.

3. "More than Land or Sky" traveled to museums throughout Appalachia after its Washington debut. See Barbara Shissler Nosanow, *More than Land or Sky: Art from Appalachia*, exh. cat., National Museum of American Art and other venues (Washington, D.C.: Published for the National Museum of American Art by the Smithsonian Institution Press, 1981).

4. "Black Folk Art in America, 1930–1980" traveled to the Brooklyn Museum of Art (1982) and five other U.S. museums through 1983, and "Black Art, Ancestral Legacy" traveled to four American institutions in 1990–91. See Jane Livingston and John Beardsley, *Black Folk Art in America, 1930–1980*, exh. cat., Corcoran Gallery of Art, Washington, D.C., and other venues (Jackson: University Press of Mississippi; [Oxford, Miss.]: Center for the Study of Southern Culture, 1982). See also Alvia J. Wardlaw et al., *Black Art, Ancestral Legacy: The African Impulse in African-American Art*, exh. cat., Dallas Museum of Art and other venues (New York: Harry N. Abrams, 1990).

5. Robert Farris Thompson, "The Song That Named the Land: The Visionary Presence of African-American Art," in Wardlaw et al., *Black Art, Ancestral Legacy*, pp. 97–141.

6. Thornton Dial had several museum exhibitions devoted to his work during his lifetime, including the major retrospective "Hard Truths: The Art of Thornton Dial" (2011), organized by the Indianapolis Museum of Art and which traveled to the New Orleans Museum of Art (2012); the Mint Museum, Charlotte (2012); and the High Museum of Art (2012–13); see Joanne Cubbs and Eugene W. Metcalf, eds., *Hard Truths: The Art of Thornton Dial*, exh. cat. (Indianapolis: Indianapolis Museum of Art; Munich: Delmonico Books/Prestel, 2011). The subject of numerous group exhibitions, Dial also was selected for the 2000 Whitney Biennial, and his work has been published widely in a number of exhibition catalogues.

7. "The Quilts of Gee's Bend" opened at the Museum of Fine Arts (MFA), Houston, in 2002 and toured twelve museums across the country into 2008. Organized by the MFA, Houston, "Gee's Bend" traveled to eight museums and also ended its run in 2008. See John Beardsley et al., *Gee's Bend: The Women and Their Quilts*, exh. cat., Museum of Fine Arts, Houston, and other venues (Atlanta: Tinwood Books, in association with the Museum of Fine Arts, Houston, 2002); William Arnett et al., *Gee's Bend: The Architecture of the Quilt*, exh. cat., Museum of Fine Arts, Houston, and other venues (Atlanta: Tinwood Books, 2006).

8. Michael Kimmelman, "Jazzy Geometry, Cool Quilters," *New York Times*, Nov. 29, 2002, p. E33.

9. See, for example, Alisa LaGamma and Christine Giuntini, *The Essential Art of African Textiles: Design without End*, exh. cat. (New York: The Metropolitan Museum of Art, 2008).

10. See Leslie Umberger, "Bill Traylor," in Smithsonian American Art Museum, https://americanart.si.edu/artist/bill-traylor-4852 (accessed Dec. 8, 2017).

11. See Gladys-Marie Fry, *Stitched from the Soul: Slave Quilts from the Ante-Bellum South*, exh. cat., Museum of American Folk Art, New York, and other venues (New York: Dutton Studio Books, in association with the Museum of American Folk Art, 1990).

12. The quilters of Gee's Bend are discussed at length in the fourth-grade textbook *Social Studies Alive! Regions of Our Country* (Palo Alto, Calif.: Teachers Curriculum Institute, 2010); see chap. 6, "A Boat and Bus Tour of the Southeast," pp. 98–101. In addition to discussing the region from which the quilters hailed, this segment illustrates examples of the quilts on U.S. postage stamps, an early twentieth- century photograph of the ferry used to get to and from Gee's Bend, a portrait of Arlzonia Pettway, and an installation photograph of the quilts in one of the touring exhibitions. See also a recent book on the Gee's Bend quilters for young audiences; Susan Goldman Rubin, *The Quilts of Gee's Bend* (New York: Abrams Books for Young Readers, 2017). The United States Postal Service issued *Quilts of Gee's Bend* commemorative stamps in 2006 as part of its American Treasures series. Featured on the stamps were ten quilts created between about 1940 and 2001.

13. Birmingham was the site of key tragic and pivotal events of the Civil Rights struggle, including the bombing of the Sixteenth Street Baptist Church by white supremacists on Sept. 15, 1963. In Memphis, on Feb. 12, 1968, black sanitation workers took to the streets in what was known as the Memphis Sanitation Workers' Strike to demand better pay, safer working conditions, and the right to unionize. Their efforts were memorialized in a dramatic image by Memphis photographer Ernest C. Withers, in which a phalanx of more than one thousand protesters carried placards affirming "I AM A MAN." In recent years, that now-iconic image has been reimagined for our own times by conceptual artists harnessing a mnemonic aesthetic such as Glenn Ligon (born 1960)—see the oil and enamel on canvas *Untitled (I Am A Man)* (1988), and the diptych *Condition Report* (2000)—and Hank Willis Thomas (born 1976)—see the Liquitex on canvas *I Am A Man* (2009).

14. Scholar-activist Angela Y. Davis describes the prison industrial complex as follows: "Taking into account the structural similarities and profitability of business-government linkages in the realms of military production and public punishment, the expanding penal system can now be characterized as a 'prison industrial complex.'" See Angela Y. Davis, "Masked Racism: Reflections on the Prison Industrial Complex," *Colorlines*, Fall 1998, p. 12.

15. Thompson, "Song That Named the Land," p. 131.

16. See Kellie Jones, *South of Pico: African American Artists in Los Angeles in the 1960s and 1970s* (Durham, N.C.: Duke University

Press, 2017), especially pp. 70–90, for an extensive discussion of Purifoy's work and practice.
17. See Robert Farris Thompson's discussion of West African textile designs in his seminal study *Flash of the Spirit: African and Afro-American Art and Philosophy* (New York: Random House, 1983).

Self-Taught and Modern
1. On the scholarly debates about this terminology, see Lynne Cooke, "Orthodoxies Undermined," in *"Great and Mighty Things": Outsider Art from the Jill and Sheldon Bonovitz Collection*, ed. Ann Percy, with Cara Zimmerman, exh. cat. (Philadelphia: Philadelphia Museum of Art, 2013), pp. 204–15. See also Gary Alan Fine, *Everyday Genius: Self-Taught Art and the Culture of Authenticity* (Chicago: University of Chicago Press, 2004), chap. 1, "Creating Boundaries," pp. 18–53.
2. See Didi Barrett, *Muffled Voices: Folk Artists in Contemporary America*, exh. cat., PaineWebber Art Gallery, New York (New York: Museum of American Folk Art, 1986).
3. Jane Livingston and John Beardsley, *Black Folk Art in America, 1930–1980,* exh. cat., Corcoran Gallery of Art, Washington, D.C., and other venues (Jackson: University Press of Mississippi; [Oxford, Miss.]: Center for the Study of Southern Culture, 1982).
4. Jane Livingston, "What It Is," ibid., p. 13. It bears noting that Livingston then considered quilting, perhaps the most highly regarded practice in rural Southern art making, as craft, not art per se.
5. For Dubuffet's impact on the reception of the work of untrained artists, see, among other sources, John Beardsley, "Imagining the Outsider," in *Vernacular Visionaries: International Outsider Art*, ed. Annie Carlano, exh. cat. (New Haven, Conn.: Yale University Press, in association with the Museum of International Folk Art, Santa Fe, N.M., 2003), pp. 10–17.
6. See Roger Cardinal, "Vernacular Art: A Palpable Expression," in *Souls Grown Deep: African American Vernacular Art of the South*, vol. 1, ed. Paul Arnett and William Arnett (Atlanta: Tinwood Books, in association with the Schomburg Center for Research in Black Culture, New York Public Library, 2000), pp. 13–15 (quotation on p. 13).
7. Ibid., p. 13.
8. Robert Hughes, "Pulling the Fuse on Culture," *Time*, Aug. 7, 1995, pp. 60–68 (quotation on p. 62).
9. Paul D. Moreno, *Black Americans and Organized Labor: A New History* (Baton Rouge: Louisiana State University Press, 2006).
10. This reading of Holley's *African Mask* diverges somewhat from the artist's comments on the work: "It's about the spirit of something that is coming with you, or it's with you, but can you call upon it and can it be subject to your use again? We all have the power to call on something." Lonnie Holley, in "From the Mind of Lonnie Holley," *Garden & Gun*, Oct.–Nov. 2015, pp. 146, 147, no. 5.
11. Judith A. Carney and Richard Nicholas Rosomoff, *In the Shadow of Slavery: Africa's Botanical Legacy in the Atlantic World* (Berkeley: University of California Press, 2009).
12. Bernard D. Headley, *The Atlanta Youth Murders and the Politics of Race* (Carbondale: Southern Illinois University Press, 1998).
13. The iconography of the tiger in Dial's art is explored in *Thornton Dial: Image of the Tiger*, exh. cat. (New York: Harry N. Abrams, in association with the Museum of American Folk Art, New York; New Museum of Contemporary Art, New York; and American Center, Paris, 1993); see pp. 16–17 in particular.
14. Joyce Henri Robinson, "Nellie Mae Rowe," in *Wos Up Man? Selections from the Joseph D. and Janet M. Shein Collection of Self-Taught Art*, exh. cat. (University Park: Palmer Museum of Art, Pennsylvania State University, 2005), p. 30.
15. William Arnett, "Nellie Mae Rowe (1900–1982): Inside the Perimeter," in P. Arnett and W. Arnett, *Souls Grown Deep*, pp. 290–307. Arnett's discussion of *Nellie's Birthday* appears on pp. 302, 304.
16. "'Black Man of the Jewish Faith': Told by Joe Light," in *Souls Grown Deep: African American Vernacular Art of the South*, vol. 2, ed. William Arnett and Paul Arnett (Atlanta: Tinwood Books, 2001), pp. 302–19, especially p. 304.
17. Holley, in "From the Mind of Lonnie Holley," pp. 146, 147, no. 1.
18. See Carol Crown and Charles Russell, eds., *Sacred and Profane: Voice and Vision in Southern Self-Taught Art* (Jackson: University Press of Mississippi, 2007).
19. Sharon Patton, "Spiritual Visions and Allegory in Contemporary African-American Folk Painting," in *Self-Taught Art: The Culture and Aesthetics of American Vernacular Art,* ed. Charles Russell (Jackson: University Press of Mississippi, 2001), pp. 129–45 (quotation on p. 131).
20. "'I Believe in My Mission': Told by Mary Proctor," in W. Arnett and P. Arnett, *Souls Grown Deep*, vol. 2, pp. 448–53 (quotation on p. 451).

Quilt/Art: Deconstructing the Gee's Bend Quilt Phenomenon
1. In the exhibition catalogue, William Arnett was listed as collector and author, and his son Paul Arnett as the cocurator of the Arnett Collection; see John Beardsley et al., *Gee's Bend: The Women and Their Quilts*, exh. cat., Museum of Fine Arts, Houston, and other venues (Atlanta: Tinwood Books, in association with the Museum of Fine Arts, Houston, 2002), p. 427. Though John Beardsley was serving at the time as a senior lecturer in landscape architecture at the Graduate School of Design, Harvard University, Cambridge, Mass., he was known as the cocurator with Jane Livingston of "Black Folk Art in America, 1930–1980," which was presented at the Corcoran Gallery of Art, Washington, D.C., in 1982. Livingston was working as an independent curator at the time of the Gee's Bend show. Alvia J. Wardlaw was the curator of modern and contemporary art at the Museum of Fine Arts (MFA), Houston.
2. Rennie Young Miller, letter to the editor, *Artforum*, Mar. 2004, pp. 22, 30. Miller's letter was written in response to Thelma Golden's comments about the Whitney exhibition; see Thelma Golden, "The Quilts of Gee's Bend," *Artforum*, Dec. 2003, p. 126.
3. Tara Dooley, "2 Gee's Bend Quilters Say They Were Cheated," *Houston Chronicle*, June 16, 2007; Shaila Dewan, "Handmade Alabama Quilts Find Fame and Controversy," *New York Times*, July 29, 2007, p. 14.
4. For more information on African American quilters and the wide variety of styles, see Cuesta Benberry, *Always There: The African-American Presence in American Quilts* (Louisville: Kentucky Quilt Project, 1992); Roland L. Freeman, *A Communion of the Spirits: African-American Quilters, Preservers, and Their Stories* (Nashville, Tenn.: Rutledge Hill Press, 1996).

5. Louisiana P. Bendolph, "A New Generation of 'Housetops,'" in William Arnett et al., *Gee's Bend: The Architecture of the Quilt*, exh. cat., Museum of Fine Arts, Houston, and other venues (Atlanta: Tinwood Books, 2006), pp. 189–95.
6. For a comprehensive history of collecting and interpreting quilts made by African Americans, see Patricia A. Turner, *Crafted Lives: Stories and Studies of African American Quilters* (Jackson: University of Mississippi Press, 2009); Bridget R. Cooks, *Exhibiting Blackness: African Americans and the American Art Museum* (Amherst: University of Massachusetts Press, 2011), especially chap. 5, "Back to the Future: The Quilts of Gee's Bend, 2002," pp. 135–54. For more information on William Arnett and his folk-art collecting, see Andrew Dietz, *The Last Folk Hero: A True Story of Race and Art, Power and Profit* (Atlanta: Ellis Lane Press, 2006).
7. Walter moved at a particularly notable time. The Civil Rights Act of 1964 ended segregation in public places and banned employment discrimination on the basis of race, color, religion, sex, or national origin. The Voting Rights Act, which protected African American citizens' right to vote, was proposed in Mar. 1965 and passed in Aug. 1965. On Mar. 21–25, 1965, Dr. Martin Luther King Jr. had led 25,000 marchers from Selma to Montgomery in support of the act.
8. Nancy Callahan, *The Freedom Quilting Bee* (Tuscaloosa: University of Alabama Press, 1987), p. 3.
9. Ibid., pp. 13–14, 18, 19.
10. Ibid., p. 21. Emphasis in the original.
11. Ibid., p. 26.
12. "The Responsive Eye," the first exhibition to introduce the concept of Op art, was on view Feb. 23–Apr. 25, 1965. See William C. Seitz, *The Responsive Eye*, exh. cat., Museum of Modern Art (New York, 1965).
13. See, for example, "Scene-shifting for Summer," *Vogue*, May 1968, p. 169; "Unsweetened Quilting . . . New Decorating Idea," *Vogue*, Aug. 1, 1968, p. 69; "Patchwork Explosion," *Vogue*, June 1969, p. 77.
14. Lee Krasner, quoted in Callahan, *Freedom Quilting Bee*, p. 62; see also pp. 60–61.
15. Ibid., pp. 62–63.
16. Henry Geldzahler, quoted in ibid., p. 62.
17. In 1968, the Freedom Quilting Bee received a $20,000 contract to sell its quilts through Bloomingdale's, and the quilts were advertised in major newspapers, such as the *New York Times*. See Callahan, *Freedom Quilting Bee*, pp. 66, 71.
18. Annie Mae Young, interview with William Arnett, Oct. 1999, quoted in William Arnett and Paul Arnett, "On the Map," in Beardsley et al., *Gee's Bend: The Women and Their Quilts*, pp. 46, 422, n. 10.
19. Jonathan Holstein, *Abstract Design in American Quilts*, exh. cat. (New York: Whitney Museum of American Art, 1971).
20. Jonathan Holstein, *Abstract Design in American Quilts: A Biography of an Exhibition* (Louisville: Kentucky Quilt Project, 1991), p. 17.
21. The exhibition and catalogue of *Abstract Design in American Quilts* were dedicated to Newman, who died in 1970, a year before the show opened. Newman was a leading Abstract Expressionist and a renowned Color Field painter.
22. Holstein, *Abstract Design in American Quilts* (1991), p. 20.
23. Ibid., pp. 20–21.
24. Ibid., p. 26.
25. Ibid., p. 34.
26. Hilton Kramer, "Art: Quilts Find a Place at the Whitney" (review of the exhibition "Abstract Design in American Quilts"), *New York Times*, July 3, 1971, p. 22.
27. There is a long tradition in American quilting of making "show" or "best" quilts that were meant to display the artistry of their maker, rather than being used day to day. They might be laid out on a bed to be admired but were not subject to the hard wear of constant use. The Museum owns many examples of nineteenth-century quilts in immaculate condition that were treasured in this way.
28. In 1945, the Museum purchased a newly made small appliquéd quilt with designs taken from the story of Alice in Wonderland (45.38). It was one of a group of Storybook quilts made by Marion Whiteside Newton. Not intended for display in the galleries, it was meant only for study purposes. The reason for its purchase was explained in a memo: "The Textile Study Room receives constant inquiries about quilting. As we have no examples of contemporary work, this purchase would provide a useful piece for study purposes." Memorandum, Feb. 28, 1945, American Wing departmental files.
29. Marilynn Johnson Bordes, *12 Great Quilts from the American Wing*, exh. cat. (New York: The Metropolitan Museum of Art, 1974).
30. After opening at the MFA, Houston, in Sept. 2002, the exhibition visited eleven other museums around the country, finally ending its run six years later at the Museum of Art in Fort Lauderdale in Jan. 2008. It was followed by a second show, "Gee's Bend: The Architecture of the Quilt," which highlighted many of the same quilts and was again organized by the MFA, Houston, with the Tinwood Alliance. Between June 2006 and Dec. 2008, it traveled to eight museums.
31. Arnett's African art collection was shown at the High Museum of Art, Atlanta, in 1978, and he coauthored, with Marcilene K. Wittmer, the related exhibition catalogue *Three Rivers of Nigeria: Art of the Lower Niger, Cross, and Benue from the Collection of William and Robert Arnett*. In 1994, he donated a large part of the collection to the Michael C. Carlos Museum at Emory University, Atlanta. For more information on Thornton Dial and Lonnie Holley, see Randall R. Griffey, "Self-Taught and Modern," pp. 21–51, in this volume.
32. W. Arnett and P. Arnett, "On the Map," p. 37.
33. Ibid.
34. Ibid.
35. Robert Farris Thompson, *Flash of the Spirit: African and Afro-American Art and Philosophy* (New York: Random House, 1983), pp. 207–23.
36. Maude Southwell Wahlman, *Signs & Symbols: African Images in African American Quilts*, rev. ed. (1993; Atlanta: Tinwood Books, 2001), p. 33.
37. Ibid., p. 85.
38. Ibid., p. 45.
39. Both Thompson and Wahlman are white academics. For some perspective on their ideas by African American quilt scholars, see Benberry, *Always There,* pp. 14–16; Turner, *Crafted Lives*, pp. 172–202.
40. Jane Livingston, "Reflections on the Art of Gee's Bend," in Beardsley et al., *Gee's Bend: The Women and Their Quilts*, p. 52.
41. Ibid. Emphasis in the original.
42. Alvia J. Wardlaw, "Introduction: The Quilts of Gee's Bend," in Beardsley et al., *Gee's Bend: The Women and Their Quilts*, p. 10. Emphasis mine.
43. Ibid., p. 11.

44. Maxwell L. Anderson, then-Director of the Whitney, partnered with Director Peter Marzio of the MFA, Houston, to mount the Gee's Bend exhibition. Anderson had ties to Bill Arnett; he had been Director of the Michael C. Carlos Museum when Arnett had donated his African art collection. After leaving the Whitney in 2003, Anderson held several other museum positions, and on June 23, 2016, it was announced that he was appointed President of the Souls Grown Deep Foundation.
45. Michael Kimmelman, "Jazzy Geometry, Cool Quilters," *New York Times*, Nov. 29, 2002, pp. E33, E37.
46. Michael J. Prokopow, "Material Truths: *The Quilts of Gee's Bend* at the Whitney Museum of Art; an Exhibition Review," *Winterthur Portfolio* 38, no. 1 (Spring 2003), p. 60.
47. What may also imbue the work-clothes quilts with an extra measure of emotion is that the clothes used were sometimes owned by deceased loved ones. In 1941, when Missouri Pettway lost her husband, she said, "I'm going to take his work clothes, shape them into a quilt to remember him, and cover up under it for love." See Amei Wallach, "Fabric of Their Lives," *Smithsonian* 37, no. 7 (Oct. 2006), pp. 66–75 (quotation on p. 72).
48. Prokopow, "Material Truths," p. 61.
49. Ulysses Grant Dietz, "From under the Bedcovers: A Culture Curator's Perspective," in Roderick Kiracofe, *Unconventional & Unexpected: American Quilts below the Radar, 1950–2000* (New York: Stewart, Tabori & Chang, 2014), p. 143.
50. Mary Lee Bendolph, "Mama's Song," in W. Arnett et al., *Gee's Bend: The Architecture of the Quilt*, p. 178.
51. William Arnett, "Gee's Bend: The Architecture of the Quilt," in W. Arnett et al., *Gee's Bend: The Architecture of the Quilt*, p. 46, ill. p. 47.
52. Annie Mae Young, quoted in Beardsley et al., *Gee's Bend: The Women and Their Quilts*, p. 104.
53. Gearldine Westbrook and Mary L. Bennett, quoted in the introduction by Shelly Zegart and Paul Arnett to "My Way," ibid., p. 88.

The Old Country

1. Bernice Kelly Harris, "Tore Up and a-Movin'," in Federal Writers' Project, *These Are Our Lives, as Told by the People and Written by Members of the Federal Writers' Project of the Works Progress Administration in North Carolina, Tennessee and Georgia* (Chapel Hill: University of North Carolina Press, 1939), p. 20.
2. Zora Neale Hurston, *Mules and Men* (Philadelphia: J. B. Lippincott, 1935).
3. Sterling Brown, "Old Time Tales" (review of *Mules and Men*, by Zora Neale Hurston), *New Masses*, Feb. 25, 1936, pp. 24–25.
4. W. T. Couch, preface to Federal Writers' Project, *These Are Our Lives*, p. xii.
5. Richard Wright, *Black Boy: A Record of Childhood and Youth* (New York: Harper & Brothers, 1945).
6. Ralph Ellison, "Remembering Richard Wright" (lecture presented at the Institute for Afro-American Culture, University of Iowa, Iowa City, July 18, 1971), in *Going to the Territory* (New York: Random House, 1986), pp. 211–13 (quotation on p. 211).
7. John Lewis, with Michael D'Orso, *Walking with the Wind: A Memoir of the Movement* (New York: Simon & Schuster, 1998), p. 259.
8. Anne Moody, *Coming of Age in Mississippi* (New York: Dial Press, 1968).
9. LeRoi Jones [Amiri Baraka], *Blues People: Negro Music in White America* (New York: William Morrow, 1963).
10. Ralph Ellison, "The Blues," *New York Review of Books*, Feb. 6, 1964, pp. 5–7.
11. Zora Neale Hurston, "Characteristics of Negro Expression," in *Negro*, comp. Nancy Cunard (London: Wishart, 1934), pp. 39–41.
12. W. E. B. Du Bois, "Criteria of Negro Art," *Crisis* 32 (Oct. 1926), pp. 290–97 (quotation on p. 292).
13. U.S. Census Bureau, *Supplementary Analysis and Derivative Tables: Twelfth Census of the United States, 1900*, Special Reports (Washington, D.C.: Government Printing Office, 1906), p. 185; U.S. Census Bureau, *Demographic Trends in the 20th Century*, prepared by Frank Hobbs and Nicole Stoops, Census 2000 Special Reports, ser. CENSR-4 (Washington, D.C.: U.S. Government Printing Office, 2002), p. 82, and p. 83, fig. 3–8.

LIST OF FIGURES

Joseph H. Hazen Foundation Purchase Fund, 1997 (1997.4a, b)
Page 27

16. **Thomas Hart Benton**
American, Neosho, Missouri, 1889–1975 Kansas City, Missouri
Deep South panel from *America Today*, 1930–31
Egg tempera with oil glazing over Permalba on gesso on linen, mounted to wood panel with a honeycomb interior
92 in. × 9 ft. 9 in. (233.7 × 297.2 cm)
The Metropolitan Museum of Art, New York, Gift of AXA Equitable, 2012 (2012.478d)
Page 32

17. **Dox Thrash**
American, Griffin, Georgia, 1893–1965 Philadelphia
The Welder, ca. 1936–41
Carborundum mezzotint, sheet: 10 × 6 in. (25.4 × 15.2 cm)
The Metropolitan Museum of Art, New York, Gift of Reba and Dave Williams, 1999 (1999.529.167)
Page 32

18. **Thomas Ruff**
German, born Zell am Harmersbach 1958
jpeg ny02, 2004
Chromogenic print, 105 15/16 in. × 11 ft. 11 5/16 in. (269 × 364 cm)
The Metropolitan Museum of Art, New York, Purchase, Denise and Andrew Saul Gift; Marlene Nathan Meyerson Gift, in memory of Andrew H. Golkin; Pamela and Arthur Sanders, The Robert A. and Renée E. Belfer Family Foundation and Neil C. S. Hirsch Gifts; and Marian and James H. Cohen Gift, in memory of their son, Michael Harrison Cohen, 2006 (2006.92)
Page 39

19. **Ellen Morton Littlejohn**
American, 1826–1899
and **Margaret Morton Bibb**
American, ca. 1832–ca. 1900/1910
Star of Bethlehem quilt, The Knob, near Russellville, Kentucky, ca. 1837–50
Silk and cotton, 88 1/4 × 87 1/8 in. (224.2 × 221.3 cm)
The Metropolitan Museum of Art, New York, Gift of Roger Morton and Dr. Paul C. Morton, 1962 (62.144)
Page 54

20. **Barnett Newman**
American, New York 1905–1970 New York
Concord, 1949
Oil and masking tape on canvas, 89 3/4 × 53 5/8 in. (228 × 136.2 cm)
The Metropolitan Museum of Art, New York, George A. Hearn Fund, 1968 (68.178)
Page 56

21. Boldly patterned quilts on a clothesline, Wilcox County, Alabama
Page 58

22. **Victor Vasarely**
French, born Pecs, Hungary, 1908–1997 Paris
Eridan III, mid-1950s
Tempera on paperboard, 20 1/8 × 15 5/8 in. (51.1 × 39.7 cm)
The Metropolitan Museum of Art, New York, Bequest of William S. Lieberman, 2005 (2007.49.95)
Page 58

23. Diana Vreeland's Freedom Quilting Bee quilt (1966) by Lucy Mingo in Vreeland's living room, New York
Page 60

24. Lee Krasner's Freedom Quilting Bee quilt (late 1960s) by an unknown artist in Krasner's living room, New York
Page 60

25. Freedom Quilting Bee brochure, 1980s
Page 61

26. **Amish maker**
Sunshine and Shadow quilt, Lancaster County, Pennsylvania, ca. 1930
Wool and cotton, 81 × 76 1/2 in. (205.7 × 194.3 cm)
The Metropolitan Museum of Art, New York, Purchase, Eva Gebhard-Gourgaud Foundation Gift, 1973 (1973.94)
Page 64

27. **Elizabeth Van Horne Clarkson**
American, 1771–1852
Honeycomb quilt, New York, ca. 1830
Cotton, 107 5/8 × 98 1/4 in. (273.4 × 249.6 cm)
The Metropolitan Museum of Art, New York, Gift of Mr. and Mrs. William A. Moore, 1923 (23.80.75)
Page 64

28. Wilcox County quilter Annie Mae Young and her great-granddaughter Shaquetta Young, 1993
Page 65

29. **Arthur Rothstein**
American, New York 1915–1985 New Rochelle, New York
Girl at Gee's Bend (*Artelia Bendolph*), April 1937
Negative, approx. 3 1/4 × 4 1/4 in. (8.3 × 10.8 cm)
Prints and Photographs Division, Library of Congress, Washington, D.C.
Page 69

30. **Unknown maker**
Log Cabin quilt, possibly Pennsylvania, ca. 1865
Wool and cotton, 92 1/2 × 80 in. (235 × 203.2 cm)
The Metropolitan Museum of Art, New York, Purchase, Eva Gebhard-Gourgaud Foundation Gift, 1973 (1973.159)
Page 70

31. **Unknown maker, possibly Mennonite**
Log Cabin quilt, Pennsylvania, ca. 1900
Cotton and wool, 85 3/8 × 67 in. (216.9 × 170.2 cm)
The Metropolitan Museum of Art, New York, Gift of Jack Ellenberger, 2004 (2004.418.1)
Page 70

32. **Julia Perry Brigham**
American, 1830?–1871
Roman Stripes quilt (or decorative throw), Wyoming County, New York, ca. 1865
Silk, silk velvet, and cotton, 61 × 52 1/2 in. (154.9 × 133.4 cm)
The Metropolitan Museum of Art, New York, Gift of Katharine Brigham, 1979 (1979.22)
Page 75

33. **Unknown maker**
Strip quilt, New Hampshire, ca. 1840
Cotton, 79 × 62 1/2 in. (200.7 × 158.8 cm)
The Metropolitan Museum of Art, New York, Purchase, Mrs. Roger Brunschwig Gift, 1990 (1990.40.1)
Page 75

34. **Amish maker**
Split Bars quilt, Lancaster County, Pennsylvania, ca. 1930
Wool and cotton, 87 × 77 in. (221 × 195.6 cm)
The Metropolitan Museum of Art, New York, Purchase, Jan P. Adelson and Joyce B. Cowin Gifts, 2004 (2004.26)
Page 79

35. **Mary Malvina Cook Taft**
American, 1812–1905
Chintz appliquéd quilt, Sag Harbor, New York ca. 1835–40
Cotton, 9 ft. 2 1/4 in. × 92 1/2 in. (280 × 235 cm)
The Metropolitan Museum of Art, New York, Gift of Miss Elsey R. Taft, 1970 (1970.288)
Page 79

36. **Unknown maker**
Flying Geese quilt, ca. 1840–50
Cotton, 9 ft. 4 1/2 in. × 9 ft. 6 5/8 in. (285.8 × 291.1 cm)
The Metropolitan Museum of Art, New York, Gift of Mr. and Mrs. Sidney Hosmer, 1948 (48.134.2)
Page 83

37. **Susan Reed Ruddick**
American, 1839–1869
Wild Goose Chase quilt, Forestburgh, New York, 1851
Cotton, 86 1/4 × 73 in. (219.1 × 185.4 cm)
The Metropolitan Museum of Art, New York, Gift of Mrs. William Rhinelander Stewart, 1976 (1976.198.1)
Page 83

38. **Annie E. Freshour Schaeffer**
American, 1851–1928
Birds in Air quilt, Lewistown, Maryland, before 1891
Cotton, 77 1/8 × 74 3/4 in. (195.9 × 189.9 cm)
The Metropolitan Museum of Art, New York, Purchase, Mrs. Roger Brunschwig Gift, 1990 (1990.40.2)
Page 83

39. **Unknown maker, probably Quaker**
Crazy quilt, Pennsylvania, ca. 1885–1900
Silk, silk velvet, and wool, 75 3/4 × 73 3/8 in. (192.4 × 186.4 cm)
The Metropolitan Museum of Art, New York, Purchase, Virginia H. Groomes Gift, in memory of her mother, Mary W. Groomes, 1974 (1974.34)
Page 89

40. **Unidentified photographer**
River Baptism, Citronella, Alabama, 1907
Gelatin silver print, 4 3/8 × 3 3/8 in. (11.1 × 8.6 cm)
International Center of Photography, New York, Daniel Cowin Collection, Museum purchase, 2005
Page 94

41. Cotton fields ready for harvest
Page 95

42. **Unidentified photographer**
The Lynching of Dick Robinson and a Man Named Thompson, Pritchard Station, Alabama, October 6, 1906
Gelatin silver print, mounted to cardstock, 5 × 7 in. (12.7 × 17.8 cm)
Page 96

WORKS IN THE SOULS GROWN DEEP FOUNDATION GIFT

This list is organized alphabetically by artist's last name, followed by artwork title. An asterisk indicates works that are not illustrated in this volume.

Willie "Ma Willie" Abrams
American, Rehoboth, Alabama, 1897–1987
Rehoboth
Roman Stripes quilt, ca. 1975
Top: cotton; back: cotton-polyester blend; binding: self-bound, back turned over front and stitched, 93 1/4 × 70 in. (236.9 × 177.8 cm)
Gift of Souls Grown Deep Foundation from the William S. Arnett Collection, 2014 (2014.548.38)
Detail, page 52; plate 29, page 62

Annie Bendolph
American, Boykin, Alabama, 1900–1981
Boykin
Thousand Pyramids quilt, ca. 1930
Top: cotton and cotton-polyester blend; back: cotton; binding: self-bound, back turned over front and stitched, 85 × 71 1/2 in. (215.9 × 181.6 cm)
Gift of Souls Grown Deep Foundation from the William S. Arnett Collection, 2014 (2014.548.39)
Plate 41, page 84

Wild Goose Chase with Flying Geese border quilt, ca. 1930
Top and back: cotton; binding: self-bound, back turned over front and stitched, 78 1/4 × 71 1/2 in. (198.8 × 181.6 cm)
Gift of Souls Grown Deep Foundation from the William S. Arnett Collection, 2014 (2014.548.40)
Plate 42, page 85

Louisiana P. Bendolph
American, born Boykin, Alabama, 1960
Housetop quilt, 2003
Top and back: cotton-polyester blend; binding: self-bound, front turned over back and stitched, 98 × 66 5/8 in. (248.9 × 169.2 cm)
Gift of Souls Grown Deep Foundation from the William S. Arnett Collection, 2014 (2014.548.41)
Plate 27, page 55

Linda Diane Bennett
American, Boykin, Alabama, 1955–1988
Boykin
Bricklayer quilt, ca. 1970
Top and back: cotton-polyester blend; binding: front turned over back and stitched, 80 1/2 × 64 1/2 in. (204.5 × 163.8 cm)
Gift of Souls Grown Deep Foundation from the William S. Arnett Collection, 2014 (2014.548.42)
Plate 31, page 71

Emma Lee Pettway Campbell
American, Boykin, Alabama, 1928–2002
Boykin
Blocks and Strips work-clothes quilt, ca. 1950
Top: cotton and cotton-polyester blend; back: cotton and polyester; binding: self-bound, front turned over back and stitched, 90 3/4 × 68 3/4 in. (230.5 × 174.6 cm)
Gift of Souls Grown Deep Foundation from the William S. Arnett Collection, 2014 (2014.548.43)
Plate 36, page 77

Thornton Dial
American, Emelle, Alabama, 1928–2016
McCalla, Alabama
African Athlete, 1998
Graphite, charcoal, and pastel on paper, 44 × 30 in. (111.8 × 76.2 cm)
Gift of Souls Grown Deep Foundation from the William S. Arnett Collection, 2014 (2014.548.23)
Plate 11, page 36

**Celebration*, 2004
Graphite, pastel, watercolor, and gouache on paper, 29 × 41 in. (73.7 × 104.1 cm)
Gift of Souls Grown Deep Foundation from the William S. Arnett Collection, 2014 (2014.548.24)

The End of November: The Birds That Didn't Learn How to Fly, 2007
Quilt, wire, fabric, and enamel on canvas on wood, 72 × 72 in. (182.9 × 182.9 cm)
Gift of Souls Grown Deep Foundation from the William S. Arnett Collection, 2014 (2014.548.5)
Plate 22, page 49

History Refused to Die, 2004
Okra stalks and roots, clothing, collaged drawings, tin, wire, steel, Masonite, steel chain, enamel, and spray paint, H. 102 in. (259.1 cm), W. 87 in. (221 cm), D. 23 in. (58.4 cm)
Gift of Souls Grown Deep Foundation from the William S. Arnett Collection, 2014 (2014.548.1)
Plate 8, page 33

January 20, 2009, 2009
Graphite, pastel, and coffee on paper, 44 1/4 × 30 5/8 in. (112.4 × 77.8 cm)
Gift of Souls Grown Deep Foundation from the William S. Arnett Collection, 2014 (2014.548.25)
Detail, page 12; plate 12, page 37

9/11: Interrupting the Morning News, 2002
Graphite, charcoal, and watercolor on paper, 41 × 29 in. (104.1 × 73.7 cm)
Gift of Souls Grown Deep Foundation from the William S. Arnett Collection, 2014 (2014.548.22)
Plate 13, page 38

Out of the Darkness, the Lord Gave Us Light, 2003
Carpet, cloth, two-part epoxy putty, enamel, and spray paint on canvas on wood, H. 72 1/2 in. (184.2 cm), W. 74 in. (188 cm), D. 3 in. (7.6 cm)
Gift of Souls Grown Deep Foundation from the William S. Arnett Collection, 2014 (2014.548.2)
Plate 21, page 48

**Powder Plant*, 2013
Sheet metal, sawdust, commercial paint, and adhesive on canvas on wood, H. 66 in. (167.6 cm), W. 60 in. (152.4 cm), D. 3 in. (7.6 cm)
Gift of Souls Grown Deep Foundation from the William S. Arnett Collection, 2014 (2014.548.3)

**Shadows of the Field*, 2008
String, twine, synthetic cotton batting, wood, burlap, sheet metal, cloth rags, nails, staples, and enamel on canvas on wood, H. 79 in. (200.7 cm), W. 105 in. (266.7 cm), D. 5 in. (12.7 cm)

Gift of Souls Grown Deep Foundation from the William S. Arnett Collection, 2014 (2014.548.4)

Victory in Iraq, 2004
Mannequin head, barbed wire, steel, clothing, tin, electrical wire, wheels, stuffed animals, toy cars and figurines, plastic spoons, wood, basket, oil, enamel, spray paint, and two-part epoxy putty on canvas on wood, H. 83 1/2 in. (212.1 cm), W. 11 ft. 3 in. (342.9 cm), D. 16 in. (40.6 cm)
Gift of Souls Grown Deep Foundation from the William S. Arnett Collection, 2014 (2014.548.6)
Detail, page 2; plate 14, pages 40–41

Lonnie Holley
American, born Birmingham 1950
African Mask, 2004
Automobile tires, welder's mask, electrical outlets, electrical cord, door lock, and lace fabric, H. 42 in. (106.7 cm), W. 38 in. (96.5 cm), D. 10 in. (25.4 cm)
Gift of Souls Grown Deep Foundation from the William S. Arnett Collection, 2014 (2014.548.7)
Plate 7, page 31

Grown Together in the Midst of the Foundation, 1994
Cottonwood, steel, metal wire, concrete, and PVC pipe, H. 96 1/2 in. (245.1 cm), W. 37 in. (94 cm), D. 29 in. (73.7 cm)
Gift of Souls Grown Deep Foundation from the William S. Arnett Collection, 2014 (2014.548.8)
Plate 9, page 34

Ruling for the Child, 1982
Investment casting materials, H. 20 in. (50.8 cm), W. 19 1/2 in. (49.5 cm), D. 15 in. (38.1 cm)
Gift of Souls Grown Deep Foundation from the William S. Arnett Collection, 2014 (2014.548.9)
Plate 20, page 46

Mary Elizabeth Kennedy
American, Boykin, Alabama, 1911–1991 Boykin
Log Cabin quilt, ca. 1935
Top: cotton and rayon; back: cotton and rayon; binding: self-bound, back turned over front and stitched, 81 1/4 × 79 1/2 in. (206.4 × 201.9 cm)
Gift of Souls Grown Deep Foundation from the William S. Arnett Collection, 2014 (2014.548.44)
Plate 32, page 72

Nettie Jane Kennedy
American, Boykin, Alabama, 1916–2002 Boykin
Basket-Weave quilt, 1973
Top: cotton; back: cotton-polyester blend; binding: self-bound, back turned over front and stitched, 80 1/8 × 80 3/4 in. (203.5 × 205.1 cm)
Gift of Souls Grown Deep Foundation from the William S. Arnett Collection, 2014 (2014.548.45)
Plate 35, page 76

Joe Light
American, Dyersburg, Tennessee, 1934–2005 Memphis
Hobo # Birdman, 1988
Place mats, glass, enamel, and spray paint on plywood, 48 × 96 in. (121.9 × 243.8 cm)
Gift of Souls Grown Deep Foundation from the William S. Arnett Collection, 2014 (2014.548.20)
Plate 18, page 44

Pony, 1988
Enamel on plywood, 36 × 38 in. (91.4 × 96.5 cm)
Gift of Souls Grown Deep Foundation from the William S. Arnett Collection, 2014 (2014.548.15)
Plate 19, page 45

Ronald Lockett
American, Bessemer, Alabama, 1965–1998 Bessemer
The Enemy Amongst Us, 1995
Commercial paint, pine needles, metal, and nails on plywood, H. 50 in. (127 cm), W. 53 in. (134.6 cm), D. 3 in. (7.6 cm)
Gift of Souls Grown Deep Foundation from the William S. Arnett Collection, 2014 (2014.548.10)
Plate 3, page 25

Lucy Mingo
American, born Rehoboth, Alabama, 1931
Blocks and Strips work-clothes quilt, 1959
Top and back: cotton; binding: self-bound, back turned over front and stitched, 80 5/8 × 69 1/2 in. (204.8 × 176.5 cm)
Gift of Souls Grown Deep Foundation from the William S. Arnett Collection, 2014 (2014.548.46)
Detail, page 8; plate 30, page 68

Joe Minter
American, born Birmingham 1943
Four Hundred Years of Free Labor, 1995
Welded found metal, H. 105 in. (266.7 cm), W. 85 in. (215.9 cm), D. 54 in. (137.2 cm)
Gift of Souls Grown Deep Foundation from the William S. Arnett Collection, 2014 (2014.548.11)
Plate 6, page 30

John B. Murray
American, Mitchell, Georgia, 1908–1998 Sandersville, Georgia
Untitled, early 1980s
Tempera, ink marker, and ink on paper, 24 × 18 in. (61 × 45.7 cm)
Gift of Souls Grown Deep Foundation from the William S. Arnett Collection, 2014 (2014.548.27)
Plate 25, page 50

Untitled, early 1980s
Watercolor, crayon, marker, and graphite on paper, 24 × 18 in. (61 × 45.7 cm)
Gift of Souls Grown Deep Foundation from the William S. Arnett Collection, 2014 (2014.548.28)
Plate 23, page 50

Untitled, 1987
Marker, metallic marker, watercolor, and gouache on paper, 23 3/4 × 17 3/4 in. (60.3 × 45.1 cm)
Gift of Souls Grown Deep Foundation from the William S. Arnett Collection, 2014 (2014.548.26)
Plate 24, page 50

Mertlene Perkins
American, Gastonburg, Alabama, 1917–2015 Alberta, Alabama
Birds in Flight quilt, 1940s
Top and back: cotton; binding: self-bound, back turned over front and stitched 85 5/8 × 68 3/4 in. (217.5 × 174.6 cm)
Gift of Souls Grown Deep Foundation from the William S. Arnett Collection, 2014 (2014.548.47)
Plate 43, page 86

Lola Pettway
American, born Boykin, Alabama, 1941
Eight-Block Housetop quilt, ca. 1975
Top: cotton; back: cotton and cotton-polyester blend; binding: self-bound, edges turned into each other and stitched together, 84 1/2 × 71 in. (214.6 × 180.3 cm)
Gift of Souls Grown Deep Foundation from the William S. Arnett Collection, 2014 (2014.548.48)
Plate 39, page 81

Loretta Pettway
American, born Boykin, Alabama, 1942
Housetop quilt, 1963
Top: cotton and polyester; back: cotton and rayon; binding: self-bound, back turned over front and stitched, 77 1/4 × 73 1/2 in. (196.2 × 186.7 cm)
Gift of Souls Grown Deep Foundation from the William S. Arnett Collection, 2014 (2014.548.49)
Plate 38, page 80

Lazy Gal Bars quilt, ca. 1965
Top: cotton and cotton-polyester blend; back: polyester; binding: self-bound, back turned over front and stitched, 80 1/2 × 68 1/2 in. (204.5 × 174 cm)
Gift of Souls Grown Deep Foundation from the William S. Arnett Collection, 2014 (2014.548.50)
Plate 28, page 57

Medallion quilt, ca. 1960
Top: cotton and rayon-acetate blend; back: cotton; binding: self-bound, back turned over front and stitched, 81 3/4 × 70 in. (207.6 × 177.8 cm)
Gift of Souls Grown Deep Foundation from the William S. Arnett Collection, 2014 (2014.548.51)
Plate 46, page 90

Lucy T. Pettway
American, Boykin, Alabama, 1921–2004 Boykin
Housetop and Bricklayer with Bars quilt, ca. 1955
Top and back: cotton and acetate; binding: self-bound, edges turned into each other and stitched together, 91 3/8 × 80 1/8 in. (232.1 × 203.5 cm)
Gift of Souls Grown Deep Foundation from the William S. Arnett Collection, 2014 (2014.548.52)
Plate 34, page 74

Martha Pettway
American, Alberta, Alabama, 1911–2005 Mobile, Alabama
Log Cabin quilt, 1930s
Top: cotton and acetate; back: cotton; binding: self-bound, back turned over front and stitched, 82 1/4 × 74 1/2 in. (208.9 × 189.2 cm)
Gift of Souls Grown Deep Foundation from the William S. Arnett Collection, 2014 (2014.548.54)
Plate 33, page 73

Nine-Block quilt, 1930s
Top: cotton and acetate; back: cotton; binding: self-bound, back turned over front and stitched, 82 1/4 × 73 1/2 in. (208.9 × 186.7 cm)
Gift of Souls Grown Deep Foundation from the William S. Arnett Collection, 2014 (2014.548.53)
Plate 45, page 88

Pearlie Kennedy Pettway
American, Boykin, Alabama, 1920–1982 Boykin
Triangles quilt, ca. 1960
Top: cotton and cotton-polyester blend; back: cotton; binding: self-bound, back turned over front and stitched, 77 × 75 in. (195.6 × 190.5 cm)
Gift of Souls Grown Deep Foundation from the William S. Arnett Collection, 2014 (2014.548.55)
Plate 44, page 87

Mary Proctor
American, born Lloyd, Florida, 1960
The Keys, 1996
Hollowcore door, plywood, keys, glass cabochons, buttons, watch faces, beads, toys, and commercial paint, H. 80 in. (203.2 cm), W. 30 in. (76.2 cm), D. 2 1/4 in. (5.7 cm)
Gift of Souls Grown Deep Foundation from the William S. Arnett Collection, 2014 (2014.548.12)
Detail, page 20; plate 26, page 51

Nellie Mae Rowe
American, Fayetteville, Georgia, 1900–1982 Smyrna, Georgia
Atlanta's Missing Children, 1981
Commercial paint, crayon, oil pastel, graphite, ink marker, and cut and pasted paper on paperboard, 32 × 30 in. (81.3 × 76.2 cm)
Gift of Souls Grown Deep Foundation from the William S. Arnett Collection, 2014 (2014.548.30)
Plate 10, page 35

Empty Chair, 1981
Graphite, crayon, and pastel on paper, 18 × 23 3/4 in. (45.7 × 60.3 cm)
Gift of Souls Grown Deep Foundation from the William S. Arnett Collection, 2014 (2014.548.32)
Plate 16, page 43

Nellie's Birthday, 1981
Colored pencil, crayon, and graphite on paper, 18 × 24 in. (45.7 × 61 cm)
Gift of Souls Grown Deep Foundation from the William S. Arnett Collection, 2014 (2014.548.31)
Plate 15, page 42

Woman Scolding Her Companion, 1981
Oil pastel, crayon, colored pencil, ink marker, and graphite on paperboard, 29 1/4 × 32 in. (74.3 × 81.3 cm)
Gift of Souls Grown Deep Foundation from the William S. Arnett Collection, 2014 (2014.548.29)
Detail, page 6; plate 17, page 44

Sue Willie Seltzer
American, Alberta, Alabama, 1922–2010 Alberta
Nine-Block Housetop quilt, ca. 1955
Top: cotton and cotton-polyester blend, rayon, and acetate; back: cotton-polyester blend; binding: self-bound, edges turned into each other and stitched together, 83 × 77 1/2 in. (210.8 × 196.9 cm)
Gift of Souls Grown Deep Foundation from the William S. Arnett Collection, 2014 (2014.548.56)
Plate 40, page 82

Emmer Sewell
American, born Marion, Alabama, 1934
Untitled, early 1990s
Automobile tire, plastic chair, and cinderblock, H. 43 in. (109.2 cm), W. 28 1/2 in. (72.4 cm), D. 22 in. (55.9 cm)
Gift of Souls Grown Deep Foundation from the William S. Arnett Collection, 2014 (2014.548.13a–c)
Plate 2, page 24

Mary T. Smith
American, Hazlehurst, Mississippi, 1905–1995 Hazlehurst
**Untitled*, 1987
Commercial paint on plywood, 48 × 32 in. (121.9 × 81.3 cm)
Gift of Souls Grown Deep Foundation from the William S. Arnett Collection, 2014 (2014.548.16a, b)

**Untitled Self-Portrait*, 1988
Commercial paint on plywood, 48 × 32 in. (121.9 × 81.3 cm)
Gift of Souls Grown Deep Foundation from the William S. Arnett Collection, 2014 (2014.548.17)

Georgia Speller
American, Aberdeen, Mississippi, 1931–1988 Memphis
**Dancing People in a Line*, 1986
Tempera and graphite on paper, 18 × 24 in. (45.7 × 61 cm)
Gift of Souls Grown Deep Foundation from the William S. Arnett Collection, 2014 (2014.548.35)

**Head of the Penitentiary*, 1986
Tempera and graphite on paper, 17 3/4 × 23 3/4 in. (45.1 × 60.3 cm)
Gift of Souls Grown Deep Foundation from the William S. Arnett Collection, 2014 (2014.548.36)

Minnie and Her Friends, 1987
Tempera and graphite on paper, 17 3/4 × 23 3/4 in. (45.1 × 60.3 cm)
Gift of Souls Grown Deep Foundation from the William S. Arnett Collection, 2014 (2014.548.37)
Plate 4, page 28

Henry Speller
American, Rolling Fork, Mississippi, 1903–1997 Memphis
**Boat on the Mississippi*, 1987
Marker, crayon, and graphite on paper, 18 × 24 in. (45.7 × 61 cm)
Gift of Souls Grown Deep Foundation from the William S. Arnett Collection, 2014 (2014.548.34)

Untitled, 1985
Colored pencil, crayon, and graphite on paper, 24 × 18 in. (61 × 45.7 cm)
Gift of Souls Grown Deep Foundation from the William S. Arnett Collection, 2014 (2014.548.33)
Plate 5, page 29

Mose Tolliver
American, Montgomery County, Alabama, 1924–2006 Montgomery
Bill Traylor People, 1987
Housepaint on plywood, 29 1/4 × 23 1/2 in. (74.3 × 59.7 cm)
Gift of Souls Grown Deep Foundation from the William S. Arnett Collection, 2014 (2014.548.18)
Plate 1, page 21

**Untitled Self-Portrait*, 1987
Commercial paint on plywood, H. 27 3/4 × 27 7/8 in. (70.5 × 70.8 cm)
Gift of Souls Grown Deep Foundation from the William S. Arnett Collection, 2014 (2014.548.21)

Annie Mae Young
American, Boykin, Alabama, 1928–2012 Alberta, Alabama
Strip Medallion quilt, 1976
Top: cotton and cotton-polyester blend; back: cotton-polyester blend; binding: self-bound, back turned over front and stitched, 104 1/2 × 77 in. (265.4 × 195.6 cm)
Gift of Souls Grown Deep Foundation from the William S. Arnett Collection, 2014 (2014.548.57)
Plate 37, page 78

Purvis Young
American, Liberty, Missouri, 1943–2010 Miami
Locked Up Their Minds, 1972
Commercial paint on plywood, 84 × 84 in. (213.4 × 213.4 cm)
Gift of Souls Grown Deep Foundation from the William S. Arnett Collection, 2014 (2014.548.14)
Detail, page 10

**Ocean*, ca. 1975
Commercial paint and wood on commercial wall paneling, 16 × 14 1/4 in. (40.6 × 36.2 cm)
Gift of Souls Grown Deep Foundation from the William S. Arnett Collection, 2014 (2014.548.19)

SELECTED READINGS

Artists

Arnett, Paul, and Eugene W. Metcalf, eds. *Mary Lee Bendolph, Gee's Bend Quilts, and Beyond*. Exh. cat. With essays by Joanne Cubbs, "The Life and Art of Mary Lee Bendolph," pp. 8–33, 69; Matt Arnett, "Wrapped in the Blanket of Time," pp. 34–49, 69; and Dana Friis-Hansen, "Beyond Gee's Bend: The Future of Art, pp. 50–68, 69." Atlanta: Tinwood Books; Austin, Tex.: Austin Museum of Art, 2006.

Arnett, William. "Mary T. Smith: Her Name Is Someone." *Raw Vision*, no. 31 (Summer 2000), pp. 24–31.

Binelli, Mark. "Lonnie Holley: The Insider's Outsider." *New York Times Magazine*, Jan. 26, 2014, pp. 32–37.

Borum, Jenifer P. "Ted Degener: Exposing the Faces." *Raw Vision*, no. 38 (Spring 2002), pp. 48–53.

Brown, Nic. "Southern Masters: Lonnie Holley." *Garden & Gun*, Oct.–Nov. 2015, pp. 142–47.

Cubbs, Joanne, and Eugene W. Metcalf, eds. *Hard Truths: The Art of Thornton Dial*. Exh. cat. With essays by David C. Driskell, "Giving In to the Visionary Dream: A Visit with Thornton Dial," pp. 13–21; Greg Tate, "Thornton Dial: Free, Black, and Brightening Up the Darkness of the World," pp. 23–35; and Joanne Cubbs, "Hard Truths: The Art of Thornton Dial," pp. 37–85. Indianapolis Museum of Art and other venues; 2011–13. Indianapolis: Indianapolis Museum of Art; Munich: Delmonico Books/Prestel, 2011.

Griffin, Roberta T. *Abstraction in the Art of Thornton Dial*. Exh. cat. Marietta, Ga.: Kennesaw State College, 1995.

Haardt, Anton. "Mose Tolliver Goes to Washington." *Raw Vision*, no. 12 (Summer 1995), pp. 22–29.

Herman, Bernard L., ed. *Fever Within: The Art of Ronald Lockett*. Chapel Hill: University of North Carolina Press, 2016.

Kistulentz, Steve. "Mary Proctor's Vision." *Raw Vision*, no. 29 (Winter 1999/2000), pp. 32–37.

Kogan, Lee. *The Art of Nellie Mae Rowe: Ninety-Nine and a Half Won't Do*. Exh. cat. Museum of American Folk Art, New York; High Museum of Art, Atlanta; and African American Museum, Dallas; 1999–2000. New York: Museum of American Folk Art, 1998.

Metcalf, Eugene W., Jr. "Bill Arnett, Thornton Dial and the Myth of America." *Raw Vision*, no. 55 (Summer 2006), pp. 24–30.

Moreno, Gean. "Purvis Young's Predicament." *Raw Vision*, no. 36 (Fall 2001), pp. 34–38.

Murphy, Jay. "Cultural Recycling: The Work of Lonnie Holley." *Raw Vision*, no. 7 (Summer 1999), pp. 20–23.

Nellie Mae Rowe. Exh. cat. With an essay by Xenia Zed, "Nellie's Hagiography," pp. 15–25. Augusta, Ga.: Morris Museum of Art, 1996.

Nellie Mae Rowe: Visionary Artist, 1900–1982. Exh. cat. Atlanta: Southern Arts Federation, 1983.

Padgelek, Mary G. *In the Hand of the Holy Spirit: The Art of J. B. Murray*. Macon, Ga.: Mercer University Press, 2000.

———. "J. B. Murray: 'This Well Is Deep, and Never Go Dry.'" *Raw Vision*, no. 58 (Spring 2007), pp. 42–49.

Puchner, Edward M. "Henry Speller: Bodies of the Blues." *Raw Vision*, no. 65 (Winter 2008–9), pp. 24–29.

Purvis Young. Exh. cat. With an essay by Paula Harper, "Art as a Matter of Life and Death." Miami: Joy Moos Gallery, 1993.

Purvis Young: Painting the Blues. Springfield, Ohio: Springfield Museum of Art, 1998.

Russell, Charles. "Joe Minter: The Stations of the African American Passion." *Raw Vision*, no. 68 (Winter 2009–10), pp. 42–45.

———. "Thornton Dial: Vernacular Art and the 'New' South." *Raw Vision*, no. 43 (Summer 2003), pp. 20–27.

Sloan, Mark, ed. *Something to Take My Place: The Art of Lonnie Holley*. With essays by Mark Sloan et al. Exh. cat. Charleston, S.C.: Halsey Institute of Contemporary Art, College of Charleston, School of the Arts, 2015.

Thornton Dial: His Spoken Dreams. Exh. cat.; 1998–99. With an essay by Thomas McEvilley, "Thornton Dial: Brinksman," pp. 3–5. New York: Ricco/Maresca Gallery, 1998.

Thornton Dial: Image of the Tiger. Exh. cat.; 1993–94. With essays by Thomas McEvilley, "Proud-Stepping Tiger: History as Struggle in the Work of Thornton Dial," pp. 8–31; and Amiri Baraka (LeRoi Jones), "Fearful Symmetry: The Art of Thornton Dial," pp. 32–64; and contributions by Paul Arnett and William Arnett. New York: Harry N. Abrams, in association with the Museum of American Folk Art, New York; New Museum of Contemporary Art, New York; and American Center, Paris, 1993.

Thornton Dial: Strategy of the World. With an essay by Paul Arnett, "The Strategy of Thornton Dial," pp. 5–9. Jamaica, N.Y.: Southern Queens Park Association, 1990.

Thornton Dial in the 21st Century. Exh. cat.; 2005–6. With essays by Joanne Cubbs et al. Atlanta: Tinwood Books, in association with the Museum of Fine Arts, Houston, 2005.

Two Black Folk Artists: Clementine Hunter, Nellie Mae Rowe. Exh. cat. Oxford, Ohio: Miami University Art Museum, 1986.

Welborn, Braden. "Thornton Dial's Blood and Meat: Survival for the World." *Prairie Schooner* 79, no. 4 (Winter 2005), pp. 58–59.

Zed, Xenia. "Nellie Mae Rowe: Makin' a Way Outta No Way." *Raw Vision*, no. 32 (Fall 2000), pp. 24–31.

Zimmerman, Cara. "Ronald Lockett's Roses." *Raw Vision*, no. 84 (Winter 2014–15), pp. 34–39.

———. "Thornton Dial." *Raw Vision* 74 (Winter 2011–12), pp. 52–55.

African American Art

Arnett, Paul, and William Arnett, eds. *Souls Grown Deep: African American Vernacular Art of the South*. Vol. 1, *The Tree Gave the Dove a Leaf*. Atlanta: Tinwood Books, in association with the Schomburg Center for Research in Black Culture, New York Public Library, 2000.

Arnett, William, and Paul Arnett, eds. *Souls Grown Deep: African American Vernacular Art of the South*. Vol. 2, *Once That River Starts to Flow*. Atlanta: Tinwood Books, 2001.

Ashe: Improvisation & Recycling in African-American Visionary Art. Exh. cat. Winston-Salem, N.C.: Diggs Gallery at Winston-Salem State University, 1993.

Cooks, Bridget R. *Exhibiting Blackness: African Americans and the American Art Museum*. Amherst: University of Massachusetts Press, 2011.

Davis, Gerald L. "What Are African American Folk Arts? The Importance of Presenting,

Preserving, and Promoting African American Aesthetic Traditions." In *The Arts of Black Folk: The Arts of Black Folk Conference for Community Organizations; Presenting African American Folk Arts,* pp. 20–27. New York: Schomburg Center for Research in Black Culture, New York Public Library, 1991.

Driskell, David C., ed. *African American Visual Aesthetics: A Postmodernist View.* Washington, D.C.: Smithsonian Institution Press, 1995.

Farrington, Lisa. *African-American Art: A Visual and Cultural History.* New York: Oxford University Press, 2017.

Hartigan, Lynda Roscoe. "Recent Challenges in the Study of African American Folk Art." *International Review of African American Art* 11, no. 3 (1994), pp. 27–29, 60–63. [Issue titled "Image and Identity: The African American Experience in 20th Century American Art."]

History Refused to Die: The Enduring Legacy of the African American Art of Alabama. Exh. cat. With essays by William Arnett et al. [Montgomery, Ala.]: [Montgomery Museum of Fine Arts]; [Mobile]: [Alabama Contemporary Arts Center], 2015.

Livingston, Jane, and John Beardsley. *Black Folk Art in America, 1930–1980.* Exh. cat. Corcoran Gallery of Art, Washington, D.C., and other venues; 1982–83. Jackson: University Press of Mississippi; [Oxford, Miss.]: Center for the Study of Southern Culture, 1982.

Metcalf, Eugene W., Jr. "Black Art, Folk Art, and Social Control." *Winterthur Portfolio* 18, no. 4 (Winter 1983), pp. 271–89.

Next Generation: Southern Black Aesthetic. With essays by Lowery S. Sims et al. Exh. cat. Winston-Salem, N.C.: Southeastern Center for Contemporary Art, 1990.

Powell, Richard J. *Black Art and Culture in the 20th Century.* London: Thames and Hudson, 1997.

Vlach, John Michael. *The Afro-American Tradition in Decorative Arts.* Athens: University of Georgia Press, 1990.

African American History and Culture in the South

Alexander, Michelle. *The New Jim Crow: Mass Incarceration in the Age of Colorblindness.* New York: New Press, 2010.

Branch, Taylor. *At Canaan's Edge: America in the King Years, 1965–68.* New York: Simon & Schuster, 2006.

———. *Parting the Waters: America in the King Years, 1954–63.* New York: Simon & Schuster, 1989.

———. *Pillar of Fire: America in the King Years, 1963–65.* New York: Simon & Schuster, 1998.

Federal Writers' Project. *These Are Our Lives, as Told by the People and Written by Members of the Federal Writers' Project of the Works Progress Administration in North Carolina, Tennessee and Georgia.* Chapel Hill: University of North Carolina Press, 1939.

Griffin, Larry J., and Don H. Doyle, eds. *The South as an American Problem.* Athens: University of Georgia Press, 1995.

Hurston, Zora Neale. *Mules and Men.* Philadelphia: J. B. Lippincott, 1935.

Jones, LeRoi [Amiri Baraka]. *Blues People: Negro Music in White America.* New York: William Morrow, 1963.

Katznelson, Ira. *When Affirmative Action Was White: An Untold History of Racial Inequality in Twentieth-Century America.* New York: W. W. Norton, 2005.

Rourke, Constance. *American Humor: A Study of the National Character.* New York: Harcourt, Brace and Company, 1931.

Wilkerson, Isabel. *The Warmth of Other Suns: The Epic Story of America's Great Migration.* New York: Random House, 2010.

Environments, Installations, and Architecture

Beardsley, John. *Gardens of Revelation: Environments by Visionary Artists.* New York: Abbeville Press, 1995.

Gundaker, Grey. "Tradition and Innovation in African-American Yards." *African Arts* 26, no. 2 (Apr. 1993), pp. 58–71, 94–96.

Manley, Roger, and Mark Sloan. *Self-Made Worlds: Visionary Folk Art Environments.* New York: Aperture, 1997.

Rousseau, Valérie. "The Object's Potentiality: At the Source of Outsider Art Environments." In *Used/Goods*, edited by Giselle Amantea, Lorraine Oades, and Kim Sawchuck, pp. 177–89. Montreal: Cut Rate Collective, 2009.

Umberger, Leslie. *Sublime Spaces & Visionary Worlds: Built Environments of Vernacular Artists.* Exh. cat.; 2007–8. With contributions by Erika Doss et al. New York: Princeton Architectural Press; Sheboygan, Wisc.: John Michael Kohler Arts Center, 2007.

Ward, Daniel Franklin, ed. *Personal Places: Perspectives on Informal Art Environments.* Bowling Green, Ohio: Bowling Green State University Popular Press, 1984.

Westmacott, Richard. *African-American Gardens and Yards in the Rural South.* Knoxville: University of Tennessee Press, 1992.

Quilts

Arnett, William, et al. *Gee's Bend: The Architecture of the Quilt.* Exh. cat. Museum of Fine Arts, Houston, and other venues; 2006–8. Atlanta: Tinwood Books, 2006.

Beardsley, John, et al. *Gee's Bend: The Women and Their Quilts*. Exh. cat. Museum of Fine Arts, Houston, and other venues; 2002–8. Atlanta: Tinwood Books, in association with the Museum of Fine Arts, Houston, 2002.

Benberry, Cuesta. *Always There: The African-American Presence in American Quilts.* Louisville: Kentucky Quilt Project, 1992.

Callahan, Nancy. *The Freedom Quilting Bee.* Tuscaloosa: University of Alabama Press, 1987.

Freeman, Roland L. *A Communion of the Spirits: African-American Quilters, Preservers, and Their Stories*. Nashville, Tenn.: Rutledge Hill Press, 1996.

Holstein, Jonathan. *Abstract Design in American Quilts: A Biography of an Exhibition.* Louisville: Kentucky Quilt Project, 1991.

Just How I Picture It in My Mind: Contemporary African American Quilts from the Montgomery Museum of Fine Arts. Exh. cat. With an essay by Mary Elizabeth Johnson Huff. Montgomery, Ala.: Montgomery Museum of Fine Arts, 2006.

Kiracofe, Roderick. *Unconventional & Unexpected: American Quilts below the Radar, 1950–2000*. New York: Stewart, Tabori & Chang, 2014.

Peck, Amelia. *American Quilts & Coverlets in The Metropolitan Museum of Art*. Rev. ed. With the assistance of Cynthia V. A. Schaffner. New York: The Metropolitan Museum of Art, 2007.

Prokopow, Michael J. "Material Truths: *The Quilts of Gee's Bend* at the Whitney Museum of Art; an Exhibition Review." *Winterthur Portfolio* 38, no. 1 (Spring 2003), pp. 57–66.

Turner, Patricia A. *Crafted Lives: Stories and Studies of African American Quilters.* Jackson: University of Mississippi Press, 2009.

Self-Taught Art

Barrett, Didi. *Muffled Voices: Folk Artists in Contemporary America.* Exh. cat. PaineWebber Art Gallery, New York. New York: Museum of American Folk Art, 1986.

Cardinal, Roger. *Outsider Art.* London: Studio Vista, 1972.

Cerny, Charlene, and Suzanne Seriff, eds. *Recycled, Re-Seen: Folk Art from the Global Scrap Heap.* Exh. cat. New York: Harry N. Abrams, in association with the Museum of International Folk Art, Santa Fe, 1996.

Conwill, Kinshasha. "In Search of An 'Authentic' Vision: Decoding the Appeal of the Self-Taught African-American Artist." *American Art* 5, no. 4 (Autumn 1991), pp. 2–9.

Conwill, Kinshasha, et al. *Testimony: Vernacular Art of the African-American South. The Ronald and June Shelp Collection.* Exh. cat. Kalamazoo Institute of Arts, Kalamazoo, Mich., and other venues; 2000–2004. New York: Harry N. Abrams, in association with Exhibitions International and the Schomburg Center for Research in Black Culture, 2001.

Cooke, Lynne. "Orthodoxies Undermined." In *"Great and Mighty Things": Outsider Art from the Jill and Sheldon Bonovitz Collection*, edited by Ann Percy, with Cara Zimmerman, pp. 204–15. Exh. cat. Philadelphia: Philadelphia Museum of Art, 2013.

Crow, Thomas. "Folk into Art: A Phenomenon of Class and Culture in Twentieth-Century America." In *Harry Smith: The Avant-Garde in the American Vernacular*, edited by Andrew Perchuk and Rani Singh, pp. 205–23. Issues & Debates. Los Angeles: Getty Research Institute, 2010.

Crown, Carol, and Cheryl Rivers, eds. *Folk Art*. Vol. 23 of *The New Encyclopedia of Southern Culture*. Center for the Study of Southern Culture, University of Mississippi, Oxford. Chapel Hill: University of North Carolina Press, 2013.

Crown, Carol, and Charles Russell, eds. *Sacred and Profane: Voice and Vision in Southern Self-Taught Art.* Jackson: University Press of Mississippi, 2007.

Danto, Arthur C. "Outsider Art." *Nation*, Mar. 10, 1997, pp. 33–36.

Fine, Gary Alan. *Everyday Genius: Self-Taught Art and the Culture of Authenticity.* Chicago: University of Chicago Press, 2004.

Hall, Michael D. "The Mythic Outsider: Handmaiden to the Modern Muse." *New Art Examiner* 19, no. 1 (Sept. 1991), pp. 16–21.

Hall, Michael D., and Eugene W. Metcalf Jr., eds., with Roger Cardinal. *The Artist Outsider: Creativity and the Boundaries of Culture.* Washington, D.C.: Smithsonian Institution Press, 1994.

Hartigan, Lynda Roscoe. "Going Urban: American Folk Art and the Great Migration." *American Art* 14, no. 2 (Summer 2000), pp. 26–51.

Hollander, Stacy C., and Valérie Rousseau. *Self-Taught Genius: Treasures from the American Folk Art Museum.* Exh. cat. American Folk Art Museum and other venues; 2014–17. New York: American Folk Art Museum, 2014.

Jacobs, Joseph. *A World of Their Own: Twentieth-Century American Folk Art.* Exh. cat. Newark, N.J.: Newark Museum, 1995.

König, Kasper, and Falk Wolf, eds. *The Shadow of the Avant-Garde: Rousseau and the Forgotten Masters.* Exh. cat. Museum Folkwang, Essen; 2015–16. Ostfildern: Hatje/Cantz, 2015.

Lippard, Lucy R. *Mixed Blessings: New Art in a Multicultural America.* New York: Pantheon Books, 1990.

Maizels, John. *Raw Creation: Outsider Art and Beyond.* Introduction by Roger Cardinal. London: Phaidon Press, 1996.

Manley, Roger. "Separating the Folk from Their Art." *New Art Examiner* 19, no. 1 (Sept. 1991), pp. 25–28.

Maresca, Frank, and Roger Ricco, with Lyle Rexer. *American Self-Taught: Paintings and Drawings by Outsider Artists.* New York: Alfred A. Knopf, 1993.

Quart, Alissa. *Republic of Outsiders: The Power of Amateurs, Dreamers, and Rebels.* New York: New Press, 2013.

Rousseau, Valérie, et al. *When the Curtain Never Comes Down: Performance Art and the Alter Ego.* Exh. cat. New York: American Folk Art Museum, 2015.

Russell, Charles, ed. *Groundwaters: A Century of Self-Taught and Outsider Artists*. London: Prestel, 2011.

———. *Self-Taught Art: The Culture and Aesthetics of American Vernacular Art.* Jackson: University Press of Mississippi, 2001.

Self-Taught Artists of the 20th Century: An American Anthology. Exh. cat. With essays by Arthur C. Danto, "The Artworld and Its Outsiders," pp. 18–27; Maurice Berger, "Critical Fictions: Race, 'Outsiders,' and the Construction of Art History," pp. 28–37; and Gerald L. Davis, "The Presence of Mind in the Production of American Folk Art," pp. 38–43; and contributions by Carol Millsom Studer et al. Philadelphia Museum of Art and other venues; 1998–99. San Francisco: Chronicle Books, 1998.

Sellen, Betty-Carol, with Cynthia J. Johanson. *20th Century American Folk, Self-Taught, and Outsider Art.* New York: Neal-Schuman Publishers, 1993.

Stillinger, Elizabeth. *A Kind of Archeology: Collecting American Folk Art, 1876–1976.* Amherst: University of Massachusetts Press, 2011.

Transmitters: The Isolate Artist in America. Foreword by Elsa S. Weiner [Longhauser]. Exh. cat. Philadelphia: Philadelphia College of Art, 1981.

Tuchman, Maurice, and Carol S. Eliel. *Parallel Visions: Modern Artists and Outsider Art.* Exh. cat.; 1992–93. With contributions by Barbara Freeman et al. Los Angeles: Los Angeles County Museum of Art: Princeton, N.J.: Princeton University Press, 1992.

Vlach, John Michael. *Plain Painters: Making Sense of American Folk Art.* Washington, D.C.: Smithsonian Institution Press, 1988.

Yelen, Alice Rae. *Passionate Visions of the American South: Self-Taught Artists from 1940 to the Present.* Exh. cat. With essays by William Ferris et al. New Orleans Museum of Art and other venues; 1993–95. New Orleans: New Orleans Museum of Art, 1993.

INDEX

Page numbers in bold refer to images.

PHOTOGRAPH CREDITS

Front cover: © 2018 Estate of Thornton Dial/Artists Rights Society (ARS), New York. Photo: Steve Pitkin/Pitkin Studios; back cover: © 2018 Estate of Lucy T. Pettway/Artists Rights Society (ARS), New York. Photo: Steve Pitkin/ Pitkin Studios

By page number

Pp. 2, 12: © 2018 Estate of Thornton Dial/Artists Rights Society (ARS), New York. Photo: Steve Pitkin/Pitkin Studios; p. 6: © 2018 Estate of Nellie Mae Rowe/Artists Rights Society (ARS), New York. Photo: Steve Pitkin/Pitkin Studios; p. 8: © Estate of Emma Lee Pettway Campbell. Photo: Steve Pitkin/ Pitkin Studios; p. 10: © 2018 Estate of Ronald Lockett/Artists Rights Society (ARS), New York. Photo: Steve Pitkin/Pitkin Studios; p. 20: © Mary Proctor. Image © Metropolitan Museum of Art. Photo: Juan Trujillo; p. 52: © 2018 Estate of Willie "Ma Willie" Abrams/Artists Rights Society (ARS), New York. Photo: Steve Pitkin/Pitkin Studios; p. 92: © Walker Evans Archive, The Metropolitan Museum of Art

By figure number

Fig. 1: © El Anatsui. Courtesy of the artist and Jack Shainman Gallery, New York; fig. 2: © Bill Traylor Family Trust; fig. 3: © 2018 Lonnie Holley/Artists Rights Society (ARS), New York. Photo: William Arnett; figs. 4–5: © 2018 Emmer Sewell/Artists Rights Society (ARS), New York. Photo: William Arnett; fig. 6: Courtesy of Noah Purifoy Foundation © 2018; fig. 7: © The Museum of Modern Art/Licensed by SCALA/Art Resource, NY; figs. 8, 22: © 2018 Artists Rights Society (ARS), New York/ADAGP, Paris; fig. 12: Image © Metropolitan Museum of Art. Photo: Juan Trujillo; fig. 13: © Robert Rauschenberg Foundation; fig. 14: © 2018 Jim Dine/Artists Rights Society (ARS), New York; fig. 15: © Anselm Kiefer: fig. 18: © 2018 Artists Rights Society (ARS), New York/ VG Bild-Kunst, Bonn; fig. 20: © 2018 The Barnett Newman Foundation, New York/Artists Rights Society (ARS), New York; fig. 21: Birmingham, Alabama, Public Library Archives; fig. 23: © 2018 Lucy Mingo/Artists Rights Society (ARS), New York. Photo: Nancy Callahan; fig. 24: Photo: Nancy Callahan; fig. 25: Courtesy of The International Quilt Study Center & Museum; fig. 28: Photo © 2018 Roland L. Freeman; fig. 29: Library of Congress, Prints & Photographs Division, FSA/OWI Collection, LC-DIG-fsa-8b35942; fig. 32: Image © Metropolitan Museum of Art. Photo: Bruce Schwarz; fig. 40: International Center of Photography, Daniel Cowin Collection, Museum Purchase, 2005; fig. 41: © Barna Tanko, Shutterstock; fig. 42: Reproduced with the Permission of the National Center for Civil and Human Rights

By plate number

Pl. 1: © 2018 Estate of Mose Tolliver/Artists Rights Society (ARS), New York. Photo: Steve Pitkin/Pitkin Studios; pl. 2: © 2018 Emmer Sewell/Artists Rights Society (ARS), New York. Photo: Steve Pitkin/Pitkin Studios; pl. 3: © 2018 Estate of Ronald Lockett/Artists Rights Society (ARS), New York. Photo: Steve Pitkin/Pitkin Studios; pl. 6: © 2018 Joe Minter/Artists Rights Society (ARS), New York. Photo: Steve Pitkin/Pitkin Studios; pls. 7, 9: © 2018 Lonnie Holley/ Artists Rights Society (ARS), New York. Photo: Steve Pitkin/Pitkin Studios; Pls. 8, 11–14, 21–22: © 2018 Estate of Thornton Dial/Artists Rights Society (ARS), New York. Photo: Steve Pitkin/Pitkin Studios; pls. 10, 15–17: © 2018 Estate of Nellie Mae Rowe/Artists Rights Society (ARS), New York. Photo: Steve Pitkin/Pitkin Studios; pls. 18–19: © 2018 Estate of Joe Light/Artists Rights Society (ARS), New York. Photo: Steve Pitkin/Pitkin Studios; pl. 20: © 2018 Lonnie Holley/Artists Rights Society (ARS), New York; pls. 23–25: © 2018 Estate of John Bunion ("J. B.") Murray/Artists Rights Society (ARS), New York. Photo: Steve Pitkin/Pitkin Studios; pl. 26: © Mary Proctor. Image © Metropolitan Museum of Art. Photo: Juan Trujillo; pl. 27: © Louisiana P. Bendolph. Photo: Steve Pitkin/Pitkin Studios; pls. 28, 38, 46: © 2018 Loretta Pettway/Artists Rights Society (ARS), New York. Photo: Steve Pitkin/Pitkin Studios; pl. 29: © 2018 Estate of Willie "Ma Willie" Abrams/Artists Rights Society (ARS), New York. Photo: Steve Pitkin/Pitkin Studios; pl. 30: © 2018 Lucy Mingo/Artists Rights Society (ARS), New York. Photo: Steve Pitkin/Pitkin Studios; pl. 31: © Estate of Linda Diane Bennett. Photo: Steve Pitkin/Pitkin Studios; pl. 32: © Estate of Mary Elizabeth Kennedy. Photo: Steve Pitkin/Pitkin Studios; pls. 33, 45: © 2018 Estate of Martha Pettway/Artists Rights Society (ARS), New York. Photo: Steve Pitkin/Pitkin Studios; pl. 34: © 2018 Estate of Lucy T. Pettway/ Artists Rights Society (ARS), New York. Photo: Steve Pitkin/Pitkin Studios; pl. 35: © 2018 Estate of Nettie Jane Kennedy/Artists Rights Society (ARS), New York. Photo: Steve Pitkin/Pitkin Studios; pl. 36: © Estate of Emma Lee Pettway Campbell. Photo: Steve Pitkin/Pitkin Studios; pl. 39: © 2018 Lola Pettway/Artists Rights Society (ARS), New York. Photo: Steve Pitkin/Pitkin Studios; pl. 40: © Estate of Sue Willie Seltzer. Photo: Steve Pitkin/Pitkin Studios; pls. 41–42: © Estate of Annie Bendolph. Photo: Steve Pitkin/Pitkin Studios; pl. 43: © 2018 Estate of Mertlene Perkins/Artists Rights Society (ARS), New York. Photo: Steve Pitkin/Pitkin Studios; pl. 44: © 2018 Estate of Pearlie Kennedy Pettway/Artists Rights Society (ARS), New York. Photo: Steve Pitkin/Pitkin Studios